It's All Coming Back

On love after the war

Jon Kahn

Copyright © Jon Kahn, 2017
Published by I_AM Self-Publishing, 2017.

The right of Jon Kahn to be identified as the Author of the Work has been asserted by him in accordance with the Copyright, Designs and Patents Act 1988.

All rights reserved.

ISBN 978-1-912145-62-1

This book is sold subject to the condition it shall not, by way of trade or otherwise, be circulated in any form or by any means, electronic or otherwise without the publisher's prior consent.

@iamselfpub
www.iamselfpublishing.com

A novel set the year following WW II; when people had to learn how to build a new life under the shadow of the recent past. Based on real people.

The novel is a further development of the novel in Swedish 'En osannolik kärlekshistoria' by the same author.
 The Swedish library service wrote: 'En osannolik kärlekshistoria' is a story of life and its complexity, a story of family bonds and how they shape us. Jon Kahn has written an emotional and very humane novel, well worth to be read by a broad group of readers.'

Translation by the author

Contents

Copenhagen April 1946 9

I. AFTERWARDS

2000–1946

Stockholm 2000 19
New York 1994 21
Stockholm 1990 25
Stockholm 1967 29
Heilbronn 1962 33
Uppland, north of Stockholm 1955 39
Clymping, near Littlehampton, Sussex 1955 41

II. A TREMBLING AFFAIR

Bromma, outside Stockholm September 1945 49
Bromma, November 1945 55
Gothenburg and Stockholm November and December 1945 ... 59
Christmas and New Year's Eve 1945 to 1946 61
Umeå 1919 63
Umeå 1924 73
Christmas and New Year's Eve 1945 to 1946 cont. 77
Berlin 1924 79
Mesnalien, near Lillehammer, January to March 1946 85

Belsize Park, London March 1946 89
Hampstead, London March 1946 95
Heilbronn 1938-1939 99
Stockholm and London 1939 113
Belsize Park, London, March 1946 123
Eva's story 125
Amsterdam and Westerbork 1943-1944 133
Bergen-Belsen 1944 147
Somewhere in Sweden 1944 155
Bergen-Belsen 1945 161
London, last week of March, 1946 167
Hampstead, London 29 March 1946 169
Hampstead and Belsize Park, London 30 March 1946 173
Königsberg 1917 179
Berlin 1919 189
London 1 April 1946 195

III. SWEDISH SPRING

Arvidsjaur, in the north of Sweden spring 1946 199
Umeå, in the north of Sweden March 1946 211

IV. HONEYMOON

Copenhagen, beginning of April 1946 Day 1 217
Day 2 223
Day 3 227
Day 4 231

Rügen 1936 237
Day 4 cont. 245
Umeå and Luleå 1941 247
Day 4 cont. 251
Day 5 253
Stockholm and Copenhagen 1943 261
Day 5 cont. 267
Umeå 1933 277
Day 5 cont. 285
Day 6 293
London 1935 297
The night between days 6 and 7 303
Day 7 307
Day 8 317
Day 9 319

V. REFLECTIONS AND FACTS

Afterthoughts 331
What I know and do not know 343
Thanks 347
My Chronology of the first 45 years of the
    twentieth century 349
Persons occurring in the book 353

Copenhagen April 1946

Anne-Marie knows that she has to tell Helmut the hard facts. She blushes, even though she is alone in the hotel room, when she realizes that she should have done it long ago. At least before the wedding. But Helmut is so happy and loving, and they've been so occupied with it all, that they haven't had time for the deep conversation that she knows they must have.

A honeymoon may not be the best time for it; but when is the best time? They haven't had time for more than exploring each other's bodies and each other's views about life and politics, for laughing at each other's jokes and realizing how well they fit together.

It's true that they have talked about most things: the most intimate things. They talk about everything. And yet, they have skipped some of the essentials.

She has begun to get to know his family. She doesn't know everything about them, but she loves his mother and, amazingly enough, his sister has become her very best friend, just a week after they first met.

The fact that his family is Jewish is something new to her, something curious. *Oh well*, she thinks, *his folks are just like anybody, but better.*

She smiles into the small mirror over the washbasin. Oh, how happy she looks, even though her hair is a mess. It really is unbelievable the way they have rushed into this, but they had to, it was – *it is* – the chance of their lives: they both know it.

She sits on the only chair, picks up her small pocket mirror and tries to get it to stand on the bedcover in the little hotel room, the better to see herself. She reapplies her lipstick, puts on some rouge as well, and tidies the unruly mess that is her hair right now. Normally she puts it up, but now she hesitates, she could have it hanging down over her high cheekbones on the one side and comb it back on the other. She wants to look her best when he comes back.

As she waits, her frustration grows that she hasn't ventured to make even some vague remarks that could have led him in the right direction. Her sister has probably said nothing to him about their father, about Sven. Her brother Björn might have said some of it, but in case Helmut knew it all he would have been much more annoyed and she would have noticed it. The problem now would be telling Helmut this late; that would just add to any upset he might feel. But it would be so much worse if he found out by himself, later. She realizes she has put herself in an awkward, almost impossible situation.

She sits, worrying, while struggling to plait her hair into pigtails. She finds that as difficult as the prospect of speaking to her husband. She lets her hair be.

Helmut comes in again, a very much brighter man than when he left the shabby hotel ten minutes ago. He had gone for a short walk to get some air – he has been sick and needs to restore that big body of his to its normal self.

He has also been preoccupied with thoughts of her family and how he could get to know them better not only that ex-communist-now-Mormon brother of hers, but also her sister and her nieces and nephews. He has fantasies of how he hopes it will be, but at the same time, it really doesn't matter if her father, the lawyer, is a dull man or a harsh, a quiet fellow or somebody to sit down with and smoke cigars and have intellectual conversations. He just knows he loves *her* and that her family aren't going to change that, however they turn out to be. He goes straight to her now, and her hesitancy and uneasiness are blown away.

'I love you so much,' he says, making her whole body feel warm. 'I've been thinking: why don't we invite your father... why don't we invite Sven to the new flat in Stockholm as soon as possible, or even ask to him to come here, to Copenhagen? You said he likes this town. Perhaps we could all meet here before we go home?'

'Wouldn't you like me to see our new apartment first? I have to feel at ease there. I'll love it; you've said I will love it, and so I know I will. I like that new modern part of Stockholm. Oh, it will be so wonderful!' She puts her head on his lap and looks up at his face, his brown eyes, the gap between his front teeth; she caresses his chin. 'But please let us get there first, before we invite him. I mean, you don't know him... There are so many things I have to tell you about him first: there is so much you don't know.'

Helmut frowns gently down at her.

'I know, but meeting someone is so much better than just hearing about them. Just telling someone about a person can give strange images. No, I want to meet him myself, and soon.'

She tries to smile but she suddenly doesn't know how to.

Perhaps this is how it was on their honeymoon. It could well have been. I know everything and yet nothing.

My father and mother, Anne-Marie and Helmut, married in a wink of an eye in 1946 after having been together for a week or two over the course of four months, neither of them really knowing anything about the other, neither realising that their respective families had so many strange and some of them awful memories. Their histories were covering both sides of the thirties and the war. The war being such a recent experience they had to sort out all the memories and shortcomings, losses of friends and foes, at the same time as a future had to be planned. All of it really and at once. Therefore this is a story both of love and of loss. It is also a story of how to tell the awkward, almost impossible, to your partner. During the Second World War you had to sort out who was enemy and who was friend. This was true even after the war when the air was full of stories, told and untold and myths and tales, all had to be told and most of the time this was a difficult process.

The question is if whom you had sided with could be forgotten the moment the war had ended. My father and mother had so diverting backgrounds and their kinfolks were even more far apart. And yet, they both knew, as so many did after the war, that they just had to start life anew and take their chances. If they had known the other's full story from the start they would perhaps never have tried. I am glad that they did, but their improbable love story is sometimes hard to capture. This story is about real things and real people; people who existed in real life. Of course, I don't know how they felt at the time or what was on their minds or what they said. But I knew them well and my guess is a best guess. The story is however true in the most significant way: it is all based on historic facts. They actually were at the places I describe – I know that much. And from there, I have filled in the colours between those black and white lines. I tried to collect stories of the past, the strange and often dark past: I snatched them when flying by.

I wanted to know.

I had to know.

Through the small streams of historic fact, the rivers of what I later discovered, the showers and storms of my imagination sprinkled over it all, this story has come to life.

Therefore this book is a story as true as the stories my stout father told when he sat down at the dining table and looked at me with his big, round eyes, and shared one of his anecdotes: you noticed the degree of truth in how his moustache vibrated.

And then, my grandmother Emmy's tales, told in broken English: 'You will not believe it, but it is the trrruth, quite true!' – and she would smile inscrutably with her deep brown eyes and then came that disarming laughter.

I didn't know what to believe. Mother's hints of things, my parents interrupting each other to tell their own version of what really happened: they interrupted, and argued, and even shouted.

And he always got the last word.

But this is not just his story.

My parents talked and talked and explained a lot of things but very seldom did they talk about the really important matters from the past. Even though all those stories existed somewhere, most of the time there was silence when it came to the things I really wanted to know all about. That was why I tried to catch clues, sometimes standing mouth agape, as if to swallow what facts I could glean. Their way of telling tales without catching the heart of the matter made me a sceptic: and now when I write this I don't know if I even can trust my own memories.

This is a story of a fantastic and terrible century, when so many things developed, so many inventions, new ways of communicating, new materials. But it was also a century of horror, when we all lost our innocence.

And this is a tale about people in the midst of it all, touched by it all.

It's All Coming Back

What remains are fragments.

Parts of two lives conveyed at broken-off dinner conversations, while children were crying, or during short visits. Imprints of guilt, infamy, love, scorn, care and reckless joy that in small, frail pieces reach the survivors' ears and starts to grow.

Fragments of glances and quiet content; hints of viewpoints once forgotten but never forgiven – all this is perceived anew and brought together; bragging, hypocrisies and tall tales are sieved away and then that space filled up again with things that no longer exist.

With the help of photographs that have become yellow and well-read manuscripts, this all becomes a story, a tale; it takes on its own life, evolves into the saga of these lives.

That is where the past joins the present. The fresh creation of what has already happened, the story of my pre-history.

And feelings arise anew, like tender echoes of bygone instruments. You hear them over and over again and they can never fully fade away.

1.
Afterwards

2000–1946

Stockholm 2000

The past is hidden in the most peculiar places. You have to know where to look to find the traces, the small pieces of leftovers that can deliver a message to the present, to those of us living now, who have only heard a part of what's gone before. We build our images of how it was based on the information we have; it's like looking into the mist or down through the ocean - you bump half-blind into previously unknown features that forever change your idea of how things are or might have been.

It was odd for me, but also exciting that it turned out that the place to look for traces of my nearest kin was in the archives of the Swedish secret police. I had realised that my maternal grandfather's strange political views might have meant that he had a file there. Maybe, it occurred to me, they might also have some information that would be new to me, regarding what my father did in Copenhagen during the war.

My hope when I went there was that whatever I might find would provide a clearer picture of all the historic facts that evaded me for so long, and that some things may even perhaps be settled once and for all.

This part of the archives was situated far north of the centre of Stockholm, in a modern building next to a shopping centre. I had to identify myself to get the files; fair enough, they might contain very important and classified material.

As it turned out they had hardly anything about my grandfather – in fact, overall, a lot less than what I knew already. However, there was one very relevant new fact - that he was classified as a security risk during World War II. This rang true to me. Of course he was. That fact would, to my mind, have led to a deeper investigation of his activities than what I could read in the files.

The information about my father was much more interesting. They had nothing on him being in Denmark. What they had was details of an investigation that had arisen because a woman cleaning his office became suspicious of what he and some other people, of disparate backgrounds, were doing in his office at odd times. She suspected that my father was engaged in some kind of spy network. I sat and read, drinking in every word, that the secret police had sent someone under cover to the Stockholm suburb Bromma, where he was living with a friend. The police officer managed to get into my father's house and meet with him and his friend; in the report he wrote that the two men weren't German-friendly whatever else they were. In fact to his mind they seemed left-wing in their views.

My father had told him that the meetings at his office were to listen to the BBC and discuss the war in a group comprised of refugees and friends. This was all news to me.

I've tried to find out what that was. A centre for aid to refugees was situated in the Old Town; a voluntary activity set up by mainly left leaning people, of which at least one was my father's close friend. The activity that my father was doing and which the Secret Service writes about had perhaps something to do with that. These two activities were happening in the same neighbourhood. I do not know. My father never mentioned it.

The information from the files gave me new things to think about, as did most things in this story. I tried to find answers but found only new loose ends.

New York 1994

When you meet relatives that you've never met before and will perhaps never meet again, there's a sort of belonging: and you sit there, as if you have never done anything else, even if it is just half an hour in the middle of your life.

I thought it would be difficult to recognize him.

I was in New York for only two days, for meetings at the UN, but had taken the time to look in the telephone directory for a Stephan Kahn. My father had so many cousins, not least in the U.S., that I had never had met. The book was packed with Kahns, and yet I managed to find him after a couple of tries.

'Of course you're right! I'm your father's cousin!' he said in the most natural voice when I called him, and we decided to meet.

It wasn't difficult finding him at the far end of the Mediterranean-style diner at the bottom of Beekman Tower close to the UN building. I don't know if it was the familiar eyes or the way he flirted with the waitress, but I knew at once that this was him. He was humble and modest and made the staff feel beautiful and meaningful.

'The weather's going to be great this weekend, your boyfriend really has something to look forward to!' he smiled as he looked the dark waitress up and down, but warmly. 'What do you think me and my young cousin from overseas should have?' And then he began to talk to me, very present looking at me all the time except when the waitress was near, not about his own life as the manager of a big tobacco company in the US, but about my part of the family.

'I remember your father's father, Sigmund. He was a ladies' man: I think he had other children outside his marriage than you lot here and there. You look like him. Helmut, your father, was sort of the same; the women fell for the eyes and his way of telling stories.' He hesitated for a while as if he waited for a reply and just as I was to say something he continued.

"That was true of them both. Yeah, I think it was that: it didn't matter that Aga was big, and stout. He was called Aga wasn't he? You may not remember, but he looked like Aga Khan, the playboy. I mostly met him when we were young, down in the south of Germany. He went hiking with another cousin… oh we were a big family; all the cousins used to know each other so well then, there were so many of us and there was always somebody to play with.'

His eyes were looking inward, focused on the past – I could tell he was back there, reliving it all. Then he was present again.

'The last time I saw Helmut was when we were in our twenties; maybe he calmed down.'

I tried to protest, to say that he didn't ever calm down, not in that respect anyhow, but I had begun to eat the pastry that he and the waitress had recommended, crispy with apple in it, and could only make a snort as an answer before he began again.

'I remember Sigmund's wife Emmy. She was beautiful, grand, and rather imperious; but she cared about us children. It must be sixty years since I saw her… I'm sad to think that I won't meet her again. I understand that she is gone too now?' For a short moment he was quiet as he waited for me to confirm what he'd said: I nodded. He sighed. 'I know nothing about your mother. I never met her. Pity. Is she alive?'

I shook my head.

'What was her name?"

'Anne-Marie.'

'Was she German?'

'No, Swedish.'

'Jewish?'

I swallowed. 'No, she wasn't. Well… to some degree, but her father, my maternal grandfather, he was on the other side… I don't know how to put it.'

I suddenly hesitated, unsure about how to present my mother and her family. Why? Was there something that should be concealed and not said? Was I ashamed, or did I want to tell it as a funny anecdote? I had never before been confronted with the matter so openly.

'Really? Indeed.' Stephan quietly noted what I'd said, paused briefly, looked at me again with those big brown eyes and then continued.

'I also have to tell you about the war, about the camps.'

What did he know about that part of the story? My purpose in meeting Stephan was merely to establish a contact with the American part of the family, all the cousins my father had told me about and of whom I had only met one or two. He sat there and poured out details I had never known. All the time concentrating on me except when the waitress came by or stood nearby.

'You know I came to the US in the mid-thirties, years before anyone else from the family, and I joined the army at the beginning of the war. I was only just twenty, and I was with the first American troops that went to Germany when the war was coming to an end after the D-day invasion. It felt strange: the Germany of my childhood... it was terrible to be there and meet all those people, the victims and the offenders. They were all tired... they were all victims in a way – all happy that it had come to an end. I became a translator and so I came to know more than most. We went to Bergen-Belsen... well, the British were there first, but we arrived soon after them. You have probably heard the stories? They're true. It was just like that: no colours, only different shades of grey and so damn terrible, just anguished misery everywhere. People were lying dead or almost dead all over. A few were stumbling around. The stink you can't imagine... it was all so alien and unreal. We couldn't understand. We wanted to help everyone. I looked at the lists of the dead. The Nazis were orderly when it came to registers. I looked to see if I could find any relatives. And then I saw my uncle Karl's name; Karl was married to my father's and your grandfather's little sister, he worked as a psychoanalyst. Have you heard of him?' I nodded.' But I found no one else; no other relatives, not even Karl's wife or children, my cousins. There I was, not knowing what could have happened to them.'

His speech was very much to the point, very focussed, and I could only hum for my answer. The way it is at the dentist's. He talked and I could only sit there, numb.

There was no time for much more. I had to hurry to an important meeting and he to something else.

The goodbye was short, and I made my way out into the New York traffic. The sun was shining over the UN, where I was supposed to go back to a meeting about the environment, sustainable development and the future of the planet, and where I had to learn to listen to other countries. I didn't manage to go directly there.

Quickly crossing 1st Avenue in-between a small truck and a yellow cab, I felt choked; I just had to get through all the thoughts overwhelming me. Some of the drivers opened their windows and yelled, but I was so filled up with the images of the past that my recent conversation had evoked that the New York reality became a backdrop. The magnolias were in full bloom, but I didn't see them anymore.

I went into a small department store, remembering that there was something I needed to buy - but when I got in there, I had forgotten what it was.

I couldn't concentrate, however hard I tried. I had known already that Karl had died in that camp, but the way that Stephan told me about it had made it all come to life, full of smells and images.

But it was also then I realized that I knew nothing.

Stockholm 1990

The Swedish authorities had prevented my great uncle Karl from establishing his life in Sweden. It was there in black and white in the Swedish newspaper from 1933, *Nya Dagligt Allehanda*.

My father had never told me that.

I had gone to the newspaper department of the Stockholm City Library in Hagagatan – the old reading machines were lined up. Some of it was on microfilm; other material could be handed out in print on a short loan to be carefully read on-site.

People sat making painstaking notes with small pencils, determined, concentrated without showing what they were doing there: looking for material for an essay or an exam; reading about relatives from the past, what their parents had done and not told them, why and how people had died, great and small, sensitive, intimate or just boring. They had put fruit and thermos bottles on one side very neatly, and just sat quietly and wrote in their notebooks.

I had come because I wanted to read what my maternal grandfather Sven had written about the court case in Germany concerning the fire at the Reichstag in 1933.

I wanted to know more about this grandfather and what it really meant that he was supporting the other side, the wrong side. He was the only Swede covering the case against the suspected arsonist Manfred van der Lubbe, in person from the courts in Berlin and Leipzig. In other European countries this was first page material.

Granddad was an attorney in Umeå in northern Sweden and had been a conservative, but this year, he was seriously considering whether he would side with the new, the forceful and determined men who had taken power in Germany and showed no softness in the fight against bolshevism, which was very important to Sven, and no remorse in fighting what they considered other weaknesses. This same year he had been hired by the *Nya Dagligt Allehanda* to cover the most important case at that time. He wrote roughly one article a week, sometimes more. He had been allowed to meet the accused arsonist van der Lubbe in his cell, and wrote a lot about his perceptions of him and his character. He even pretended that there was new evidence to be found, he had talked to van der Lubbe in his cell. The entire autumn of 1933 he obviously went back and forth to Germany from his base in northern Sweden.

I tried to focus on my reading but my concentration dropped for a minute and my eyes flickered around over the ink. I rubbed them, not knowing whether I should call it a day or not. Hungry, I began peeling the orange I had brought, trying not to let anyone see it, and not stain the paper or the reading machine. I ate slowly and imagined my very tall and very bald grandfather, in search of the German spirit, wanting to take part and still trying to be objective in what he wrote.

I ate segment after segment of the orange and finally decided to leave; there was no more to read. I collected my notes and before I went to hand back what I had borrowed I gave the newspaper a final glance.

Then I happened to look at the opposite side of the same spread: a psychoanalyst was not going to be allowed to live in Sweden. I looked closer.

The psychoanalyst they were writing about was my father's uncle Karl.

I sat down again. The article was full of information. There was a picture of this uncle with a sharp, slightly bent nose; he looked focused and relaxed. Imagine seeing this here!

I had never seen a photo of him before, so I concentrated on that first: then I started reading.

In the spring of 1933 he was invited to lecture about psychoanalysis in Stockholm. The Royal Medical Board was asked for their views on whether he should be given permission to do so or not and if he would be allowed to be a doctor practising psychoanalysis on Swedish patients. The answer was a long time coming.

It's All Coming Back

Here it was in black and white: he was welcome to lecture but they could not allow him to practise as a doctor. But he wanted to do exactly that. So he decided to go on, to Amsterdam, where he was also invited, instead. He talked of America, that was where he really wanted to go, but Holland was an acceptable option for him. He seemed calm and content even though he could not be near his relatives in Stockholm.

I was puzzled and angry. My father had never said anything at all about his Uncle Karl coming to Stockholm. Dad had often spoken about Karl; he had said that he'd learnt a lot from him, and years later he had told me several times what had happened; Dad claimed that he himself had played a role in helping to rescue some of the family from the camps and yet he'd said nothing about any possibility of Karl's family coming to Stockholm a decade earlier.

Why had he never told me this about Karl in Stockholm?

I headed home in the slush, past where the Metropol restaurant used to be; now it's the Hard Rock Café.

Had Karl really been in Stockholm? Did they sit there in that restaurant, as it was then, talking about the Royal Medical Board while eating herring and cheese and butter? Did they talk about how Sweden treated the Jews, how Germany had become what it was? I turned down Sveavägen past the City Library and the Grand cinema. All those things that were new and at the height of fashion in 1933. Swedish policies were cowardly then.

The ground rocked under my feet: I suddenly didn't know what all those stories I had heard over the years were really worth – so many questions were buzzing around in my head: didn't they understand anything in 1933? Should they have understood?

And the most important question: did the authorities stop him because he was Jewish? Later in the thirties they stopped Jewish doctors from practising in Sweden: a dark chapter in our history. Perhaps they had already started that kind of reasoning in 1933. Nothing was said about that.

My two relatives were on the two opposite pages of the newspaper: one of them tried to find the great, the new and Germanic while the other was fleeing from the same reality.

I went down Sveavägen, decisively, measured, without caring about the people around me. I bumped into some, and finally went down to the tube.

Stockholm 1967

My uncle and aunt were coming to visit in the summer.

I still lived with my parents in their small house in a Stockholm suburb, where we had lived since 1951. We seldom had any guests, sometime an English cousin or two came to stay for a while, and once a year or so my mother's aunt had come from Germany. I remember that she and my father had talked all night. I think she was the only one in her family who he really liked.

My mother on the other hand loved his family, all of them. That was why we went to England so often.

We seldom saw her brother, my uncle Björn who lived in London, but now he was coming here. Their visit was decided on short notice, and then, very quickly, we all ended up in our small garden.

This was where my father had his black and red currant bushes and his peach tree which was unique at our latitude and which he pollinated himself with a small brush, and the small Hillman car, which my mother had smashed on both sides. She was the one who drove, I never saw him driving, but I heard he had driven a lot in his youth. Of course, there were also all the cats.

So, Björn arrived with his wife Lolo and we all sat in our garden, he with his baldhead and peering big brown eyes. I learnt then that Lolo was also Jewish, which I had never known before. I don't know why my father and Björn never really got close; they could have. Perhaps they both wanted to have the upper hand and be the one to lecture everyone else, when they met. I did learn that he had been a die-hard communist in his younger years; that he had worked for the youth league and the newspaper, but had changed his views as the war grew closer. He had then fled his party, left his first wife and his son and gone to England to work for the Swedish radio.

Jon Kahn

Now he was talking about Biafra. He was very convinced, he said, that the Biafrans were right to break out of Nigeria – and he had even met Ojukwu. He talked at length about the famine, and the injustices that were being carried out. I remember I was very impressed by his clear stance, and I agreed with him: I, too, cared about what happened to minorities.

I listened to him that time as I had done when we had met before.

He often talked about his foreign travels for Swedish newspapers, and I remember being impressed by his passport so full of stamps.

I was myself very engaged by what was happening in Biafra at the time.

My interest in politics started early. In 1962 I walked in my first Anti-apartheid demonstration in Trafalgar Square with an English second cousin on my father's side of the family. By 1967 I had been rallying against the US war in Vietnam for a couple of years. I don't know today if it was right to support Biafra or not, but it definitively felt like the right stand then.

I don't know if I got my interest in politics from my parents.

On my mother's side of the family, they leaned more to the right than to the left. But there were also some liberals there. My mother's sister's husband was a very engaging and social man who was working for the Union of Industries, and we he and I had our arguments over Vietnam. My mother's other uncle was a military man who had funny caricatures of right and centre party politicians hanging in the privy.

My mother was a liberal, a member of a party and all. She thought her family conservative.

My father was very hard to get a handle on when it came to politics. I remember following him to the ballot box when Sweden had a referendum on shifting to driving on the right side of the road. I must have been seven at the time. He cast a blank ballot paper, which I at the time found extremely strange. He said he sometimes decided whom to vote for on his way to the school where the ballot box was put.

It's All Coming Back

By the time that Uncle Björn came to visit, all my friends were socialists and I joined them when it came to what happened in the world. I was more critical to central state power however, and became a centrist. At that time, I didn't know all about that party's pre-war history and some strange racist beliefs. That summer day I made connections, and joined the dots about family and politics, while eating sandwiches and drinking coffee. But it was also a day that really set me thinking about politics, and soon after, I was a member of the centre party.

Heilbronn 1962

You could see it in her eyes that strong feelings were welling up when she started to tell us. She had to recall memories that were so strong that her body was numbed, that her senses had to be partly shut off in order for her to make room for her story. The story that came from her guts, close to the heart. Every detail so strong that she had to catch her breath before telling it. She stood there straight, and we listened.

She was thin with lank black hair and she wore something that looked like a housecoat. She didn't sit down. She stood, full of pain, by the old petrol station, reliving it all, telling us how it really was, us strangers. She had stayed in the same neighbourhood in spite of all that had happened, stayed so that the memories would remind her every time she went shopping in town. She was the only one they could think of who really had taken part.

We had wandered around Heilbronn all day, and my father had kept looking for something, something that would remind him of his childhood. He never lived there, but held it very dear as it was his father's birthplace and where all his uncles and cousins lived. But hardly anything seemed to be as before.

We found an old factory, closed and in a neglected state. Helmut got out of the car to see if he could pick up any faint smell of tobacco, if he could somehow sense if this was where his uncles had had their cigar business, if this was the shop that had been guarded by the seven boxer dogs that he used to love. He didn't know if it was: he never found out.

We had almost forced him to come with us to his father's homeland.

Dad was not the sentimental type; he didn't want to relive. He hardly wanted to know. What had been had been, full stop – at least when it came to Germany. Or rather of his birthplace Berlin or of Heilbronn. Or when it came to the war.

On the other hand, when we were out travelling, my parents sometimes did what they called 'to Mona Lisa': after the painting was stolen, and for many years afterwards, everyone went to the spot at the Louvre where the Mona Lisa used to hang, and look at the empty space. So when we came to a place where they, or somebody else for that matter, had had intense experiences in the past, they would find a pathway to the past, kiss as they did then, listen to the sea as they did then, taste Danish sandwiches as they did then. They *Mona Lisa'd*. My sister and me didn't understand and didn't feel involved.

But this desire of my father's to recapture a sense of the past was never applicable to the war or to his childhood. That was too sensitive, too difficult, and just too hard on him in some strange way.

He didn't want to go to Heilbronn at first but somehow especially us kids made him go in order for him to tell us something more about the family history. I was thirteen and we had gone, my parents, my two sisters and me, in our old Volkswagen van with the spare tyre in front, on a horror ride by Autobahn from Stockholm. Outside Hamburg we had a flat tyre - mother, driving, managed to avoid crashing by the skin of her teeth - but that spare jumped loose and rolled away over the Autobahn, miraculously without hurting anyone. Dad was quiet during this frightening episode, remarkably enough; usually he yelled and cursed about her driving. But finally we arrived in Heilbronn: his father's Heilbronn.

When we had had a look at that factory, we were all getting tired and didn't know what to do or where to go next. We went to fill up the car and my father told the garage attendant what we were doing there. And that is when he called an old lady living nearby, and that is when she stood there, shaking as her story slowly developed.

'We were at school, and then the alarm went off. "Run to your homes!" the teacher said, but no one made it, and that was just as well.

A friend and I ran past the indoor swimming pool and tried to find refuge there. Maybe the water could save us, maybe we could dive in when the worst came.

But the big pool was empty when we got there. We climbed down and sat together in a corner at the bottom with blue tiles all around us and held hands, hard, hard. We didn't know if anybody would be injured or even die: we were very frightened, scared to the bone. As a child one does not understand very much, life is so obvious, but we understood that this could mean the end, that this was the judgement – our hearts were pounding and it hurt.

The roar and the rumbling came closer and all of a sudden it was extremely light and very, very hot. The entire building came crashing down. I don't know if we screamed or were quiet, just that we kept holding hands. Then it was all black and filled with soot and planks and bricks and we just huddled amidst the debris for hours.

Finally we dared to get up and out and it was all quiet – no birds flying, no leaves on the trees, no people, only houses in ruins everywhere. We couldn't find our way. We used to play there every day, but nothing was as before – anyone who wasn't there can't imagine it. It took a long time before we found anyone to talk to and we didn't know if it was a friend or foe. There was no one, do you understand?'

Now she seemed to be accusing us.

'Nobody, nobody!' she repeated, 'Finally I managed to get to some aunts outside the town, and there I stayed. It was worst for those that died, but it was not easy to survive either – perhaps you can't imagine.'

At this point she began to cry for the first time and mother tried to hold her but she didn't want that.

'Why this havoc? They could have managed to win the war anyhow, why kill all those people?'

Her voice had risen to a falsetto but then she went quiet. Pulling her coat closely around her body she suddenly laughed and asked if she could go home. My parents wanted to know how she had managed during the rest of the war but she made it clear that she had told us what she was able to, and wanted no more of this.

When we arrived back in Sweden, Dad settled into the withdrawn state that he always adopted when only the immediate family was present. It wasn't that he didn't want us around, but he was deeply involved in his own activities and his own mind. He often spent time in the garden or the basement.

When you entered our untidy house by the basement you entered a different world. A damp smell, rich with old mortar and cat pee, old preserved vegetables, drying laundry, musty books, coke for the boiler and the warm steamy air from all the fish tanks. It all mixed, and today when I open my old books I can still catch the odd mixture of cats and tobacco smoke. Sometimes there was a flood in the basement after a sudden rain; it occurred because roots from the peach tree had found their way under the house, blocking the sewage pipe, and the effluent added an extra spice to the odours down below. The basement was his territory. It was full of lumber and history. Sometimes we weren't allowed down there. It was when a woman was involved, I believe. He was always hunting.

I don't know what the women saw in him. He was very fat and walked with a stick because of an accident in the late 40's: perhaps it was his eyes that attracted them, the gap between his front teeth, or his way of telling stories.

What was he running away from? Did he have any dreams left, any hope? Upstairs he had a study smelling of cigars. There he rested on his knees in a chair, with his arms on big books, and combed his moustache. Then he was in another world.

I remember him best raking mosquito larvae for his fish to eat out of our small lake; then he was engaged and active and did not hesitate even if a strand or two of reed was in the way. I used to wish that he had been that way more often. Perhaps that ardour was what the women were allowed to see.

We lived in the southern suburbs of Stockholm, but my parents were born elsewhere and always longed to be in other places, not Germany or northern Sweden where they were born - where we had to drag them - they longed for England and Denmark.

It's All Coming Back

Well, we passed Germany at times and Dad got out of the carriage at Hamburger Hauptbahnhof to smell trains and city and sauerkraut and Weißbier and German cakes; and he listened to the loudspeakers - something about them attracted him. He spoke to anybody on the platform, and if they asked if he came from Berlin he smiled and said, *Ne das war da schon seit länge.* A long time ago. He never did go to Berlin though. Heilbronn was more important to him, probably because of all his older cousins who taught him things about life there, how to walk long distances, drink beer and make passes at girls. Heilbronn was one of the cities that were entirely destroyed at the end of the war by the allied carpet-bombing. Why? The war was closing in.

That day in Heilbronn I saw my father first trying to comfort us and the lady, and then when we were alone he showed that he thought it was all hopeless, how disillusioned he was. After her story and a stop at a Bäckerei for some strudels from his youth - there were none of course but there was something close - we went back to the factory.

It was one of the very few buildings that had been saved, but not as a Jewish family-owned factory; it was taken over, placed in German hands, Aryanised. Nowadays it is a cultural centre called Zigarre, but when we were there it was still in a mess.

'Evil doesn't show on the façade.' That was one of the things the old lady in Heilbronn had also said. 'We weren't Nazis: why didn't they just kill them?'

In the evening Dad talked for a long time about collaborators, and who was to blame for what, and said that we all shared some part of the guilt. We children didn't understand much more than the scared eyes of the woman.

Uppland, north of Stockholm 1955

My grandfather Sven asked me to come and hug him. As if I would have wanted to. As if I should have had those sorts of feelings towards him. I seldom hugged anybody, and he was no exception. I mean, he was hardly there, close by, during my childhood. We rarely met those older relatives.

My friends met their grandparents on both sides often; I heard them speaking about car trips to the parents of their parents, about coffee parties and visits to amusement parks.

I didn't meet my grandmother Emmy in England until I was starting school. We had those two: Sven my mother's father, and Emmy my father's mother.

We met Sven a few times. He gallantly invited all our cousins and us to his birthdays at the big Bern's restaurant in Stockholm a couple of times; it was grand. I remember Caterina Valente or Max Hansen performing in the big hall while we had a three-course meal. But one did not get close to him; there were many people round the table.

Once we met at the Copenhagen train station: he was wearing a brown beret, a long coat and a Swedish flag on his blazer. There was a picture taken outside the station of us all, Grandfather almost two metres tall and myself as a child of five or six, my older sister, Sven's new wife and my mother and father. In fact, most of us had berets on. He looked like a giant compared to us. Very pleased with the situation, it seemed.

A couple of times we went to visit him in Umeå and once a year he came to Stockholm.

This time, I had come to Uppland with my mother to visit him. Mummy, who was always so volatile, always wanting to move on to something else, would take the time to see her old father and wanted us to come along.

She was the professional woman who also tried to be a housewife, as well as taking an active part in all sorts of organizations: who also wished to be on speaking terms with her family, both close and distant. So she brought us along. She knew that Sven wanted to meet his grandchildren, that he thought he had neglected us, that he wanted to make up for something, and yet he was so ill by then that he mainly only had the strength to care about himself. And we became 'an apron' for her feelings; an excuse to go there, or something to talk about with him, or for them to talk to.

At first I was happy. In our world with no TV and no car there were not so many excursions except the obligatory mushroom picking with the family at the weekends (a very Swedish pastime). But by the time we arrived at the pension where he was on rehabilitation in Upplands-Bro it was not fun anymore. We had gone by bus, train and bus again.

Dad wasn't with us: I don't know if it was Granddad who asked that only Mummy should come, or Dad who did not want to go.

Outdoors it was just as grey, and there was nowhere to play. We went for a short walk with him. He needed it, he said. He wanted to talk to me but didn't quite know what to say to a six year old. He had a suit of grey wool, and I remember the damp smell. Now he wanted a hug, to hold me. He probably knew that he would die soon. We had nothing to say to each other and he did not even have the compulsory five-crown coin. He received no hug that time. I do not remember ever giving him one.

I knew nothing then of the background to his story, I just felt a distance. I sensed that my grandfather was not like other children's – I simply had not sat in his lap often enough when I was a small child. And yet I now understand that he liked children, liked to teach and talk to children. But I was not an easy one. I do not know if it was his fault or mine.

Clymping, near Littlehampton, Sussex 1955

Seeing my grandmother Emmy for the first time was quite an experience.

My older sister and I were six and eight when our family travelled by train to Esbjerg in Denmark, then by boat to Harwich and on by train to Liverpool Street Station in London, where Emmy met us with a car.

She was short and rotund with red hair and wore heavy make-up and strong perfume. She had a bracelet with lots of jangling discs hanging from it.

I remember driving down to Sussex in the old car with seats in the back opposite each other, and the roads were green all around, branches of trees hanging over the narrow way almost for the whole route, and the landscape so hilly that the perspective looking back through the rear window changed all the time; you did not know what was close-by or further off. Granny talked all the time, warm, overly friendly, strange.

And the place she lived, Bailiffscourt, the hotel she ran in a tiny village in West Sussex called Clymping, right by the sea, was magical.

Emmy and her second husband, Hans, had taken on this extraordinary property after the war, with no experience of running a hotel, but with a certainty that they could make it work.

The main building was a quadrangle of golden stone, big stones brought from France, built around a central courtyard. Dotted around the sprawling green grounds there were walled gardens, and many authentic or semi-authentic mediaeval buildings, which had been transported to this new site from their original locations in the 1920s. The place had been standing empty when my grandmother and Hans took it on in 1947 – and now, the wear and tear of misuse for so long was really beginning to show. The tennis courts, tucked away off the wooded driveway, were, like the beach hut on the shore nearby, in a terrible state, but they were good for advertising.

In the grounds, there was also an old chapel, of truly Norman origin, which had stood there since the days of William The Conqueror. Inside it, the ashes of Lord and Lady Moyne, who built the place, were kept. Lord Moyne had been a British diplomat killed by Jewish terrorists in Palestine before it was Israel. Bailiffscourt was the dream and creation of his inspired second wife. And now they were resting there, after an exciting life.

I knew nothing of this then. I knew nothing of politics. I liked standing in the wind and flying a kite with my father on the beach and watching the horses in the stable, and playing by the billiards table and trying the bicycles without a foot break. I tried them but fell over because I was used to quite another bike.

'I never had the opportunity to meet your grandfather, Anne-Marie's father. They haven't spoken too much about him; your parents I mean. Is he nice?'

She had followed my sister and me down to the beach-hut by the choppy waters of the Channel. Those were the days when she still managed to walk the few hundred yards down across the field to the beach and feel the salty winds coming in. She didn't dare step on the stones that formed a slope down to the waves.

The shingle began at the top of the beach closest to the farmland that lay between the sea and the hotel. The stones moved when you stepped on them with a clattering, tapping, and clopping sound and also moved according to the weather, the currents and the phases of the moon.

The sea didn't come up onto the fields except during the November storms, and I have never been there at that time of year to experience how it was when the sea invaded the land.

A very poor concrete wall had been built for protection between the farmland and the beach, and the beach hut was placed right there, on that wall. The hut was of old masonry and had a straw roof that had not been well kept. The interior was a mess; none of the staff ever thought it worthwhile to go down and tidy it and they knew that Emmy wouldn't look.

But she did that day, because of us. The hut and the wall were not large, but for a six-year-old they seemed huge.

The tide was something quite astonishing for me. The sea going kilometres out and leaving a sandy beach with crabs and the especially fascinating sand worms with their coiling heaps of sand poo, and the barnacles who waved their fronds to get food. And then the salty, frothy water coming in at full speed and rushing up to the beach hut, stopping at that section of flint and chalk and shells which moved under your feet, and which Granny was scared to put her small feet on.

It was my first time in England. It was the first time I met my granny, my father's mother, in front of whom he changed character and was, all of a sudden, timid. She fascinated me. Not just the place she lived in and managed, this old, mediaeval-looking hotel with posh guests and luxurious food. It was her whole presence. And she hugged us, something I was not very used to. And she told people what to do, not my father so much, but everybody else. She was quite different from anything I had seen so far.

So: my grandmother had followed us to the beach. I don't know what our parents were doing, but she followed us, and chattered away in a very strange Swedish. I didn't realize then that this was the Swedish that she had learned over 20 years before, and she hadn't used it for that long either.

She asked us about my mother's father while trying to find somewhere for us, or rather for her, to sit on in the jammed heap of lumber, old stools and umbrellas and all sorts of unsorted stuff that cluttered up the small hut.

How could we say anything to her about him? We did not see much of him either. And he was so different from her. Another distance, another kind of dignity, hers very close and his more reserved.

'There's something I've never understood, or they say I would never understand, about his politics.' She continued, pressing us with careful insistence for a response. 'I don't know what that could be. The poor man: he lost his first wife, Anne-Marie's mother, and everything.'

We had not thought much about our grandmother on my mother's side. She was dead, and just a picture in a frame. And we did not know anything about Emmy's first husband Sigmund, our grandfather, either. He wasn't even a picture.

'I'm so sorry I haven't got to know your grandpa, your *morfar*. I'll ask Anne-Marie if he can come here. With the hotel to run, I can't go to Sweden. It's a pity.'

'Ask Mummy and Daddy,' I –' or was it my sister – suggested. And then we'd had enough. 'I like the wind!' I said. 'Granny, can we go fossil hunting? Daddy has shown me how to do it!'

I ran off down the stones and out on to the long stretch of sand that was growing bigger and bigger as the water withdrew, the sea soon far out but yet still present in the drops of salt coming up from the waves with the wind. It was June, but a strong breeze blew across the Channel towards us.

'Come on!' I shouted, while Granny and my sister stood above the rocks and looked utterly helpless.

I ran around exploring the rock pools and the sand for strange stones where traces of a long distant past could be seen, while Emmy wondered if she should have brought us down to the shore. Her shoes, almost always too small and frail but very pretty, didn't do well in the salt and wet sand.

The beach was very good for marketing the hotel but she knew nothing of it and neither did her husband, but they did tell potential guests about it, hoping they wouldn't try to explore it for themselves.

Hans was an Austrian who had been confined to a wheelchair for many years, an old injury from the first war finally catching up with him. I knew nothing of family, and was not interested. It seemed to me that my grandmother knew too little about children. She sometimes treated us as if we were very small, giving us shovels and buckets for the sand, and sometimes she asked us grown-up questions like these about my mother's father. I wanted to play, and she asked us impossible questions. And when we knew nothing, and she found the beach-hut's interior impossible for her to get in order she wanted to go back to the hotel. We wanted to play, but she insisted and tried to lead us on by talking about food.

That was another amazing thing about that place, all the food: cakes, sandwiches, Knickerbocker glories and the rest. And we ate and we grew. It was, after all, more amazing than knowing about my grandfather. And the grandfather in Sweden had nothing to do with the English family. It didn't matter how much my granny tried to connect it all.

We went there at least every second year after this first time, I guess it was because we were not so rich that it wasn't more often. Emmy loved having family around. When she was eighty she closed the hotel for Christmas and invited all her children and grandchildren and her brother's children and grandchildren. We met a lot of other relatives at Bailiffscourt from France, USA or Israel. That is how I saw them, as relatives and not as Jewish refugees or migrants.

II.
A trembling affair

Bromma, outside Stockholm September 1945

Summer is over and war is ending, now not only in Europe. Helmut is reading the paper: the Japanese have signed surrender documents aboard the USS Missouri in the Pacific. He is relieved. It's over; it's finally over. Now it's time to decide about the future.

For the last six years, or perhaps even ten, a person engaged in politics like he is has had to live from hand to mouth or from day to day, reading the news and then deciding how to act upon it; if it would be best to flee, hide or involve yourself.

Peace has come at last, but only because the atomic bomb was dropped, and he is happy and sad at the same time. Something entirely new has come to the world, but he hasn't yet decided if it is good or bad. He realizes that he has become disillusioned: by the war or by growing older, he isn't sure. He isn't that old, just passed thirty, but a lot of experience has been packed into that relatively short time.

Everybody is looking for somebody to hold on to, for old and new friends; so many at the end of the war realize that they need someone. Perhaps he should as well? He has luck with girls, but realizes that the right ones perhaps won't want to settle down with him. Or maybe his obesity might be an issue.

Helmut looks up from the paper. Sitting in his house in Ängby in the south of Bromma with a lit cigar in hand and a cup of coffee, and a cat at his leg waiting for a cuddle, it's clear that he somehow has to build a new life, but he isn't quite sure how. The fellow from Berlin he has shared the house with during the last years of the war will look after his own concerns now; his Estonian wife and their children will be his only priority. Helmut had met this man in a bar one evening, and they had immediately realized that they were on the same wavelength. Two Helmuts in Stockholm but born in Berlin, with a similar taste for political reasoning; open to all ideas but still much more left than right; both with a love of good cigars and for women.

So Helmut, who had thought already about moving out of the inner city had decided there and then to exchange his flat for a house in Bromma, and invited his new friend to live there with him. And they had had a wonderful time during the war there, growing vegetables and raising rabbits to eat, because everything was rationed. Now this has to end.

His thinking is interrupted when one of his friend's children comes in with a letter.

'Aga, it's for you, from Holland. Can I have the stamp?'

'Indeed you can; just let me read first.'

As he opens it quickly, he realizes that this too is a post-war thing – letters come once more from where they are stamped, not, as they have done for the past few years, having to go around the world to be delivered, if they reached the addressee at all. He reads and he can feel there is a tear welling in his eye. How silly; he has been overcome by feelings all by a sudden. Not like him. He looks up to see if anyone can see him.

The letter is from his cousin, Eva. He has already heard that she and her mother Lins are back in Amsterdam, although not with her father, Uncle Karl, and he has sent them a package, with no idea if it would reach them or not. He had been very worried about what happened to them during the war. Now here is a letter; she is alive and back in Amsterdam and his parcel reached its destination. The address he had written was enough. His eyes are wide open and he lights a cigarette. He reads it trembling. It has a former address of theirs in it, perhaps they live with friends there now, the house they lived in before the deportation probably being occupied by someone else.

Amsterdam 1.9.45
Grevelingenstraat 22.

Lieber Helmut,

Your consignment is still partially unopened in the room but I must say at once how much we have rejoiced. We have had several packages from America in the last fortnight but yours is the first that we have been truly happy about. It has been put together with so much love; there is nothing there that we cannot use at once, nothing that we have not longed for. And we have especially relished the groceries.

KLM came to the house with it all, mother went down and, all upset, called for help as she could not drag it upstairs herself. Though Suse was out, we started unpacking at once contrary to our rule that the three of us should unpack all things together. For instance just yesterday we had talked of asking someone for a wool blanket.

Do you have a wife after all? The things have been selected with such understanding - a man could hardly have done that alone. (You should see mother all dressed up in Swedish clothes!)

Where did you get our address? Have you heard about us from London? I recently made a summary of our fate over the last four years, I have no carbon copy left, which is why I write so superfluously about that time as I do not want to talk about these things again. You probably know that Father, mother and I were in Bergen-Belsen, that father died 27 January, that Suse lived in disguise here, with false papers as a servant girl with foreign people. Unfortunately she was in Arnhem, the city that was almost completely devastated and she had many terrible experiences there. Paulus fled and came via Belgium, France and Spain (as a Dutch worker) to Palestine. Although he is only nineteen, he seems to have become very mature and grown up.

It is funny, but with your parcel in the room, I can imagine the two of us on a bus and you showing me London. That was ten years ago! Sometimes I have problems being kind to people, but the things you have sent have touched me to the core and I know that bonds that were once forged between us cannot be broken entirely even though we haven't met for years.

Hearty greetings, write to us and tell us about your life and tell me if you wish to know more.

Viel Liebes,

Dein Eva

The above is written on a typewriter, the rest of the letter below in ink on the same piece of paper.

Dear Helmut,

I cannot express in words what I felt when I unpacked your parcel. You should have seen how we enjoyed it; you made us happy. It was as if it came from heaven. Sometimes you get sentimental feelings when receiving something, but that was not the case with what you sent. It is put together with so much wisdom. We have often talked about you and how you made it through the war. You were close to Karl's heart and he liked you very much. I wrote you some letters earlier from Holland and

> was worried when I did not get an answer. I will enjoy writing again to you and your family ...
>
> Lassen wir nochmals herzlich danken und grüßen
>
> Von deine
>
> Tante Lins

It's only when he finds himself sitting heavily back down again that he realises that he has been reading standing up. He stays still in the chair for a long while. Eventually, his friend who he has shared so much with during the past few years comes and asks if he's alright – he takes the letter proffered to him and reads it too, sighing.

'So much has happened during the years of war; people have been exposed to horror, killed, relocated,' his friend says. Helmut cannot find the right way to answer, he just snaps the letter and walks away and his friend taps his arm. 'Now it's time to get it all clear and find the guilty,' he says.

News of the atrocities in the concentration camps had begun to filter into Swedish households via the press. Helmut has feared the worst, even *known* inside, and still he is completely overwhelmed by the terror when he sees it as it has truly been.

But the autumn of 1945 is also a time when many people want to start anew, to build new lives from scratch with new partners. He does not yet know if that will happen to him.

Time flies that autumn when everything should be new and different but isn't really. At least he gets his business going fully again and he spends time looking for a flat and getting in contact with people from different backgrounds that have come to Sweden. He has a new girlfriend, a pretty girl born in Romania and adopted in Sweden. She has a slight handicap following the polio she suffered when she was younger. The relationship isn't really very sexual, it's more of a friendship, a connection. Will it be them? He isn't sure. He isn't sure of anything any longer.

Bromma, November 1945

Anne-Marie is in her best mood though it is cold, grey and misty in Stockholm. There is peace on earth and all that's old should be cleansed and put away – now the issue at stake is rebuilding. Rebuilding Europe, rebuilding relations, starting anew.

Soon she will be free from tuberculosis. Soon she will have finished her studies.

Throughout the entire damned wartime she has been studying and coughing, but now things are turning round. She is going for a couple of long cures over the winter, but she feels almost healed. It may be a hard few months, she knows that. But she has decided to make the best of it; things can only go up now.

While waiting for the next cure she works in Stockholm and lives with her sister Harriet and her family in the old vicarage in Bromma, a couple of miles west of the city centre, that Harriet's family have rented. She sits in her room wearing her nice dress made from parachute silk. That is the thing these days; to use war surplus material. She puts her hair up, hairpin after hairpin, and puts on a nice necklace. The record she has chosen is playing in the corner of the room, and she sings along to *Rum and Coca Cola*, dancing with her arms. Tonight, despite the rationing of food and liquor, they have been invited to a party! The event is being held by some friends of Harriet's and her husband, but she has been invited too this time, and she really wants to, especially as her sister has managed to get a baby-sitter; a baby-sitter other than her.

There are usually nice people at these parties, and she knows she will enjoy it – but she has no intention of forgetting her Norwegian fiancé. A nice and kind and slender boy with undulating hair, looking a bit like herself but not half as daring as she is. They have been together for quite a while and now he is very keen to take the next step. He hasn't proposed yet but it is implicit. He calls her 'my clover' and sends poetry books but she's not quite sure, she just can't be certain that she wants to get married, to share her whole life with him. The record has finished and the player crackles. The last hairpin is in her hand and Norway and young men are on her mind.

She is 28 now, and something has to get serious soon.

Helmut is still living in Ängby in south Bromma. He likes to have people around him, to sit through the night discussing politics and the war; he thrives on the intense discussions and detailed analyses.

There is a hatred of Nazism and a disappointment about socialism that unites them, but this is also a starting-point for new discussions. They had a séance of a sort yesterday and they had red wine and rabbit, just like they did during the war. Now he feels a slight hangover, the discussions have been intense: he rubs his eyes. There is a party again tonight. He cannot go on like this. He pours a glass of water and drinks it down in one gulp. He fills it up again and brushes his teeth, checks that he has combed back his hair so that it is as smooth as it can be. He lathers soap for his shave. The party is on and everyone will bring their ration of liquor and wine - alcohol has been rationed since the '20s but the hosts will provide food; you have to be a bit of a fixer to make good meals these days as everything is still rationed. But this family always serves good things to eat.

The host is a new friend of Helmut's. He works in film and has ideas for scripts that he would like to discuss. Maybe film could be his calling, Helmut muses; the old tobacco business is really paying nothing, and importing and selling tobacco is a no-go with the more rigorous state monopoly. Plus it's just no fun anymore. But he needs an income. He will be 32 soon and must work out what to do with his life; he feels great, but at this age you have to start planning your future. He knows nothing about what could turn up next.

He shaves carefully, takes a lot of after shave, dries himself, tucks a bandanna into his collar, and combs his hair better still, plastering it firmly down with the help of hair tonic.

It's All Coming Back

Arriving at the party he greets a girl named Harriet and her husband in the hallway - he has met them here before. Then Harriet's sister is introduced to him.

Her name is Anne-Marie and there is no doubting that this is a girl who attracts his interest. He straightens his back and puts on his best smile.

Anne-Marie is just as pleased with this new acquaintance, but they only have time to exchange a couple of words over a drink before they are seated at different ends of the table. This doesn't stop them from exchanging the occasional furtive glance and smile. After the meal they make sure to sit next to one another by the sparkling fire where some of the guests are gathered, singing. Both of them come to life with the wine and the song. He sings a popular tune, funny and nostalgic, and she recites some Norwegian poems that she has received from her fiancé, poems filled with nationalism and indignation over the German occupation but also effusion and warmth.

He looks at her with those deep brown eyes. When he smiles at her he shows the gap between his front teeth. Dark and hairy with his eyebrows almost growing into each other, big and fat, urbane and exciting. The combed-back hair exposes an already high hairline over his temples.

She laughs and her blue-greyish eyes glitter in her narrow face with the pronounced cheekbones, shown clearly as her long hair has been put up. As usual she is witty, knowledgeable, alert and keen and always on the run to something else, but this time she has merely to stay in the moment. By the end of the evening, it's only the two of them. Each is looking at nothing but the other. A kiss, nothing more, and they part.

Walking home between the houses in Ängby in the dark late autumn night, he is surprised with himself not having tried harder.

She writes to a friend the first thing the next day asking about what it is like to be intimate with a Jewish man. She hasn't experienced being close to a Jewish man, though she has been engaged eleven times. In the vicarage she sings while she is packing her case. She is heading for Gothenburg again. She looks for his address in the telephone directory.

She writes the name of the road in her distinct handwriting in her address book and draws a frame around it.

Gothenburg and Stockholm November and December 1945

This is the beginning of the first warless and still misty winter. People wake up and don't really know where they are; many have been relocated over and over. They listen to the noises around them and rub their eyes, expecting to recognize the well known; the family home, hear the usual wind and birds, see the sun rise where it always does. But in fact they are somewhere else and have to concentrate to understand where and if one can feel safe. Some look for the comfort of a partner near by, someone to reach out for and hold when it feels unsafe. But for many there is nobody there.

Anne-Marie and Helmut are now far apart, each dreaming of the other. Waking-up to a feeling of belonging together and yet being so far apart. They don't care so much about the weather this winter, they are heated up and worrying and full of desire.

He is still in the Ängby house but is preparing to move – there's a lot on his mind. His friend has found another place to live, and Helmut is returning to the city centre. He spends his time looking through the housing ads. Often Anne-Marie fills his thoughts; he hopes all the time that he'll hear from her.

She has left for Gothenburg; to get care for her tuberculosis, and to finally sit her exams after all the long war years filled with coughing and studying and being in sanatoriums. This big man she has met, that she's only really just got a glance of – the gap between his teeth, the joined eyebrows, the warm brown eyes that look so intensely at her – he fills her all up. She has nothing else on her mind, and very soon, yes, she writes him a letter:

> The Renström hospital, Gothenburg 25.11.45
>
> After for a week having fought with myself about how fit it would be for a young lady to, without further ado, write to a gentleman, I can no longer care for what is fit. I just have to send Winnie the Pooh to you...

And he replies fast:

> Ängby 2 December 1945... It is always a great pleasure when somebody you have been attached to does not give in to conventional feelings of inferiority, but is so uninhibitedly nice as the impulse may show. Therefore: Thank you!.. It was such a pity that we did not have the ability to meet once more here. If you get the opportunity to get up here, please call me. And write. If there is nothing to write about, write about that...

Anne-Marie now writes a long letter to Aga, she has already learnt this is his nickname, she starts with *Mon cher!* and ends with *So long!*

Christmas and New Year's Eve 1945 to 1946

There are no letters between December and January, or at least I haven't found any, so they must have been together then, probably in Stockholm and probably in his office.

They feel that their life together is more important than anything else and that not a moment can be missed and they abandon what they had planned for the days after Christmas so that they can be together. She of course has some obligations. Several Christmases now have been spent with her sister in Bromma. Her stepmother Siri, who she loved a lot, is no longer with them. Last Christmas the older woman had been in Saltsjöbaden, near Stockholm, recovering from a broken leg and from her life with Anne-Marie's father Sven. And then she had died there and then on her way from Saltsjöbaden to Harriet's place where Anne-Marie, Harriet, her husband and children were waiting for the Christmas party.

So yes, Anne-Marie has to go to Harriet's this year, for comfort, and also to remember Siri. They spend some time with Harriet's family and some with the friend he still is living with in Ängby and his family. But most of the time they are just focusing on each other, going for long walks, exploring each other's interests and habits, exploring each other's body.

The day before New Years Eve they are sitting in a restaurant in Kungsgatan, the street where seven months ago they had both celebrated the coming of peace, whilst being completely unaware of each other. There had been so much confetti, so many cars and people, *everybody*, it seemed, in fact, and they talked about it on the walk there.

When seated at their table, he points out to her which window he was in then and she, where she had walked. They've decided not to speak so much about family, to try to get to know each other first, but he is curious about her mother or rather her *mothers*, as she calls them both 'Mamma'. She has to tell him both how her own mother died and how Mamma Siri came into the family.

'It was a long time ago… I don't know how to put this,' and her long blond hair falls down over her face so that he can't see her eyes. He softly sweeps her locks back and looks at her in earnest. Holding her hand over the table, he offers her a cigarette.

'I think your two mothers are very important to you, so just tell me. I understand – don't feel you have to hide things from me, I want to hear everything.'

'Yes, yes, I will tell you, it'll take its time, and I don't remember it myself really… you know, I was only one and a half when she died, so I can only tell you what I've put together from bits and pieces told to me. They were strong and independent women, both of them, to begin with…'

Umeå 1919

'What I heard was that this: my second winter, was as cold as the winters we'd had the year before and all the years before that. It was March and I was 18 or 19 month old. A toddler. I try to picture it from my mother Laura's perspective, there in that small northern town by the river. The town where my father Sven was running the major law firm and was becoming renowned as somebody well known in society. Not only as a capable lawyer, but also as a man with strong, radical and – some thought – rather peculiar views. I'll tell you about that some other time. During a freezing winter like that, there was just as much activity on the river as in the town itself. But deep snow was everywhere, and it wasn't easy to be ill in that kind of weather. It wasn't easy to have five children. I was the youngest as you know.'

'Five?' Helmut asked.

'Yes; five. I had a beloved brother, who is gone now. Could we talk about him some other time?,' she says and her gaze flits away and she holds her hand to he head for a second. 'Don't let all my family stories spoil our love, please Helmut.'

'The other secrets will be kept for another time,' he agrees, touching her cheek, and she goes on.

'On the ice, Laura must have seen sledges, kick-sleds and skis, and on a cleared 'pitch' – you know, an acre from which all the snow has been swept from the frozen water – some boys were probably practising bandy, skating around with their curved sticks, hitting the red yarn ball…

*

A sledge was turning to and fro, trying to come up the riverbank. There was no risk that the undercurrents would be a threat to the ice; it was too thick. People were strolling along side by side, their hands in thick gloves or pushed into muffs. It was desperately cold, and breath streamed out like fog, but the sun had coaxed them to come out no matter how bitter the day was.

'Happy,' she sighed, looking down towards the ice. It could be so wonderfully bright up here she thought; at least on a sunny day at the beginning of March.

She couldn't stay in the house and keep away from the town, from life, not any longer, in this weather. So before long, she stepped cautiously out of the elegant red house, which was now theirs, and fluttered her eyes in the intense light.

She was ill; she had been in bed for a long time. Those dark, intense eyes could not focus. Her shoulders were bent forward; her entire small, soft, round body was tense. The long, dark hair was arranged in a knot and carefully pushed into a small, round fur hat. The cold filled her little nose and she felt her cheeks being chapped by the sun and the freezing air.

Laura was tired. She would be forty soon. She recognized that she had dedicated all her life to Sven, a capricious and unfathomable man. She could have done so much more than just having lived for him. Yet she had wanted him, longed for him, taken him back time after time.

She had followed him in her mind and in her life ever since they met that wonderful day by Lago Maggiore. They had gone travelling there at the same time. Sven: he had been so noticeable, so tall, so protective and so exciting.

And what had life given them? Five lovely children, of course; five wild children. But he hadn't changed.

She looked at the bustling people, at the bushes around the house where all the small birds had only had one thought in their heads: to be fed. Now she was frozen, and coughed so hard that it almost turned her stomach. She was terribly lonely. She had been lying on her sickbed, worrying about everything and yet without any possibility of doing anything, while the cold and the pneumonia had lingered.

Straightening up, she decided. She jumped over the snow bank that had piled up on the sidewalk and strode with decisive steps towards the town centre. The maid could manage the young ones. There was so much snow that the red wooden house was embedded on all sides by broad banks of it, and more drifted down from the roof.

The miserable feeling of being unwell didn't go; it might still be pneumonia, but she was only going to the post office with a letter. It was to her parents, telling them about her life in this wintry town. She would have liked to write about Sven too. How he invited all sorts of men back to their house for meetings without giving her any notice, and how he sometimes got very low but didn't let anyone outside the family know.

They had something in common there; she was also melancholic at times, everything an uphill struggle. She was limited by being his wife, and he was often so impulsive.

It was five years since he had had to face the court, charged with assaulting a colleague.

Perhaps it had been a little better lately, but sometimes it came back, his profound irritation at some perceived nuisance or other. She was his wife and had to keep up the façade, though she sometimes felt she couldn't bear it. His depression was her biggest problem now. It had become worse by the end of the war, when he had feared victory for the West and ravaging Bolsheviks, he feared the *Entente*. Politics was important to him: sometimes more important than she was. But she had to comfort him all the same.

He had engaged himself for the whites in the Finnish civil war, as he hated all socialism and communism. Last year's story of the assault on Tampere was the worst she had experienced of him so far. He had gone there, to Finland and the war, in order to help out with the bad state of affairs in the Swedish voluntary brigade, and he had finally taken part in the assault by the Whites on this

Red stronghold. Earlier he had advised her brother not to go; it was too dangerous, he said. Then, he didn't want to go himself, even when his own brother went. And then, suddenly, when somebody else asked him he went himself, at the end of the war, leaving her and the children. He finally used the gun he often carried; that's what he had told them, anyhow. She didn't know, she didn't want to know what he had really done during that time.

*

'The way you tell it, it is hard on your father,' Helmut says. 'I'd rather get to know him myself, without being told so much in advance – I think that's important.'

'Yes, I understand – but if you want me to tell you the story I can only tell it my way,' she replies as she takes another gulp of the wine. 'It's how I imagine *she* saw him; it's not exactly *my* view.'

Helmut frowns. 'I read what happened in Tampere,' he says sombrely. 'Two thousand of the Reds were killed, either in battle or executed, and then piled up in one long mound, body after body, like fire logs. At least two hundred Whites also died.'

*

All those dead... Laura could not even imagine the atrocities, and could only speculate in horror about what Sven might have seen and done. He had a small wound in his thigh that he made sure that everyone knew about when he came home; you would think he had lost the leg. He bragged about meeting Marshal Mannerheim and showed off his Freedom Cross, as if he was a big hero.

She was so tired of his behaviour. The way he told his cock-and-bull stories, the ones she had once laughed at, but could no longer find anything funny in. He was revived when he could extend his hospitality and care for his friends, and she valued that kindness in him; but sometimes it was too much for her to care about – and he never noticed all of her hard work, day after long day.

No, she didn't write any of that to her family. And perhaps it wouldn't have been proper to tell her parents of her present feelings for her husband. Instead, she had congratulated her father on the new translation work and asked about his stay in England. Oh, how she wished she could have gone along! She had asked him about his work in the Swedish Academy, about how things really were there. That's what she had written about; Uppsala, Stockholm, journeys – pleasant things. Not about this remote corner in the North, all the problems with the children and the nanny and a husband that rarely if ever seemed to notice how she was feeling.

She had put a photograph in the envelope. It was the five children, neatly in a row, with Björn the oldest at the far left. Then Ivar, Paul, Harriet and Anne-Marie. In the photograph she, the small one, sat still, but in fact she was never really still; Laura always had to worry about her – one-and-a-half and already so bold...

Even though the letter was so innocuous, she was glad that Sven wouldn't see it. *I could have sent it with him this morning*, she muttered to herself as she trudged on, *but I don't know; he's so jealous. Best to go myself.* And of course, it had given her a reason to leave the house.

Björn, their oldest son, would be thirteen the next day. She wanted to buy something for him, too. The troublemaker. Three years ago when he was just ten years old, he ran away. Took himself on an adventure, and rode the train from Umeå and changed at Vännäs, without any ticket. He got as far south as one can go in Sweden, to Ystad.

She could understand, though. His father was so strict, so stern, of course he wanted to kick against that. Oh yes, she could understand.

I haven't spent enough time with Björn, she thought. The others were demanding as well, not least the littlest one, toddling all over the place. Sven wanted to discipline the smallest children as well, but Laura had managed to persuade him that one couldn't do that with somebody that small. Of course there was a need for manners! But also for good times with the children. And not just good times swimming in the river, going sleigh-riding or drinking aquavit and soda with the men.

The children had gone to bed, and yet Sven had not shown up, not after work, not for dinner. He normally wanted everybody to be present for the evening meal, and also at lunch when he was home for that; everybody clean and washed, sitting up straight with their hands under the table. You couldn't manage that with the twelve-year old and less with the little ones.

He wanted them there, close-by, but if they didn't do as he told them, they had to leave the dining room. On the other hand, he certainly appreciated their games and their skills. He could sometimes give his full attention to questioning the older ones about school, about their tests, how they answered, how they had done. But too often, he would criticise. They children rarely got to bask in his encouragement.

Now Sven wasn't there, and Laura had been romping and playing with the children throughout dinner without any plan. It really wasn't proper at all. She wanted to feel them all close, today, at that moment. Their warmth and laughter, their fair, soft hands; it made her feel good. Sven would never understand; she got on the floor and played trains with them. She was the engine, with Anne-Marie on her back, and they hooted at every crossing and pretended to let out steam like a real train and blow the whistle. They laughed and cheered. The other children also thought she imitated a train letting out steam when she coughed, a very hard deep cough. Her throat was aching. She felt she had to go to bed soon. She asked the maid to help her put

Anne-Marie to bed and told the others to go up at once. They wanted to wait for their father, but she said no.

*

'Do you remember any of this?' Helmut asks, but she just shakes her head and continues.

*

It was eleven o'clock. Everybody was finally sleeping, the maid had gone home, and Sven had still not returned.

For a while Laura wandered around between bouts of coughing, and tried to see from the window if any restaurants were still open. They were too far away, even though the white snow and the bare trees made it possible to see further than usual.

She paced very slowly, and imagined the scene when he finally would come home. All her questions and all his inadequate answers. Her meticulousness and her solicitude and his stiff, hard-boiled, measured ways; no good would come of that. She would go to bed now; she turned down the light. He must understand, surely, when no one was there to bid him welcome.

She placed the pillboxes under the light on the bedside table. The ones that eased her cough, and the ones called Verinal that she had been given by the doctor once so that she could sleep.

She considered for a long while and then scooped up a handful from each box.

I must be able to sleep. I must get away, away from all this, she murmured while closing her eyes. Then she swallowed half in one go. *I don't know where. I don't care where.*

Then she slowly walked to the window, while undoing all the hard strings and bands from her body. She meditated.

She looked out over the dark city, making sure that Sven was not coming. She lifted the other handful of pills to her mouth.

She tidied up the bedside table and sat for a short while with the Red Cross accounts, and the accounts for their recent parties. At these gatherings he was always was so positive and cheerful, but then, the next day he was so low, as if he had a weight around his neck, pulling him down.

She glued an *Ex Libris*, the family one with a sheaf, inside the cover of the book she was reading, her father's history of Swedish literature.

Everything in the room was very proper; the paintings were squared, the door was shut and the window left slightly open.

She put on her nightgown, turned off the bedside light and slipped into bed. How pleasant to float away, she thought. The curtains fluttered as the cold wind found its way into the room. She felt her body slowly getting numb and it wasn't unpleasant, she felt a delight that made her shiver.

Then, no more.

*

Helmut shrugs. He looks out at the grey winter weather, the piles of grey snow on the pavement. He knows he has to say something: but what does one say? It is just so terrible. Standing, he walks to her side of the table and starts to gently massage her shoulders – but after only a moment, she asks him to sit down.

'What can I say?' he asks softly. 'What can I do? I'm so very sad for you; how can I help you?'

'It just helps that you're listening,' she replies, meeting his gaze, both of them lost for a moment in a place between the past and their present. After a moment, she gives a hardly perceptible little shudder. 'You asked about Siri. I'll tell you about when she came.'

'If you think you can face it,' he says.

She shakes her long hair, tosses it over her shoulder, and straightens her shoulders as she begins to tell him about her next mamma.

'You know,' she says, 'my mother Laura was an academic, which was very unusual for women in those days. She was educated in Uppsala, and she had to follow my father to Umeå, which was so far away, and so small. And there, she had to manage a household, and that's all that she had to do with her brain.' Anne-Marie is looking at her hands on the tablecloth, now, seeing past them to a place that she hasn't thought about for a long time. 'I think she froze to death, and I don't mean just physically.' She stirs, and meets Helmut's eyes again. 'Siri was also an academic woman and a liberal too... strange that he choose them. Oh, how I wondered how he and Siri had found each other. She had worked in a very progressive school in Stockholm, alongside suffragettes and other women who were trying to change their world; they had the idea there of educating boys and girls together. Her father was an MP for the Christian liberals.' She stops again and picks up her glass, but holds it, cradled in her hands. 'You know, there were a lot of women in our house during the years, after mamma Laura's death and before mamma Siri came into our life, women who looked after us, probably also women in his life, but we didn't love any of them. Not really.'

She raises the glass to her lips, drinks quickly, and places it back on the table. 'But then one spring, we noticed that Dad often met this woman who was working at the seminar. He didn't say anything, but my sister put two and two together.'

Umeå 1924

'She's called Siri!' Harriet told Anne-Marie one night. They asked their older brothers if they could find out if the girls at the seminar liked her. When they got the chance, they would try to catch their father and this new woman together, try to get a sense of her – try to imagine how it might be if she became part of their lives. Gradually they realized that this really might become something more. The two sisters held hands and hoped, hoped.

One day at the end of April when all the children except Björn were at home, Sven asked them to line up. They of course realised quickly what this might be about, and were unusually cooperative.

Some snow-heaps were still lying in the parts of the garden that were facing to the north, and yet the first snowdrops could be seen in the flower borders. Anne-Marie picked some of the flowers and was scolded for it; they were put in a small vase in the kitchen anyhow.

When Siri approached the house, Sven was standing upstairs looking out cautiously: he came down when he saw her, excited, less stiff than usual.

She entered with her small dog in her arms and her suitor and his four children lined up by the door to the big room.

Siri, who had been a local politician used to having her say, a speaker at meetings, and who worked at the training college for women teachers, stood there in the doorway and looked gawky. She curtsied. It was a little solemn and strange. Then the dog unexpectedly transformed the mood. It jumped from Siri's arms and ran straight to Anne-Marie, so suddenly that Siri almost toppled, and Sven caught her.

'You will all have to learn to call Siri Mother,' he said.

As summer and autumn followed, life became different in the red villa. There was somebody for the children, especially Harriet and Anne-Marie, to talk to in quite a different way than with their father, the nannies, or the maids. They were happier than they had been for a long time. Anne-Marie was wilder than before, but she was also more tolerated. Siri was interested in keeping the house light and full with art and tidy and full of flowers.

Sven worked on, worked hard, and was often away on different assignments. This, too, increased the range of possibilities for the girls. They went skiing or did their homework or played on the ice-covered river. All the boys went to boarding school in Germany for long periods.

*

Anne-Marie had talked for a long time: the food was finished and the waiter came and asked if they wanted dessert.

'You need some strong coffee, I think, and a sweet chocolate cake,' he said.

But she glared at him. 'Don't tell me what I need! What I'm trying to say is that we are strong women in our family, intelligent women! It will only end badly if we are controlled and browbeaten.'

Helmut was startled. 'That wasn't my intention! I won't patronize you, ever, or tell you what to do.'

'And you must accept that I will have my own will, and must have liberty to do things on my own!'

'Indeed: I try to be a modern man. I didn't mean anything like that.'

She took his hand again. 'I know you aren't like him,' she said. You know I was the spoilt one, I always got what I wanted. My brothers and sister were held harder.'

'Well, sometimes you talk as if he's all bad. You know I want to form my own opinion. Tell me about his good side.'

'Well: he helps people in his cases, I mean more than he has to. And he likes children.'

'Hear, hear, that sounds fine.'

'But he isn't that easy. There are aspects of him that I think you'll find difficult-or worse than that. But of course, you must meet him and find out for yourself. But remember, it's not him you're dating.'

'Dating?' he teases. 'We will do much more than 'date' together. It's Us now. And I am glad he likes children.' He twinkles at her.

Christmas and New Year's Eve 1945 to 1946 cont.

The next morning they wake up in his office where they have spent the night in his extra bed; it is the one he uses when he has stayed late in town and doesn't feel like taking the last tram home. It's a small single bed, and they've now both slept in it for several nights and it is getting less comfortable, even if they are entwined most of the time. This morning she wants her coffee fast, and coughs a lot.

'Wait!' he exclaims quickly, knowing that her coughing could be serious. He hurries out to the small pantry and comes back with a glass of very hot and aromatic liquid. It smells of cinnamon and oranges and wine.

'This is a place of resources! Leftovers can make a fantastic medicine. Now you drink this; it has never failed. And the bed is yours for the day.'

And she sips and smiles and coughs some more and snores. Before too long, she feels much better and asks him what the plan for the day is.

'I don't know,' he answers. 'I'd like to go out for a walk – perhaps we could just walk and look at the shop windows and see what they have for Christmas.'

She nods, happy. 'But we better wait until this cure has really had an effect. I want to know more about when you were young, about how it was when you came to Sweden, and all about how your family moved to England. I don't understood it all yet. It still all seems so complicated to me, and everything is still so confused – in the world and in my mind. Explain it all for me, make it all clear. Please? Come here and sit on the bed, I don't think I'm that contagious.'

He hesitates. Where should he start? What should he tell her and what isn't so important when all is said and done? What will she want to know? But she insists.

'Well… you know I came to Sweden when I was in my first years at school. And then we moved around in Stockholm every year and even went to Malmö for a while. And of course I also have to tell you that I was rather shy...' He grins at her sceptical expression. 'But in my adolescence I wasn't so interested in school and had to redo my last high school year.'

'Slow down, please! Tell me more about your childhood; tell me what it was like to move to another country. I mean, how did it feel, for you?'

'Well,' he replied, 'for a while we didn't know where to live. I'll tell you about that.'

Berlin 1924

Helmut sat leaning on his elbows and looked at her while starting his story of Berlin.

'We had moved to Stockholm but we kept our house in Berlin; in fact my father kept his business, or at least his business address, in Berlin. '*Wer weißt etwas von die Zukunft?*' he used to say: *who knows what will be?* And he had an office in Copenhagen as well. Just in case. He was trying to learn Swedish and it was going so-so: '*We have to have a safeguard. What do we know of business development, of adaptation, of politics? We could move any day.*'

This was a time of hope but also of uncertainty financially, not just for us I mean, but for everyone. Sweden had been very poor just a few years earlier but was coming along, my father hoped. Yet still he went to and fro between Stockholm, Copenhagen and Berlin. The family also had to go to and fro. Sometimes we were in Sweden and he in Berlin; sometimes it was the other way around. 'We had hardly learnt to say we lived in the '20s – we just knew that this was a decade of new opportunity, new chances.'

*

Germany still crouched low after the long misery of the first war, after the failed revolutions that came on the heels of that, and, above all, the enormous debt that the country had to bear as a result of the war.

This debt had to be paid off, and at that time, those in power knew no other way to deal with the crisis than to keep devaluing the mark – this was the currency that the debt was in, not in current purchasing value. And so the ingenious but desperate method of making more money, and thereby making each mark worth less. The printing presses were working hard and the mark was successively devalued. The effect on the citizens came second. The zeros on stamps and banknotes were multiplied. The culmination of all this was a stamp that had been overprinted with *32 million* marks.

The capital Berlin was still exhausted, five years after the fighting had ended. And yet, in spite of all the misery, there was a spark of life in many who had once been ready to give in. Perhaps – *perhaps* – Germany would flourish again.

Some wanted revenge on the French and the English, others just hoped that their country would manage its war debt and get the economy going again so that people would stop suffering. That was the talk every day in the beer cellars and cafés. But there were also those who wanted to understand their fellow men and try to help them.

Many buildings were still black after the war. There were still people living in sheds, in grinding poverty – but there were also children who played and laughed between the houses and in the yards as children always do, and other children, or maybe it was the same ones, who ran around playing pranks and making mischief. And then there were some children who mainly watched the others and played by themselves, like Helmut.

'Emmy, Emmy! Always as wonderful and beautiful!'

Helmut could hear Uncle Karl's voice from the hallway. Trautenaustrasse was sunny, and the nine year old boy stood at the balcony railing, looking towards Nikolsburger Platz. There was great activity there by the small market stall. He stood watching people, sensing the big city, the smell of coal and sauerkraut and cigars. They were living there in recently built quarters in Wilmersdorf by Kaiserallee. Best of all he liked the new pumping station in the next block by Hohenzollerndamm. He would later remember standing for ages in the shadow of the lime trees, gazing up and in through the cathedral-shaped windows of the station.

The big flywheels inside moved fast and pumped sewage on towards the River Spree. One could catch a faint smell of it. The wheels inside were huge and there were many different machines, including a big steam engine that puffed as it let the steam off.

Back at home, he read *Call of the Wild*. He felt great empathy for the dog, Buck, so lonely in the wilderness. The dog heard the wolves howling and yearned like to go to his wild relatives, but didn't dare. To be alone in the wilderness was different from being lonely in Berlin. His father was still in Stockholm and Mummy often complained about being alone, without Sigmund; he tried to comfort her.

Mummy's mother, Grandma Flora, lived nearby and often visited, and he occasionally spent time with her and Granddad Herman, who had Parkinson's disease and shook all the time.

But he liked it best when Uncle Karl came; he was the husband of Sigmund's sister, and a doctor. Karl lived in Frankfurt but often came to Berlin to meet his colleagues.

Helmut wanted to go with Karl to the zoo and watch the animals. His uncle used to tell him about all of them, how they behaved when they were in the jungle, how they played and with whom, who ate who and even how they made babies. Karl could imitate all their sounds, and just through those sounds make the male gorilla so angry that he ran to the bars, or make the birds come out of the bushes.

The most fun was when he pointed out that the goslings followed their keeper as if he was their mother – they really believed that he was: in a long line the little geese followed their tall guardian. Karl bought snacks at the Imbiss stall, when they turned into Kaiserallee on the way home. He used to whistle at the sparrows in the old lime tree there, and give them sesame seeds. That road which Helmut had walked many times with his father and mother on the way to the synagogue in Fasanenstraße on Saturdays was so much more exciting with Uncle Karl.

'Can we go to the zoo?' he asked now. 'The goslings are probably big by now. Maybe they don't follow the keeper anymore; they don't have to bother with 'Mummy keeper'. Please, can we? Something exciting may have happened. It's so long since we've been. Or maybe play chess?'

'Unfortunately Helmut, not today,' Mummy smiled. 'But miracles happen. Dad has sent money from Sweden. One Swedish crown each for you and Käthe, and ten crowns for me! Do you know how much that is? One crown is worth 50,000 Deutschmarks! Or, it was yesterday. Ach, this foolish politics and this crazy inflation! They may be able to pay off some debt, but everybody has to suffer. But we are rich today, in Swedish money. You and Käthe can go to a bakery. Buy chocolate or Mohnkuchen or whatever you want. Karl and I have a lot to talk about, and he will also examine me to see if I am pregnant again. Ilse is asleep in the other room. You don't have to stand up for her now, you little master of the house.'

Käthe was almost seven, and as they set off in search of a café, she looked at every little thing in the gutter. She spoke to black-dressed ladies and gentlemen with small caps on their heads. She approached a beggar-man and asked him why is sitting there.

Helmut took his sister by the hand and dragged her along. He had heard that German money was losing value every minute. Therefore you had to rush. '*Schlaraffenland*, the land of sweets and honey, will be a reality for us soon Käthe!' he urged. 'Chocolate and cake! Come quickly or there will be nothing!'

Finally he managed to persuade his sister walk a little faster. All the houses looked the same; stone building four or five storeys high, two apartments on each floor, and mats above the door and all balconies built into the wall – they quickly ran past it all. He found his way.

'What do you get for 100,000 marks?' he asked eagerly when they stood in front of the counter in the small bakery and café in Nikolsburger Platz. He pulled out a big envelope and extracted a bundle of notes and some coins and put them in front of the woman who sat behind the counter. A few ladies and old men were sitting on their stools, clattering their cups, and looking at the children with surprise. 'It's enough for two cups of chocolate and some almond cakes, isn't it?' he asked again.

'I am sure it is!' the waitress exclaimed, 'I have never seen so much money! Wait, I'll look at the new pricelists that came in this morning...'

She studied the paper, and her face was a picture of surprise. 'No, this can't be – two cups of chocolate and two almond cakes will be 120 000 marks! But kid, you'll get it anyway! I'll give you the last bit of cake.'

'No, let me,' a man in a green hunting outfit closest to the counter said. 'Such a young capitalist is someone to keep in with. But where did you get all that money?'

'My father sent it,' he said, 'He's in Sweden. It is much better there than here.'

'But, please, help us to make it better here as well,' the man in the hunting outfit said, while looking partly at Helmut, partly at the other customers – 'Toy money is what *we* have got, damn politicians.'

'They have real money in Sweden, and real snow and real schools! And that's where Dad is. I'm going there soon. If you are wise, you'll go to Sweden. That is what Dad told me.'

The woman gave the children chocolate with a lot of whipped cream, and two big slices of almond cake and gestured for them to sit at a small table.

'*Schlaraffenland*,' Käthe whispered.

'Sweden may be a *Schlaraffenland*,' the man grumbled, 'Where the streams are of honey and candy is growing on trees.'

'I want to go to *Schlaraffenland*!' Käthe cried when they were out in the street again. 'To Schweden – *Schlaraffenland*, where they have many cafés, and pastries. That's even better than almond cake. And fudge! Tell Mummy that we are leaving now!'

'I don't want to go without Karl,' Helmut said. 'That is what I will tell Mummy.'

'The money was just enough!' he announced quickly when they got back home. 'We have decided that we want to go now.'
'To *Schlaraffenland*,' Käthe explained.
'Where is Karl?' I asked. 'He must come along to Sweden, otherwise I won't go.'
'He had to leave,' Mummy said. 'He has a lot to do. But do you know what?' She bent down so the children can hear well. 'We *are* going to Sweden soon! Dad wants us to come to Stockholm; a cable arrived while you were out. We have to go to Sweden. He'll be very happy.' A frown flickered across her forehead so quickly that Helmut hardly had time to notice it. 'But Sweden is no *Schlaraffenland* either,' she said. 'Oh no.'

*

'And now your father is dead. It must be hard. I understand you have gone in his footsteps.' Anne-Marie holds his arm.
I really didn't want to go on with the business', Helmuth says. 'But I had no choice. And he wasn't like me. At least I do not think so. More serious I think. More German. I am glad he didn't have to see the war. '

Mesnalien, near Lillehammer, January to March 1946

After New Year Anne-Marie has to leave again, almost at once, this time for Norway, for another sanatorium.

She and Helmut find it very difficult to part; he tries to stop her from leaving but she has to go, she has no choice. There is this last cure in Norway, essential so that she doesn't suffer a relapse.

They decide just before she leaves that there's no point in hesitating; they are going to live their lives together. She lets him do all the planning. As soon as her sanatorium period is over they will make it come true.

As soon as she arrives in Norway she writes:

Oslo 9.1.46 ... Tomorrow I go on ... I want to get away from here and to a place where I can get healthy as soon as possible in order to come to You and be with You! ... At least ten times before getting to the first stop I was ready to jump off the train and go back to you. Why aren't you here right now? ...

In Oslo she meets her old fiancé, he with the undulating hair, in order to call it off.

They go to a restaurant where she first lets him hold her – he has longed for this so, he says, and he is so keen. She tries to be kind, but soon tells him that she has met another; that it is all over between them. He doesn't believe her at first, he can't grasp what she's saying: they were so much in love and so very recently too.

'My flower!' he cries, 'you're my everything, all I have hoped for: I'm not going to give in so easily. Why? Why?'

But she is rock solid no matter how he appeals to her. Her mind is full of Aga and the Norwegian finally hastens home, snuffling, after one final hug.

The next day, she travels immediately to Lillehammer by train and then by car to Mesnalien sanatorium, which turns out to be a giant wooden building above the big lake Mjösa.

There, Aga's letter awaits her:

> Stockholm 10 January 1946 .. I now have a ticket for England 2 March – and a return ticket for me and my wife on April 9! …

She is almost overwhelmed – with happiness, with all the fresh air, and with the sensation of feeling as healthy as ever; not least after having met many fellow patients whose lungs are in a much worse way than hers.

After only a short while of this joy, she realizes that her periods have stopped; she's at once both happy and anxious. She talks at length to her doctor, and finally she decides to opt for an abortion, to ensure that she is not carrying a child when she is so ill, and maybe also because she wants to wait until they are properly married.

They keep up their stream of letters, she from the sanatorium by Lillehammer, he from Ängby. A lot has to be arranged for their lives. Something quite new is starting. The weeks are filled with letter writing and plans of the future. She has major problems in arranging a visa and talks to the Swedish consul in Bergen time and time again. The main problem is that a Swede cannot go directly from Norway to England and she has no option but to go via Sweden.

He keeps on looking for a flat in Stockholm, only now it is not his home that he's searching for; it's their home. They discuss this back and forth and he decides after her advice not to take one in the west of the city but chooses a more modern one with a tiny kitchen in a new area, a bit further from the city.

They don't know when to announce their wedding to her father, to Sven.

It's All Coming Back

They discuss whether they should change their plans and get married in Stockholm: maybe her family would like them to, but they decide not to care about what they might think. They write about all this; their entire lives, their whole future, is decided by correspondence.

He goes to England when February turns into March and then, inevitably, his mother Emmy begins to intervene in the wedding planning and he lets her do so, up to a certain point.

He already knows what Anne-Marie likes and what she doesn't. He's fully occupied with seeing everyone who he hasn't seen for so many years, spending time with family and business contacts. It's tense at first, but they talk and talk days and nights alike.

She's starting to get worried when there is no letter for a couple of days, but they finally arrive and she writes once more from Norway to her beloved in London:

Mesnalien 18.3.46

My dear Aga.

Today I had two letters from You. And my worst worries and longing were stilled. Idiotic, I walk around like I don't know what, worried, nervous every day, in spite of knowing, you cannot write more often …

(… *4 pages…*)

… My dearest one, I love you so immensely. And I long for You. Our plans must become real but that would perhaps be all too good.

Your wife Annemay

P.S- I love your cardinal fault that you don't write the end of words correctly! You are so cute even in having a fault! Do You think it is true that thing about being able to love the other's faults as well? Without being irritated! We may get there in due time when we have learnt the difficult art of adaptation.

P.P.S. I have now written for 1 ½ hours without pause.

Belsize Park, London
March 1946

When Helmut arrives in North West London at the beginning of March, he and his mother sit and talk forever, it seems, about what has happened since they last met: they haven't seen each other since August 1939 more than six years ago. Emmy makes sandwiches and tea when the maid has gone home, like a mother should do.

They sit up several nights in a row until two or three in the morning talking, talking for ever.

Emmy's mother, Grandmother Flora, who will be eighty in May is there too.

A dignified white-haired woman, round and small and warm hearted, she left Germany for London at her daughter's urging in the autumn of 1933. Her husband Herman, deep in the grip of Parkinson's disease, had died in Berlin in 1933, shortly after the Nazis took power, and she had become aware of the first sparks of hatred, of the coming persecution of the Jews.

They have all lived in England, Helmut only for a year when studying at Oxford, but the others for more than five years and they most often speak English as they want to adapt to their new home. But sometimes they go back to speaking German, when they cannot find words, when they are upset or do not want others to understand, and when it is really important.

Some evenings, Helmut's sister Käthe and her husband comes along, or the other sister Ilse and her husband and daughter, or all of them at once. Helmut still can't stop himself thinking of Ilse, eight years younger than him, as his 'baby sister'. He still feels very close to her.

Throughout the war, it has been impossible to have more than occasional mail contact, and of course even then, letters were censored and didn't always reach their destination.

Jon Kahn

When he had last seen them, Ilse had been a teenager; now she has a child. Käthe was newly wed and Emmy was just widowed. Now Helmuts mother is recently remarried to Hans, another refugee, a gentleman with a strict bearing who has problems walking.

So: there is a lot to talk about, to ask each other about, and to explain.

Emmy has done voluntary work, especially at the Bloomsbury House helping to bring Jewish people fleeing the Nazis into England and for some years she Flora and Ilse were evacuated to the countryside. Back in London Emmy supported herself through the war by arranging parties and running small coffee houses, first for others when she was alone and then just by herself with Hans.

The two of them now have a business called The Cake Shop on Finchley Road, near Swiss Cottage. Business and gossip in the small café are conducted in English, French, German and Swedish, even Yiddish. It's a cheerful, vibrant place, despite the underlying sadness of the customers. This part of the Finchley Road is where most Austrian and German Jews in London live – the English bus conductors call out "Finchley *Strasse!*" with a grin when they get to the stops in this part of town.

The customers feel very at home in The Cake Shop, and Emmy loves the warm flow of the conversation about 'the Continent'; shared memories, shared experiences. She has realised that she has a real talent for this kind of work; she is very good at bringing people together and making them feel comfortable and welcome. Hans, for his part, is very good at the business side.

Sometimes as Emmy listens there is a wonderful tale of people finding each other again, of good news where there had only been bleakness, of celebration out of nowhere. But nearly every day, these are interlaced with the tales of tragedy that nearly everyone has to tell. Despite the pleasure she is finding in her new work, these are heart-breaking times for her; for everyone, as the terrible news from Europe finally begins to filter through to everybody.

At other times, she drops the business talk and suddenly transforms into a woman in front of Helmut – a view of her he has never considered before.

'Hans is so good to me!' she giggles to him late one night, when just the two of them are left up talking.

And after all – why not? he thinks. She wasn't yet 50 when she was widowed, or even when she met this new man.

'It's incredible to think,' she tells him, 'But here I am, with my second husband and my third surname and my third citizenship. Born in Germany what is now Poland, then Berlin, then Sweden and for a short while Denmark now England.'

Helmut can only stare at his mother and laugh.

'It feels like ages ago when it was Sigmund and I,' she muses, her deep eyes gazing back into the past, unseeing; 'Other lands, another time.' She sighs. 'And now I also feel like a very small human being; small in the big stream of the world. We've come through the war safe, and I'm so glad that both my daughters are married – and I am a grandmother!' She laughs again now, her easy laugh. 'And now you too, soon!'

He smiles as he lights another cigarette. 'Tell me,' he asks, 'Now that we have the time – how in the world did you end up in a little Cornish fishing village at the beginning of the war, of all places?'

She settles into her seat and crosses her hands in her lap, showing no sign of fatigue even at one thirty at night.

'Well – we had to evacuate on short notice in 1940, mother, Ilse and I. Women of no significance, with no ability to work for the war effort, had to move: it was that simple. Single women especially were moved. 'God knows what will happen if the Germans really come. You got to be safe,' they told use. Eventually we went to Polperro: yes, a tiny village in Cornwall, where Käthe spent her honeymoon in 1939. We had to go – as they say here – lock, stock and barrel.'

Helmut frowns. 'You mean helter-skelter, heads over heels?'

'*Ja,*' Emmy agrees, '*Holterdiepolter, Hals über Kopf.* Packing in a terrible rush, no time for any farewells to people.' Her hands, with their red-tipped fingernails, are helping to illustrate her emotions as the story unfolds.

'But then suddenly we were arrested!' she exclaims. 'Ilse and I were arrested in Polperro and taken to Plymouth, and really quite severely interrogated over the suspicion that we were sending information to the Germans! Us! Of all people! Why would we want to do that? !' She shakes her head and lets a small bitter laugh escape. 'They thought we were signalling to U-boats!' – Now she snorts, not hiding her scorn at this ridiculous turn of events. 'They had opened all the letters between you and I, and thought we were using some kind of secret code…'

The hard humour is gone from her voice now. Emmy's big brown eyes are wet and Helmut suddenly sees the deepened wrinkles on her forehead, behind the rouge and the powder.

'We had been teaching some people German – now I see that perhaps it was a risky thing to do, but I was so innocent! We had no reason to think it wrong! Ach…' she looks very tired now. 'It was a mess. Finally we were released. The whole thing was very hard. I was frightened for all of us.'

'I understand,' Helmut wants to hug his mother but that is something they have seldom done since he was a small boy. He just pats her arm.

Helmut takes all this in: despite their correspondence, a lot of it is news to him. But he isn't overwhelmed by it. Strange stories are delivered every day these days.

He asks what happened to all their relatives and friends after the war.

'The war has pulled everyone apart from each other,' she sighs, 'And some will never see their dear ones again. Both the war and now even this peace have created divorces. Many haven't known where to go; some just drift around, sometimes waiting for letters that never come, for people who will never show up. Many of your cousins, of my cousins, have stayed a while at the flat here next to Belsize Park tube station and gone on to America, or to try and find a new life for themselves here. Sometimes now people are finding each other: sometimes they meet. Some of these are difficult rendezvous that remind people of misery, but most at least give a sense of satisfaction, of warmth, And at the same time people are reminded that something is left, that some people are left.'

She stirs, glances at him wearily again. 'Perhaps you should ask your Uncle Fritz, about all Kahn cousins. Aren't you seeing him tomorrow?' She shifts in her chair, and he can tell that, for her, this subject is closed, at least for tonight. Eventually of course he will learn more.

She brightens herself again. 'Ilse and I will plan your wedding! Is that all right with you? Will Anne-Marie mind?'

Helmut nods without really contemplating what that could mean.

'By the way,' Emmy's eyes are suddenly even more heavily lidded as she holds her son's gaze, 'Do you have the telephone number of Anne-Marie's brother, the one who is a journalist in London?'

Helmut shifts uneasily and lights another cigarette, 'I haven't met him myself yet. Don't you think *I* should meet him first? Apparently he's a remarkable person. I should try and have lunch with him soon. Perhaps before Anne-Marie arrives.'

Emmy purses her mouth, just a little, and raises her chin – an expression that Helmut remembers well. 'Just a short call to check dates. Please.'

He recognises defeat and goes to the small shelf next to the telephone. 'Well, he's probably in the directory...' There's a short pause as he leafs through the pages. 'Here: Speedwell 2448. I'll call him now.'

Emmy is startled –Helmut has clearly lost track of the time. 'Not at two o'clock in the morning! Don't wake him up! In fact, we should all be sleeping.' She rises a little stiffly from her chair. 'Tomorrow you must tell me more of how business is in Sweden, and all you have done for the company during the past few years. And I'll tell you about the Landauers. Did you know that Eva was here?'

They are both standing now, and Helmut immediately wants to sit again to hear this new information, but his mother hushes him in a way that doesn't leave any room for argument. 'Tomorrow. Let's sleep now.'

Hampstead, London
March 1946

Next day he goes to call at the offices of the Kahn & Kahn Company where he meets his uncle Fritz and his cousin Walter. Kahn & Kahn, in the first decade of the 20th century, was his father's and Uncle Fritz's company. Then, the two of them were selling women's wear in Berlin. Later it became the name of their tobacco importing business, which Sigmund ran from Stockholm and Fritz from London. Helmut has been in charge of the Swedish side of the company since his father's illness and death before the war.

Helmut and his much younger cousin Walter, Fritz's son, sit on the desk in the small office. His uncle, a short man, is standing near them, testing some new cigars that have come from Cuba. The smoke gets annoying even for these who smoke all the time; the ventilation is broken and they have to open the window. It's a warm day, and they've removed their jackets, showing off their braces and the garters on their arms that keep their sleeves pulled up.

They're all speaking at once; they have all so much to say.

'Are you coming into the company?' Helmut asks Walter. 'You know, we could do a lot together; there's a lot of demand again after the war. In Sweden they are talking of tightening the monopoly, but even so…'

'Of course you should come into the company', Fritz looks at his son, 'but a good education would be good, as a start.' Fritz interrupts. Helmut nods – that's fair enough, he supposes.

'And you have a Swedish girlfriend?' Walter asks, happy to change the subject. 'Do you have a picture?'

Helmut happily pulls his cherished photograph of Anne-Marie from his wallet.

'Oh! Very pretty indeed!' Fritz nods in approval when he sees it. 'Of good family? Jewish?' Helmut hesitates; he is still uneasy with this question.

'Well – her grandmother was partly Jewish... but I don't know much about her family, it's very big, and I don't really care. I know her sister though; nice girl, married with children.' He gazes with warm eyes at the picture, which has now been returned to him. 'You know, Anne-Marie is a very independent woman, strong, educated. It is not her family I'm marrying.'

'Indeed?,' Walter asks, but it's clear that his attention is drifting. 'Have you heard, Helmut? My big interest has become gliding! Would you like to give it a try?' His eyes drift to the clear sky beyond the window.

'With aeroplanes?' Helmut looks alarmed. 'I don't know if I would dare!'

Hearing this confession from his older cousin, Walter grins cockily.

Fritz snorts at the two of them. 'I thought you went around in fast cars?' he asks Helmut. 'This isn't that much different! I wouldn't try either though.' He grinds out the cigar he was trying in the large ashtray in the middle of the desk. 'Let's try something a bit different' – he nods at the boxes stacked around them.

'All Cuban?' Helmut breathes in deeply the scent of the unlit cigars being offered to him before carefully selecting one and biting the end off it. Lighting it, he inhales the rich smoke deep into his throat and waits for a moment before puffing out lazy smoke rings. 'I could import this to Sweden don't you think?' he asks himself, aloud. Then he swerves one sharp eye at his cousin. ' And why did you get into gliding?'

'Well I enlisted in the RAF, learnt to fly, and gliding seemed to follow naturally.

Helmut gives a short chesty laugh. 'In the RAF indeed! I didn't know that. A Kahn was bombing our old home country or did you? Did you take part in any of those really massive bombings at the end of the war? Dresden? Even...' his voice falters for a moment. 'Even Heilbronn?'

It's All Coming Back

A cloud passes over the sunny plane of Walter's face. 'I don't want to talk about it.' He shakes his shoulders. 'We all had to take our share.'

As Helmut reaches across to give his shoulder a pat, some glowing ash falls from his cigar into the waste paper basket, and there's a flurry of activity to ensure that no fire will spread before they can continue.

Trying to keep his voice light, Helmut finally asks, 'What happened to the family? It is all blurred up for me. My cousins, uncles, aunts; all of them? What do you know, for sure? Of course, I've heard some news, of some people – but I was hoping that you might have the whole picture?'

'Well…' Fritz begins, his face now heavy, 'You don't know, then, about how they all got out? You were here in '39 for your sister Käthe's wedding, weren't you?'

'Yes of course!' Helmut agrees quickly, 'At that time, most of my other uncles, other than you, and aunt Lins and uncle Karl and all their families were in Holland. I don't know how or when most of them got out, just that they did. And really, the main thing I want to know is, if everybody else managed to get away, and saw that they had to, why did KarI and Lins stay in Holland?' This perplexes Fritz – it seems that his nephew really doesn't know very much at all.

'And I don't remember everything in detail from before then, either,' Helmut continues. 'There's been so much. You know, my father had died and I didn't know how to get back to Sweden; we all knew war was coming, didn't we? I wasn't perceptive enough, I didn't know all the evil that was to come even if there was so many things pointing in that direction. God knows, I should have seen the writing on the wall, even more than we did.'

Walter frowns. 'I'm hungry, and thirsty. Let's go to a pub and continue this conversation, if that's alright with you two?' He puts out his cigar in the ashtray now full of long crumpled butts.

They go by double-decker further into Hampstead and then walk the back alleys where they find The Holly Bush.

'This is the London pub!' Fritz announces when they have entered, 'You haven't been here before, have you?'

'New to this place, huh?' a waiter interrupts, 'It's been here for centuries. Some of London still stands.'

Helmut is very happy with his family's choice of pub. Once they're settled, he and Fritz start again to try and unravel and clarify the fate of their relatives following 1939. Helmut orders a red wine and a Welsh rarebit and then he begins to speak of his coming wife. But Fritz interrupts him almost before he has begun.

Heilbronn 1938-1939

'Let's me start,' Fritz begins. And so Helmut sits and listens."
What did your father tell you?'

'He wasn't really one so much for telling,' Helmut replies. 'I met my grandparents, Moses and Regina, though, before they died; but I was small then.'

'Well,' Fritz nods, 'It was Moses who was out most of the time, selling things, and your grandmother Regina who sat at home making the decisions and handling the money. This was in a small village near Heilbronn called Gemmingen. They had lived there for centuries, selling cattle and the like. And then my brother Anselm started a tobacco factory in Heilbronn.'

'Where did he get the money?' Walter asks.

'That's a mystery to me too! He brought in several of us brothers, and at first our sister Lins. I was in Berlin with your father at first but after he moved to Sweden I went back to work at the factory again.

We carried on after Hitler had taken power, but eventually we saw how things were going in Germany, and some of us started to leave; we had our families to think of, we had to protect ourselves. First the grown up kids left, some of them went to the U.S. and to England. At that time that was not as hard as it would be,' he sighed, 'I came out in time. Anselm left in 37 or 38. It was relatively easy for us to leave Germany at that point, but difficult to enter Britain or the USA.

'It was so awful,' Helmut intervened, 'people around the world knew that the German Jews were being harassed and whatnot and put into camps and yet they didn't do much to take any refugees. You remember the Evian conference where all countries were supposed to take a part of the refugees. All mainly silent except the Dominican Republic. Sweden was one of the worst, like Switzerland my country wanted a J to mark who was a Jew in the passports. The authorities had their views already when Karl came to Sweden in 33 and there were a lot of conservatism and fear for Germany or even collaborators. They helped the Nazi cause. we all saw the creeping for Hitler from the start.' Helmut is agitated; he lifts up his glass just to put it down again very hard so that wine pours out over the table.

'Well it kept you out of the war and camps and all,' Fritz says which makes Helmut even angrier.

'For what,' Helmut says.

'Two of my brothers were still in Heilbronn at the end of 1938; Josef and Julius' Fritz says going back to history. 'Leo was also still in Germany, in Munich. But then, he never was part of the tobacco factory in Heilbronn.'

Leaning forwards, his arms on the table, Helmut listens intently. 'I loved being at the factory,' he says now, slowly. 'I remember all the seven boxer dogs who guarded it. They were my best friends!'

'Were there seven of them?' Fritz replies. 'Perhaps, at one point in time. One or two would probably have still been alive in 1938, but they would have been old and slow.'

*

They walked slowly along Achtungstrasse. It was a Saturday morning in autumn. The leaves were piled up outside the redbrick factory with its vaults and big windows; chestnut leaves, maple leaves, oak leaves. A couple of blackbirds played along the hedge on the opposite side of the street. The sun glowed on all the beautiful russets, the golds and the browns.

Josef kicked his way through the leaves, worried but decisive. Julius was with him. It was just they two of them by now, the last two brothers left in Heilbronn: them and their wives, and most of their children.

Both around fifty and a bit stouter than they had once been, one of them with little hair, the other with a grey beard, both wearing neat coats.

It's All Coming Back

Our big brother Anselm had already left Germany for Holland, left his life's achievement; the *joint* achievement of us brothers. He used to be a member of the Synagogue board and the board of the chamber of commerce. Even when the brothers were small, Anselm was the leader of all games and pranks, and we were all perfectly happy with that, especially Josef and Julius. We the younger boys, Fritz and Sigmund, joined in sometimes – the second oldest, Leopold, not so often: he had his own ways.

All six of us looked after the smallest child, our only sister, Lins – and she, in her own way, looked after all of us. When Anselm's first wife died, Lins moved in before she herself was married, managing the household for her oldest brother while he became the director of the cigar factory. He had soon been joined by Julius; later Josef joined them, then I did, after Sigmund moved to Sweden.

The two men now walking by the factory wall had always worked together, stood by each other; it was their formula for success.

The factory had opened in 1909; it had had its twenty-five years anniversary.

*

Fritz's face was creased as he remembered. 'It was foolish to start a new venture then! But we were doing something right, because business grew steadily, and was very good for many years, with cigars like Bismark Eiche No15 and, especially, Künstler Club. It all sold well.' He looked at Helmut, his eyes baleful. 'And you know what happened at the end of the thirties?'

His nephew sat up straighter. 'Of course I do - you came abroad to England to sell tobacco, and you and my father joined businesses again although he still had some business left in Sweden. All you brothers except Leo were in tobacco in those days.' 'But I still don't know how they all came out. I was very close to Uncle Karl,' Helmut puts down his cigar and rubs the smoke from his eyes. 'He taught me a lot'

Fritz gazes at him for a moment, resists the urge to pat him gruffly on the arm. 'Anyway,' he says after ordering a new beer...

*

Mother Regina and father Moses had both passed away, and the two brothers remaining in Heilbronn had therefore collected the household goods from many homes, both heirlooms and more modern stuff. Neither of them liked getting rid of things.

They stayed in Germany in spite of all the harassment; in spite of the almost daily appeals for them to move.

They had accustomed themselves to the situation, bit by bit.

At first, when the Nazis took to the streets and entered the elections, Josef and Julius dared oppose what was happening. But since the brown shirts had taken power and exercised it more and more, it was more an issue of mere survival – of playing a very low-key game and hoping it would all pass: that all this yelling and harsh language and the new laws would eventually end.

Their task now was to stay and look after the factory. Someone had to.

They had no goal other than for the factory to do well, for people to enjoy working there, for the workers' wives and children to have a decent life. That, they agreed, was their only intention.

But others, it seemed, wanted to ruin their lives.

Adaptation had become a vital necessity, an art, and it had meant a gradual decay of human dignity and pride. They hated it, but they stuck it out: and it just kept on and on.

They had always tried to be 'more German' than the Christian citizens of that country, and the factory had sometimes been open on Saturdays, the Sabbath; shorter working days than the rest of the week, but still – not many of the workers were Jewish.

And yet, they felt more Jewish than ever in 1938.

And the factory's order book was so empty that they were closed on both Saturdays and Sundays.

Now they had come to the factory on this Saturday because somebody had called about damage again.

And it was true - all the windows along Achtungstrasse had been smashed. They gazed at the destruction. They were used to it: this was how it was every weekend, almost every day.

The saboteurs had chosen the Sabbath in order to make the Jewish owners break the day of rest, to make them abstain from their Saturday walks, from their Saturday lunches when ten people all clamoured together at the same dinner table, talking about the political situation; their little breathing space.

All the families worked in the factory; there was nothing else for Jews. The young people had had to leave their university studies and their jobs.

Julius was close to giving in. He said it was time to go soon.

Josef didn't want to.

'How we had toiled for this factory!,' he argued. 'Let us never forget what our family once was, what Moses and Regina once were, in Gemmingen with their house-to-house peddling!'

The brothers were standing outside the large, defaced building. The sun shone through the chestnut trees and picked out the red/grey bricks in brighter colours. Now they could see that somebody had daubed on the façade: '*Jude*,' '*Schwein*,' 'Murderers of Christ,' and 'You will all die'.

That would have to stay there over the weckend until they could have it washed away or painted over. Now they had to agree on a watch scheme for the weekend, and call the glaziers and arrange for the façade to be cleaned on

Monday. They could hardly afford these eternal repairs, but they were necessary.

Crying did no good. They hadn't done that for a long time. Kicking the edges of sidewalks and heaps of leaves was what they could do.

They could hear the usual Saturday Nazi parade up by the station. Soon the marchers would cross the river, cross Neckar and then turn into Moltkestrasse. Soon they would stand in City Hall Square. It was rhythmic and measured, and one's feet tended to want to march along. The Communists' demonstrations had the same effect. So damn captivating, so treacherous.

*

'I understand,' Helmut murmurs. 'I have stood there on the pavement many times. They had the music, the charisma, but no good ideas or deeds. Feet wants to move, brain says no no.'

*

The brothers agreed on who would take the first watch and that the other should go home. But just then someone came out of the factory – a man wearing a swastika armlet but also a sad face.

'Have you been working? There are no orders,' said Julius in surprise. 'Go home.' He said this, as if he was still in command. As if the Kahns still made the decisions about their Zigarrenfabrik. They did, officially; it had not yet been aryanised as was already being threatened, the shop had not yet been let to non-Jews.

But in practice, the brothers had less of a say.

It was the Union head, Herr Müller who had come out of the plant, the chairman of the new Nazi Union,

Deutsche Arbeitsfront. Soon it would be compulsory for all workers to belong to this union: the old unions would be prohibited.

This particular DAF branch was OK, they wished no ill to anyone, even though they had had to force all the workers to come along and had taken over more and more in the boardroom.

'It's very bad,' Müller shook his head, resigned. 'This factory will go bankrupt if this continues. It would be easier to go on without you, then the factory wouldn't be harassed; but I understand if you wish to stay.'

'Well, we're struggling along,' Julius replied heavily. 'They won't kill us that easily.' He chuckled.

Müller glanced around quickly, then shifted closer to the two brothers.

'You see...' he began hesitantly, 'I have heard of something huge...' He took courage. 'I don't think I am supposed to tell you this, but there's a *big* change coming. At least I think so. We are being taught how to manage the factories and others have been told to find out where all the Jews work and where they live.' He pointed to the text on the wall. 'Bigger than anything before. It may come at any time. That's what I've found out.'

He realised suddenly that the two brothers weren't taking it in, weren't hearing what he was trying to tell them.

Grasping Julius by the shoulders he cried 'This is serious!' Focusing all his powers of communication intently at them he didn't continue until he was sure that he had their full attention. 'All Jewish property will be confiscated and you will be sent away! Industry will be Aryanised – no Jews are to own anything anymore! It's coming, I'm telling you!' He tried to calm his own agitation – what if there was someone watching? He could get into terrible trouble, just for telling these poor men this.

'Promise me that you'll leave here, *promise* me. It's not possible for me to be concerned for you much longer.'

The men stood, all three shocked at the urgency of Müller words for a moment – then Julius reached out to take his former employee's hand. Shaking his head desperately, the man pulled away and disappeared as swiftly as he had come, turning into Weststrasse; probably to take part in the march where they would yell nationalistic slogans and berate the Jews and try to convince everyone else to join their clubs, the 'healthy outdoors activities' that the Nazis love to organize – for everybody but the Jews.

Josef squatted down. Julius tucked his scarf tightly around his neck and shook his head.

'He may be right… in which case, there is nothing more to do,' he said quietly, his eyes wet.

Josef still couldn't quite bear to hear what he'd been so plainly told. 'He's only talking that way to make us leave the factory, so that they can take over!' he snapped bitterly. 'It is a swindle! They want to make us run away in order to be able to confiscate our property, all we have built…'

'Na, *und*…?' Julius was weary. 'We can't discuss this for days. Either you stay or you leave. We are still able to move.'

'I know,' Josef replied reluctantly, 'But how would we even go about it? Is there a permit required? What do we have to do…?'

'Let's make a call to Karl and Lins,' Julius was suddenly decisive. 'I'm sure we'll be allowed to go to Amsterdam. This regime wants nothing better than to get rid of us. If we can only reach Amsterdam, we could eventually go to England or America.'

'No! We can't!' Josef cried, finally pulled into to the harsh reality of their present. 'I'll stay! I won't give in!' He turned up his coat collar and jutted his chin. 'They can't decide our lives.'

'Josef, we must go! Damn it that it has to end this way!' Julius picked up a rock lying in the street and aimed at the remaining unbroken window. Josef didn't try to stop him. The stone fell well before the window.

*

'Are you sure of this?' Helmut intervenes.

'I'm illustrating it. Making it alive,' Fritz replies, and Walter puts his arm on Helmut's: they both know a Kahn story is more detailed than reality itself, more alive and perhaps not correct in all details but they, too, have learned to tell their stories this way.

'Listen now,' Fritz continues.

*

'Sweden or England might be safe places to go?' Josef was thinking out loud now. 'Sigmund and Fritz seem to be managing there?'

'No!' Julius was emphatic. 'Those are both countries that are too weak when Hitler demands anything: when he shouts, Europe trembles. And remember – Karl wasn't allowed to work in Sweden. We must get further away.' He stared into the distance for a moment, lost in thought. 'Cuba may be the place; we could talk to our suppliers there, they may be able to help us. There is more than one possibility.'

'*So ist es wohl,*' Josef said coldly. '*So ist es, schlecht. So schlecht ist es. Ist alles das...*' he pointed at the plant, '*Ist alles das vorbei, alles was wir gemacht haben?* It really is this bad. Everything we have, everything we've done – is it all truly over?'

Though each of them had one child working or studying in England, Julius did decide to go to Cuba.

There were long days, discussions that went on well into the night, about what to bring along and what not. To sell stuff was hardly an option. The Jewish things, the furniture, art, their mementos and keepsakes, clothes, stamp and stone collections...

Some of the children were especially fond of a piano – they had taken lessons and played elegies until their parents screamed at them, only to immediately come and hug them. An old desk was carefully polished, a bicycle that had been taken on a final ride, a lovely pedestal was moved to and fro between the luggage and the room where things were to stay; finally they decided to let it stay.

One had time to bid a fond farewell to a lover, the young said their goodbyes to their friends.

*

'But they weren't, after all, in time. It wasn't that easy.'

Fritz can't see the cosy English pub around him, can't feel the beer-stained table beneath his hands.

'On November 10 1938, the catastrophe came. We now know it was *Kristallnacht*, Crystal Night, the night that the Nazis destroyed all that belonged to the Jews all over Germany: in Heilbronn too. The synagogue was totally destroyed. That night the carpenter who just had finished renovating a room for Julius called on that family...'

*

'Don't worry. Please go to the bedroom and stay there,' he urged them, and then they heard him, smashing everything.

They had to live through it. They tried to keep out of sight.

*

Helmut and Walter listened, transfixed.

'One day,' Fritz continued, 'Josef couldn't stand it any more: he had to go back to the factory, whatever might happen to him, to see what was going on there. He tried to look around and not be spotted, tried to look ordinary, you understand? Not as if he owned the plant.' A heavy sigh.

*

In the street outside the factory, he was arrested.

At first he didn't realise what was happening when the men in dark clothes grabbed him without a word and shoved him into a lorry, where many others were already sitting.

First they headed towards Stuttgart and then towards Munich.

Finally they realised that they were going to Dachau. They had heard of the place, they knew it was a camp for people who opposed the Nazis.

They were ushered down roughly from the loading platform, registered, their belongings taken.

Then, they were allocated a place in one of about thirty barracks with long rows of wooden bunk beds.

In the daytime it was parading and hard words and nothing to do and uncertainty. It was like a prison; or what they thought a prison would be like. There was a striped uniform for those who could wear them, but they didn't fit anybody.

Most did nothing - they lay in their bunks. You were allowed to work, but Josef didn't. After a while they were all forced to work, to labour – but Josef avoided this for as long as they could. Many thoughts preoccupied him, mostly about his wife, Erna. His children were already out, in England and the US. Where were they? Were they safe? Would he ever see them again? Was it possible for his family to get out of the country without him? And one other thing that he couldn't let go of: 'All of us always tried to be good citizens, paying our way, giving people jobs. We were more German than most, and less Jewish than most! Don't these men in power now care about any of that? Our family has probably lived in Germany for a thousand years more than that little Austrian!'

Uncertainty gnawed relentlessly at him: what did these aggressive men want to do with them?

There were, he was sure, at least a thousand people stacked into this camp. There was no room for anything but beds, and although it was reasonably clean, sanitation was getting worse all the time. Josef was certainly not feeling well at all.

And then one day, there in the camp, Josef discovered his own brother, Leo, who has been brought from Munich.

They stopped for a second while memories and questions rushed through their heads. '*Du auch*,' Leo asked, his face a mask. Josef nodded. They exchanged a few words before being parted. They didn't dare to embrace or show their feelings. Leo's story was similar to the rest of his brothers who had left it too late, who had been too trusting. Who had thought that surely, in this country that had always been their home, this couldn't happen.

After two weeks in the cold camp, that place of fear and agonizing confusion, some were suddenly released. Josef had the possibility to go.

Leopold was freed after six weeks, possibly helped by a non-Jewish friend who was a policeman.

The condition of release was that one left Germany.

Josef's wife Erna had been paralysed with uncertainty when he was taken. She had no idea what to do, what to think or hope for. She feared for the worst: she couldn't get any information at all. She tried to make a telephone call to Josef's sister-in-law Emmy in London but she couldn't get through. Finally, they were allowed to leave the country. Josef had made it home and they collected all the money there was, bought the tickets and hid any that was left over, and went by train to the Landauers in Holland late in 1938.

Julius found his way out on 3 January 1939.

They really had to leave it all; they were only allowed to take small hand luggage. They tried to pick the most important things to fill the cases and take as much as they could carry.

Lins and her husband Karl met them at the Amsterdam railway station and they arrived at their fascinating house in the new area, south of the city centre, four stories with their own entrance in a block of flats. Karl's mother was also with them.

*

'And Leo took the chance of coming to England, to Emmy in 1939; he was only allowed to bring eight mark.'

'Thanks now I recall and the puzzle starts to fit,' Helmut interrupts.

'Yes, the factory was left to its destiny,' Fritz replies. 'Leo and his family went to the US as soon as they could, and for the others, Julius to Cuba, Josef to the U.S. in April 1940, the last boat in fact shortly before the Germans came. Anselm stayed in Holland even longer and got out first in 1941 when his son Stephen had arranged for his visa. The Nazis had already occupied Holland then. Horrible having to meet the Nazis face to face again.' He stirred himself, as if shaking off such terrible memories. 'Emmy helped those coming through England. Do you want more to eat or drink?' He calls on the waiter and then he continues.

'Now, your story Helmut,' he says. 'I want to know more about Sigmund's last years. I've talked to Emmy of course, but I can never be sure if she is trying to spare my feelings in some way. I want to know it all. He was a very good big brother to me; he took me into his business in Berlin when he had the women's wear shop in Mitte, the centre, and of course we continued our collaboration in tobacco after I'd come to England. We were close, at times. *Familie, immer Familie*. And you say you were close to Karl, *mein Schwager*?'

'Indeed,' Helmut agrees while lighting a cigarette, the third during this meal.

Stockholm and London 1939

Helmut begins with the story of his father.

'Although the family was now in England – you know we moved over here in 1934, Sigmund had travelled to Sweden for business. We agreed that I could look after the business day-to-day in Stockholm, and of course we were in contact all the time, and he came back often.

And then, this time, in June '39, he had a heart attack again on the train from Copenhagen to Stockholm. He described it as a pain over the chest up into the jaw, all over the upper part of his body really. As he had had it before he knew what it was. He tried to just relax on the train but the pain didn't stop. He told the attendant, and an ambulance was waiting for him at the station. He thought, the optimist he always was, that some time in hospital would make him better. He was placed under good care at the Maria hospital in Stockholm, a small, old building on the southern island, and I took care of him...'

*

Helmut sent a cable to his mother and sisters, and they immediately travelled back, too, so that the whole family could be with Sigmund.

Then they waited, to see if he was going to make it, and if so, to see if he would recuperate enough for them to be able to go back home to England. Käthe's wedding was supposed to be in August, not so very far away: there was a lot to be planned.

But Sigmund didn't seem to be getting any better. Helmut was staying in the office on Fredsgatan near the castle, very central: he lived there now in a small room. Emmy and the girls had taken a room at the Grand Hotel.

Midsummer was coming up, the biggest and happiest festival of the year in Sweden. That year, with a war that no one seemed to be able to prevent looming on the horizon, the Swedes planned even bigger celebrations.

'Mutti, how do I look? Is this good?' Käthe, now in her early 20s, turned in her flowery pleated skirt. Her stocky body was like her mother's. She had put flowers in her hair.

'With our shape, posture is what is really vital,' Emmy used to tell her, 'And to make the most of one's face: this is the style that works for us.' Emmy, had her regal baring that made her round figure part of her allure. Käthe knew and Käthe tried. Käthe wanted to be as pretty as her sister Ilse who had inherited her looks from Sigmund's side of the family. Ilse had an hourglass figure – now 18, the men turned to look at her.

'Mother, can't we go out to celebrate Midsummer, even if Father is ill?' Ilse asked. She was engaged, a grown-up, really, though still sometimes with the selfishness of a child. She didn't normally ask her mother for permission, but considering the circumstances, she would do what she, or her father, said. Even Helmut, who was 25, was listening more deferentially to his parents.

Ilse walked to the window and looked down at the street and the water below. 'It may be the last time we are in Sweden for Midsummer.'

There can't be anything greener than Sweden in June. Below her, a long row of well-dressed people was walking, wearing light colours, happy, some clinging onto each other. The many cars she could see were also polished for the day and sometimes had birch branches mounted at the front or on the sides.

A typical Swedish midsummer.

The sun was still high, even though it was nine o'clock at night.

Helmut was quite convinced that it would be war again very soon. Emmy was not so certain. She said that everybody remembered the last time around and that surely no one was stupid enough to start something like that again, in spite of all the noise from the speakers' platforms and all the sabre-rattling. She had taken the girls, almost dragged them, to Sweden so that they could be with Sigmund. She knew that he probably didn't have much time left – those were, in fact, precisely the doctor's words on the line from Stockholm. They had had to delay the planning of Käthe's wedding, but it was still due to go ahead in August. And Ilse had to leave her love too. Käthe and Sigmund were closer, but Ilse was a mother's girl – she had never got on well, really, with her father. She thought he was disgusting, with all his love affairs.

*

'Oh, Sigmund?! But he was so charming!' Fritz intervenes.

'Perhaps not for a daughter,' Helmut replies sourly. 'But finally she came along anyhow, and yet she felt forced, uprooted; her mind was more in England with her love. She was young. I'm sure death didn't seem so real to her.'

*

'Mutti, we're going to go along with Helmut to that party; we won't be too late,' Käthe called. 'There will be herring and shrimps and salmon... all the things that we don't have in England! And we'll see friends we haven't met for all these years. Oh, how I long for this! We can, can't we? Do I look swell? Mutti?'

Her mother frowns, distracted. 'No... no, you can't go – we should go to Vati in the hospital. He would like you to be there.'

So they took a tram down to the hospital.

Big rooms, lined with heart patients... they were ushered in. But the doctor was still in there. That wasn't a good sign.

Sigmund's chest was aching, aching so much. He lay still, his face drawn.

'Oh, how warm and lovely the Swedish summer is,' Emmy said quietly, not even sure that her husband could hear her, or if she wanted him to. She put her small hand full of rings and charms to the back of her neck. 'I wouldn't mind staying here instead of grey England. Oh, if only you could live to see another Swedish summer... but of course soon we have to go back to London. Käthe, you only have a month.'

Emmy watched her husband, who, if possible, was even paler than before. Slowly he stretched his hand to hers and grabbed it. His three children stood further back. He looked at them. 'Go out, my dears,' he said, 'Enjoy yourselves. Midsummer's Night is for the living.'

'Mother? Is everything alright?' Ilse took off her shoes and rubbed her heel that hurt from so much dancing – the shoes were new and Swedish, well made, but hard. She had danced with so many partners that she had almost forgotten missing Bren for a while.

As soon as the sisters had stepped out of the cab onto the still bustling street, they got worried. They weren't that late, were they?

'Oh I have danced all night! It is so light, at two o'clock at night! But why are you up? Mother – what is the matter?'

'Mutti?' Käthe stepped forward, suddenly aware of the atmosphere in the room. 'Why do you look like that? Oh Mutter. Is it...? I mean... is he? What is it? Vati!'

'Now, children,' Emmy said, her eyes red and wet as she reached out to them. 'It is too late to cry: it's all over. The doctor just called. It is over.'

The sisters stand stunned – why had they not expected this? They knew how ill he was! But they had just seen him, this evening...

Their mother hugged them, but didn't let her emotions take her over. 'Go to bed now, girls, we have a busy day tomorrow, with all the arrangements for the funeral; there is so much to do... the synagogue, the congregation and everything... Your father wanted it all to be properly Jewish. She raises the glass to her lips, drinks quickly, and places it back on the table. We will have the service and sit Shiva, keep to the old ways, just as Father wanted it.'

'Day and night for several days?' asked Ilse, her mind already flying to how soon she could be back with Bren. And then another thought struck her, aroused by this sudden turn towards the Jewish traditions that the family had let slide, especially when Sigmund wasn't around. 'But – I mean... does that mean that we're not allowed to marry anybody non-Jewish either? I mean, I could marry Bren couldn't I?' She checked herself; she had been babbling disgracefully. 'I'm sorry Mummy, ignore me.' She held her mother. 'I promise, we will do it as he wanted it. I'm sorry. I am so tired, I am so tired and sad, poor Mother.' She was a little sad, too. She hadn't expected to be.

And yet, oddly enough Emmy slept like a log while her daughters had problems sleeping after all the wine and laughing and dancing and then the shock when they arrived home. They didn't have to jump any fences and didn't have to have any flowers under their pillows, as the Swedish girls used to at Midsummer, in order to dream of the right man. They already had their men at home waiting for them.

The men awaited them, the war awaited them in turn, but these girls were now fatherless, their mother a widow a few weeks before her 48th birthday.

Life had taken a new turn, and outside, the party was still going on as if this really was the last Midsummer. Many girls had men who would soon be drafted. They all knew this – no one was going to miss this moment. For Käthe and Ilse death had come visiting: not often very close, now they held hands and whispered quietly. Mostly, they were worried about their mother, who they had left standing stoical and forlorn in the other room

The next morning a cable arrived for Ilse from Bren. It was great news. His mother had somehow managed to buy him out of the army – now he didn't have to go to India. (As soon as war was declared he was drafted into the air force; but that was in the future now.) She ran to the telephone to dictate an answer. 'I want to send a telegram to England!' she exclaimed, delighted not only at the news, but also at the brief chance to get away from the sadness of their rooms. 'The text is: 'Wonderful news stop I am so happy stop Father died yesterday stop.' It was only when she heard the cable operator's surprised as she read it back that Ilse realised what it sounded like. She glanced over at her mother – she had overheard. At first angry and upset, Emmy quickly realised what had happened, and then even laughed a little as always; but she stopped very quickly. She was supposed to be mourning and she was. But it sounded terrible.

Sigmund's funeral at the end of June 1939 was just as Jewish as he had wished for, except they couldn't find his shawl, his tallit. It had probably been left in England. But he was well wrapped anyhow, and everybody went out to the Jewish Cemetery, where they each tipped three shovels of soil in the grave.

*

It's All Coming Back

'We didn't have much time for mourning, and none of us was any good at it. The world was in limbo...' Helmut paused, remembering. 'In truth, now that Father had died, that was preoccupying us more than our own family tragedy. And Käthe could not, did not want to postpone her marriage. She knew that her fiancé Henry might be drafted at any time once the war came. She and mother talked for a long time, about how to make time for a proper celebration. It was hard for Käthe – she was the one who was closest to Sigmund, at least of the women in the family.' He didn't speak of his own grief, or even if he felt it. 'I tried to get all the business matters in order. There were so many things I didn't know. The firm's standing was much worse than I had thought. We had to sell a lot to be able to go home to London. We had a busy time; especially those women who love to prepare parties and are keen to do so.' Fritz and Walter wondered if they should be shocked, or at least pretend to be – but no, they all knew how it was.

'In Stockholm the funeral was small and rushed, an intimate ceremony with just the family and a few friends. Quite different from Käthe's wedding. Käthe and her husband stamped on the wine glass and walked under the canopy, and I think it was a glorious party. Everyone talked to me and reminisced about Sigmund - but most of all, we talked of the future, or about our old homes in Germany; if that was our home country, when the place that you loved had been stripped of all memories.'

'I remember,' Walter says. 'The mood was almost magical – Nazis, smog and war felt very distant there and then after a short and still afternoon rain.

*

'Shortly after their wedding, I had to go back to Sweden,' Helmut says. War was racing towards us, and I didn't want to stay in England. I had so much binding me to Sweden. The business had to be managed and, still, sorted out.

I went to ferry ports and railways stations, trying to get hold of a ticket to Sweden, but it seemed quite impossible. Finally I got a ticket for a boat from Newcastle to Bergen. It proved to be the last boat, the last contact before the war between Scandinavia and England… soon isolation took hold.

The journey was rough, with bad weather and long detours; areas had been suspended for non-military traffic: the time of convoys and naval mines had begun. Vessels could no longer go where they wanted to, unaccompanied.

And then, finally I was back in the Stockholm apartment in Fredsgatan; back at work, but so lonely, so damn lonely, despite girls and friends.

Before long, I was drafted and life in the barracks was different, loneliness was different, it was greater and I had really not many to write to: the mail service to England was interrupted.

'That is why I don't know about how they got out of Holland.' Helmut cocks his melancholy eye at his uncle.

'You were left in Stockholm.' Fritz says. 'I'm glad Sweden wasn't occupied as well, I truly dread to think what might have happened then.' Another deep sigh. 'We brothers have now nearly nothing left of all we once had, but we are alive.' He nods to himself, his eyes looking deeply inward. 'But Lins, my baby sister Lins, she and Karl stayed in Holland.' He pauses, for a long time.

'But why?' Helmut asks, leaning forward and accidentally pushing the table so his drink spilled a little.

'I really don't know I tell you! The children were at school, he had his business… I think they *wanted* to go, but they stayed on. These decisions aren't easy!'

'Indeed,' Helmut agrees solemnly. 'And now we know what happened. But they must have their premonitions'

'I believe they did: indeed, I believe they did – those poor people. Well: we didn't have an easy time either! But it was so much worse for those that left it so late.'

It's All Coming Back

*

Over the last generation all of the brothers and their sister had become richer and used to a more *bourgeois* way of living.

In England they weren't allowed to work at first, and it took ten years to become a UK citizen. That's why Anselm, Leopold and Josef chose the US and Julius Cuba – countries where it was possible to start from the bottom again.

At night, they dreamed of the cigar factory, 'felt' the smell of the leaves, and woke up speaking German.

*

'But what other language did we have? It is hard to pronounce English and there are so many new words, and as for Spanish... But all my brothers and my sister are alive and safe, strangely enough. We were among the lucky ones.'

'Quite right; we are the lucky ones.' They sit still for quite some while each reflects over another pint, Fritz reflecting over how they all had come out and his dead brother, Helmut on why it was they that were saved from most of the hardships of war and the holocaust. Helmut suddenly looks at his watch, *Oh dear I have to leave*. 'We have to meet again soon, Fritz! There is so much more to talk about, and business, not least business!' He stands up and shakes his uncle's hand, at the same time trying to wipe the drinks that he has spilled from the surface of the old table. And Helmut is off in a wink, leaving the cheque for Fritz.

Belsize Park, London, March 1946

Next day he and Emmy have lunch with his cousin and Emmy's niece Trudy, a very head-on woman, working as a nurse and who is married to Helmuth's best friend from Oxford. Helmuth immediately starts telling the story of the uncles in Dachau that he heard the day before. He is upset and recapitulates it fast. 'The same for so many', his mother interrupts. 'Also my brother Erich and Gerald had to go to Sachsenhausen after the Kristallnacht.'

'Oh dear, seriously I haven't heard that, was it for long, how did they come out? Erich is in Palestine and Gerald in Argentine aren't they?

"Yes, indeed they are, it was a month or more, you perhaps have not seen Gerald's story of it all, my brave twin brother wrote it all down. I must show it to you later,' Trude says. 'But he writes this, if I remember correctly: We began to wait for the first sound of the whip. Then we started counting, each one for himself, first up to ten, to twelve, to fifteen, to twenty. Even up to fifty lashes we had to count sometimes. And there was no other sound in the whole camp. You just heard the whip falling on human flesh; you seem to see with all your mind how the man flinches under each impact, yet he does not utter a sound. First we grew pale with rage and fear; but the food they fed us left us without strength or with just enough to keep us going, but none for unnecessary emotions.'

Helmuth shakes his head.

'Terrible isn't it', Emmy adds.

'They were shaven, all their hair taken away, put in prison clothes and became numbers not names', Trude says. 'When my father and brother met in the camp Vater told Gerald "Shut up, keep your eyes open, keep moving, and if they want to kick you, put your behind before them, there it hurts least."

'And so many others never came out. I heard so many stories when I volunteered with refugees and this is my own kin', she says.

Eva's story

'Now: Eva's story, or dessert first?' Hans smiles. 'You go and look in the coffee area over there,' he points with the stick he always carries: he was wounded in the first war, a bullet in hip. 'Pastries, croissants and bitter coffee are the favourites here. They bake here themselves every day. They have *apfelstrudel* and other good things from home. A strudel for me please, and a strong coffee.'

Slightly taken aback but this sudden cheerful interjection, Helmut goes and collects desserts for Hans and for himself: Emmy doesn't want anything. The moment he returns to the table, she starts her story. She isn't one for waiting, something she expresses eloquently with a light rattle with of her bracelets.

'Well … the door opened one day to the Cake Shop. A slender young woman entered, short, thin, with sprawling black hair and lots of lipstick. I stood up and smiled, I didn't know how to react.'

Her new husband smiles at her with love. 'I remember. You gave that warm, inviting laugh, which you always use when you meet new customers or indeed new people of any kind.'

*

Emmy clapped her hands. Could it be? No, not this thin girl. But…maybe, after all? Yes - it was! *Es ist ja Eva, Karl und Lins Tochter*, Sigmund's niece!- She hurried out from behind the counter, and just held her. Hugged and hugged her. And she, this hardly recognisable young woman, so thin, and with such a curved posture hugged her back, so hard – Emmy realised that the girl was clutching on to her cardigan.

They stood like that for some time.

'*Eva! Bist es wirklich du, Eva, du lebst, du bist hier, Eva, aber wo sind Mutti und Karl und Suse und Paulus?!*' – Emmy couldn't believe it. She knew, she could *see* that this was Eva: but the young woman had changed so – grown older, grown gaunt, she remembered her as a girl.

*

'But she came to London from Holland once, don't you remember,' Helmut asked.

'Of course, yes, but I remembered her as fifteen or something, I think it was probably because she was so small.' Emmy's eyes were growing red at the memory. 'I think it was deeply moving for Eva to see me again, her aunt, *Tante Emmy*: I was the first member of the family that she had seen in England. She sat down on the Windsor chair that has been put there for the customers. I asked her about everything and everybody, of course, my words were tumbling out in such a rush – but she just looked at me; she couldn't catch her breath. I couldn't put up the 'Closed' and 'Back soon' signs because of all the customers that still had to be served. 'This is my niece, she has survived the camps, can you imagine?' – I found myself saying that to some of the customers I knew well – maybe I had to say it out loud to believe it? And when she heard it, I saw that Eva blushed a little.'

*

Eva didn't say anything for a long time. Eventually, Emmy closed the shop and took her hand, and they walked slowly back to Emmy's flat without a word. The older woman was content to be quiet for once, immersed in the simple pleasure of being able to cradle Eva's thin, narrow body. Once inside, the girl asked if she could have a bath, and was in the bathroom for what seemed like hours while Emmy went back and forth in the narrow corridor on the other side of the door, wringing her hands, so worried.

When Eva finally emerged, she apologised for using too much water. 'I scrubbed myself over and over, and then I filled the bath up to the brim – I know the English don't do it that way. I've heard they only fill it up for an inch or so and then scoop it over themselves.'

Emmy shook her head, her mouth pursed with sadness – what did it matter? But now Eva couldn't stop talking. 'I couldn't stop myself; I slid down in the water looking at this thin body, this strange body, and I don't know how I will ever get my own shape back again, my roundness – when would I ever dare to show myself to a man?'

Emmy was teary now, she had heard, through the door, Eva talking to her own body, humming. She held her hands out to her niece, taking them gently.

'Could you help me *Tante* Emmy? There was blood in the bath. Do you have any napkins? I'm so sorry, I didn't know it was going to happen – it hasn't for so long.' Her voice hiccupped to a stop, and she stared at her aunt. 'I am still alive.' And then she, too, started to cry. Emmy nodded, tried to soothe her.

'I've actually underwear with me,' Eva began again, unable to stop, now. 'Could – do you think I might borrow a drop of your perfume?'

*

'And then she said she had also been sent some from you, Helmut.' Emmy holds her son's eyes in a steady gaze.

'Yes,' he nods. 'I sent them some small things. What I thought they needed.'

'She was trying to tell me,' Emmy continues, 'But the words didn't always come the way she wished them to do.

Jon Kahn

*

Lins and Eva had been released some time before Bergen-Belsen was liberated in April 1945 and had travelled for fourteen days on a train to Berlin. Two weeks is a very long time to travel that distance. The train journey was full of stops and detours; sometimes the train was rolling but a lot changing of tracks, and uncertainty. Imagine fourteen days for a stretch that normally takes what? Maybe a day, maybe half a day. After they had been dropped off in a small village by the Elbe, they had had a terrible time; they were taken by the Americans to Leipzig, where they were abandoned again, and then managed somehow to find their way back to Holland, to Maastricht, where they were reunited with some difficulty with Eva's sister, Suse. That wasn't the end of their misery; there they were, with nothing, in that war-torn land, all anarchy, hunger and crime. But they managed somehow.

*

'Yes,' Helmut chips in. 'And Suse had been in Arnhem… you heard about the bombings and the terrible fires there?' His mother nods, her face creased. His face wears the same expression. 'It must have been awful.'
Emmy claps her small hands and continues.
'Eva didn't have the energy to tell me more at that moment, although she wanted to; she was tired of everybody feeling so sorry for her, she was so damn tired of that, she said.

*

At breakfast the next day, Eva was quiet again, just looking at her aunt. All Emmy wanted was to hug the poor girl, to cuddle her and make a fuss of her. But she sat and watched as Eva gobbled her food. She tried to slow herself down, to pause between mouthfuls, but she simply couldn't. Then she went out: she wanted to walk by herself, she said, just peacefully, taking things in. Emmy didn't have time to tell her what she had planned.   After walking for a while, Eva found herself outside a pub; it only took a moment for her to decide to go in and order a beer. She took a seat, got her breath back, and sipped it slowly. Somewhere in the background Vera Lynn was singing from a record player: *We'll meet again, don't know where, don't know when ...* Suddenly, she realised that there was a young man sitting next to her: she had chosen a table with two chairs, and he was already occupying the other one. This was certainly not a situation that she'd intended – she had assumed that there were different rooms for men and women. Picking up her glass, she looked around for another table, but he took her hand. Hesitantly, she sat down again.

'I can move!' he said, 'I think you need this seat much more than I do. I'm just taking a bit of a break from work, you know. Got to pop back soon...' He smiled at her nervously. 'But on the other hand... on the other hand, I would very much appreciate the chance to be able to sit here by you? I mean if it doesn't embarrass you? We don't need to talk or anything. If your husband isn't going to join you, of course, or your fiancé?' She smiled, lifted her glass steadily and took a gulp.

'She feels alive again and small things, human contact and interaction means a lot to her. She returned to us,' Emmy frets, even now. 'She had to start packing up her things – so I sat and talked to her while she did it.'

※

'Your perfume brings back memories,' Eva said quietly as they sat on her trunk, trying to close it.

Emmy smiled. 'Do you remember the smell? Yes, I always wore it, I would have been wearing it when we met in London and in Stockholm...' She touched her fingers to the pulse at her throat. 'I've worn the same perfume since it came out. It is intoxicating.'

Eva nodded. 'It makes me think of our home in Frankfurt, all the pomanders in the corners, all the fine ladies, Father's patients sometimes also smelled good. He had his *Psychoanalytisches Institut*...' She paused, then turned a questioning gaze on her aunt. '*Tante* Emmy, I've never understood: why didn't we move to Stockholm when the Nazis threw us out in '33?'

'Eva asked as if I knew, but how could I know all that?, 'Emmy said. 'But she really wanted an answer. 'Why didn't Karl stay there and why didn't we move there? Do you know? I know my father was very angry when they closed his Institut and then he went alone to you in Stockholm. I know he chose Stockholm as his first option.'

'There are so many questions,' Emmy agreed. 'Why did you have to go to Holland, of all places? I have so many questions to ask about your parents and your sister and brother, it is too bad we do not have time for that now. When will we get time for that?'

'I don't know about Stockholm!' Eva said. 'I was too small, I suppose, and we never had the opportunity to talk about it in the camp... My father worked with other people's minds all day. I remember when we came to Amsterdam, he was very disappointed with Sweden and he said he didn't understand why the country was so much following Germany and not wanting any Jews or Psychoanalytics.

Emmy's eyes filled. 'Your Father... Oh, poor Karl! I liked your father very much,' Emmy reached for Eva's hand. 'Who knows – I could have fallen in love with him if I hadn't met Sigmund first. He was tall and handsome and he had that voice, that soothing voice of his that no one could resist.' She gave a small, sad smile.

'The voice was all that was left by the end,' Eva whispered, her eyes closed.

'Oh...' Emmy's face was stricken. 'He was so broken already after the gas in the First War. Sigmund and all the brothers should have listened to him, and they shouldn't have gone to that war! My Sigmund could have saved his head!' She twisted her hands together as she remembered. 'There is so much coming up in my mind now. Even my first child, before Helmut.

'Another child, never heard of that.'

'He died.'

'Did you lose a child?' Eva said. 'I didn't know. So awful.'

'For us then, but not compared to what you have experienced.' Emmy stroked her hair.

*

'Eva looked very interested when she talked about you Helmut.' Emmy looks at her son, but he doesn't react.

'I told her that we hadn't seen each other for so long, you and I. I said, if only he would settle down some time, marry, you know...' She smiled at him. 'But of course, that was before this news of yours about Anne-Marie. How fast it all has developed. Oh Helmut I am so happy for you!'

'Continue with the story please, Mother,' Helmut responds, irritated.

She nods. 'I asked Eva to please, just for a short while at least, sit with me on the sofa and tell me what she could. I'd heard such different things, from different people, and none of it added up to any kind of clear picture. I even asked her, "Did you really have a fiancée in the camp?" So – we curled up tight together on my sofa, sipped some tea and ate some cakes...' Helmut watches his mother's eyes grow unfocused as she stares into the past.

'And, all the questions and answers finally came out,' she said, 'And Eva's story came too, slowly. She knew she had to talk about it, even though there were only half sentences now and then. But it had to come out and she told it all."

Amsterdam and Westerbork 1943-1944

So Emmy begins recapitulating the long and terrible story, and Helmut listens very carefully.

*

Karl, Lins and their three children were forced to take each day as it came; they were trapped in uncertainty. They would dream at times, of what they might do - fantasies were their small joy. But in reality, they had no possibility of planning anything.

The Germans had now occupied Holland for several years.

Karl was not having an easy time of it. His time was spent writing articles, holding lectures and analysing. He was dealing a great deal with narcissism in his work. About men, mainly men, who believe they are superman but yet have no real self-esteem. He was also developing his thoughts on affect, sudden anger, lack of patience and infernality without cause. And of prejudice and stupidity.

There weren't many people in his life now with which he could discuss these things. He, who was so full of words, full of a need to explain and to discuss, didn't have many contacts in the psychoanalytical world any more. He wrote of course, wrote for himself and also letters like to Max Horkheim, the man who had been his friend and collaborator, the head of the Social Institute in Frankfurt, and who had now gone to the U.S. – but Karl knew that his letters were censored before they left Holland.

He wasn't a member of the Psychoanalytical Society anymore. He had made a stupid mistake, and they had seized on the chance to expel him. He wasn't, to be sure, the first doctor who had had a love affair with an ex-patient; but he was German and Jewish. By that time, he was only allowed to have other Jews as patients. Now he was not allowed to do psychoanalysis at all.

He was trying to analyse himself, how this had come to happen and how he had been affected. His daughter Eva had gotten more and more involved in this process, and more and more interested in the subject. That was when she became determined to follow in her father's footsteps and become a psychotherapist.

They couldn't show their feelings to anybody. Not publicly and hardly even at home. It was a false situation to begin with. They were five adults – in another time the children would have started to move out at that age. But those were not normal times. Karl and Eva became close as they analysed each other, and he let her join a few sessions with the very few Jewish people he was allowed to work with.

There was a curfew through the night that began early in the evening. Lins cautioned her children over and over again to get in before the curfew began in evenings, and yet they didn't always remember. Often she went out and ordered them to come back home, despite the fact that they were all grown up. She couldn't stop the feeling that it was her responsibility – she clucked over them like a mother hen.

Theirs wasn't a particularly orthodox household, but now they took their old Jewish artefacts from cupboards and drawers for Friday night, for Sabbath in the house they inhabited since a couple of years in the south of Amsterdam. It was a nice house, relatively newly built, four stories with their own door at the bottom and a balcony at the top and trees in the street.

It just happened that just around the corner from their house was the Zentralstelle für jüdische Auswanderung, an SS-started activity for getting Jews to go to the east, to work as they were told. Around the other corner was the Expositur; Expositur was a section of the Jewish Council of Amsterdam that acted as a liaison with the Zentralstelle. At the Expositur the registration of exemptions from deportation was processed. The family was in the middle of everything really. All of this within two or three blocks of flats. Paulus worked in the Expositur, Suse, the youngest, worked near the Schouwburg in a Jewish kindergarten, Eva worked with the Jewish Council as a social worker in a school and even Karl now worked on behalf of the Jewish Council as a psychiatrist.

It was a question all the time of how much to cooperate, on how to save your own life as well as others. In May 1943, German authorities ordered 7,000 Jews, including employees of the Judenrat in Amsterdam, to assemble in an Amsterdam city square for deportation. Karl's mother was deported in May to Westerbork. They had their Sperre, not to be deported in their ID.s but who knows. They carried on and even hid people at times, those who otherwise were to be deported. Through the Jewish Council, Eva or Lins got the messages about whom to hide, sometimes whispered in the queue at the butchers or bakers. Sometimes a Gestapo man entered the shop, just as they were talking and they had to drop something or adjust the clothes to divert their interest.

They tried to help their co-victims in the midst of all the fear and anxiety. There was a lot to deal with.

Now it was Sabbath. There was a black prayer book, which Karl opened on its first page, the one at the back of the book. Then there was the adorned silver chalice, the Kiddush beaker, which came from his wealthy Munich family's home. Some of their stuff, also the Jewish stuff, was left in Frankfurt when they had to move in haste; some Karl left with Emmy and Sigmund in Stockholm.

*

'And did you hear about my grandmother, Karl's mother?' Eva said.

Emmy's face is like stone. 'I heard that she disappeared in the camps? That is so sad.'

Eva nods jerkily. 'She died in Sobibor. I recently found out, we didn't know for so long where they had taken her. She was so strong and...' And then she begins to cry silently and her story was interrupted for a while.

Emmy gently holds a handkerchief out to her, and she wipes her eyes.

'Oh how I loved her,' Eva gasps, 'you know, she was so self-assured and independent. A modern woman of that age.'

Silently, Emmy goes to fetch a candle for remembrance, and lights it. They sit silent for a long time, moving slowly, looking at the candle and at nothing at all.

'Where was I?' Eva asks after a while, and wipes her eyes again.'

'Sabbath,' Emmy replies quietly.

*

Karl had always said that he hated his Jewish ancestry, his upper class legacy, the mendacious and mincing. But now he wanted to have Sabbath again, one last time, and then get rid of all these things. He talked about his mother as well.

Lins reached out to comfort him, but he shook her off.

'What should we do with these things?' she asked. 'We have to be careful. No one must find them. They may be a burden some day.' She took a bit of bread from the cupboard and a bottle of red wine. 'This will do instead of the *challah*,' she said and put it on the table for her husband to break after he's read the Sabbath prayer.

'We must get rid of the Jewish things first, and what we want to have left if we are sent away and then come back,' Karl said while he very slowly opened the bottle and let it drop into the chalice. 'The eternal issue: should we hide or not? We have to decide.'

'I know: we have to decide,' Lins answered. 'How many times have we discussed this? Hide and maybe make it, but live like fugitives: no job, and no one else helping us. And even then, we may be discovered and then surely be sent east...' Her voice fades – there is no point in going over all of this again, and yet she feels they must.

Karl rubs his hand over his face. 'We should probably continue to live in the open but as modestly as possible; not drawing attention to ourselves. I hate it. I just want to live, get on with my life, work. I want to be able to travel – to go to the US, to London. I want to meet colleagues and to discuss things with them. I want to love you, Lins.' He looks at her, his face hollow. 'There is no obvious choice. We are trapped like mice. The trick is to be quite still, so that the trap doesn't smash us.' His knuckles whiten. 'I hate this.'

Slowly over the next few days and weeks, we moved our belongings, bit by very small bit, to the chemist on the corner who had agreed to help. Well hidden on the way there, and well hidden once there.

They tried to lead our lives as normally as possible, tried not to make a fuss. They discussed, again, for hours, if they should hide or stay quiet in their flat... and yes, continued with the latter.

The Alsatians that belonged to the Germans police were the cocks of Amsterdam in those days; mad dogs howling instead of roosters calling.

They made it throughout May and most of June while others were summoned. Many trying to escape were shot. Others just disappeared.

Karl talked endlessly about the family in England, Cuba, Sweden and the US, and about all his psychoanalyst friends in America, planning continuously for the family's departure. He had been coming up with ideas – fantasies, really – ever since he came to Holland, of where he wanted them to live. The USA was now his aim.

Even though news of the war turning came to them, they saw the starker reality. The Nazis had begun to employ a more systematic approach. They took it block by block.

'I have written about Nazism and narcissism, haven't I? Lucky for me I don't have to burn my thoughts,' Karl said, smiling. He stood more and more in front of the stove, sweeping his hand over his hair that was getting thinner by the day, and warmed himself by burning papers.

When Lins came home after her short walks, the only little excursions she dared to take, she checked meticulously to see if anybody had touched the door or been inside. She sniffed around and made sure nothing had been moved.

They had imagined the situation so many times, had gone over all the possible details. They already sensed how it would be to hear the steps, feel the smell of polished leather, hear their names being read out, feel the pistol in their backs. Karl, more than anyone else, had always known that this would be a reality, and yet he had tried to banish it from his thoughts.

*

'You had to, in order to survive.' Eva huddles into herself, remembering. 'They were getting closer again. It was very obvious that we would be reached; why not us too?'

*

It really was inevitable that the Nazis would haunt them, and find them again.

It's All Coming Back

Karl remembered every second from the last time, almost exactly ten years before, when his institute in Frankfurt was closed down.

The same men, dressed in brown and black, came screaming and crashing, though last time they were somewhat more decent - they hadn't yet learnt to shout as loud and fight as hard.

Practice makes perfect.

That first time; it wasn't as close to home, as personal. But they had come at night and taken our passports.

This time they were all much cruder. Bestiality had grown over the decade.

It was splendid, sunny weather in Amsterdam in that month of June 1943. It was the kind of weather where you just have to go out... but when they did go out they had to be on constant alert, tightly wound, tense, nervous.

One could hear the yelling from several blocks away when there was a raid on apartments and houses where Jews were living. And there were many in Amsterdam.

The family had talked about how to behave when they came, when they really came. There was no point in lying or resisting. They had to be careful not to tell about those that they had hidden of course, just tell their names and own up, when asked, to their Jewishness – they didn't feel very Jewish, but of course it was their legacy. And one could see it, notice it – those types could even smell it. They didn't even have to take down the men's underwear.

Karl was standing by the window looking at some sparrows fighting over a piece of bread. For them there were no cordons or curfews. He later told Eva about this. In his hand he held some manuscripts, articles about children with early disruption in their lives leading to neuroses. He had to read them quickly for the last time and memorize them. He couldn't publish them now; but maybe after the war. All his psychoanalytical material would be used against him and, what is worse, against his patients. What people said in confidence would be used against them. Eva never discovered what he did with everything. She didn't know if what was left when they came back was all there was, or not.

*

They didn't have much fire for the stove at the time. Perhaps he went to the stove, crumpled the papers and put them under a couple of broken cigar cases that were already there and set fire to the lot?' Eva was still trying to puzzle it out, even now.

*

One day they heard the yells and ruckus much closer. They were afraid that the Germans would come to get them now. Mother, father and Eva decided to leave the building as night fell. Lins was shivering as they walked out, if it was the cold or the fear, Karl took her arm and they walked decisively. One place to go was the Expositur; they thought it might be safer there. Paulus and Suse were out in town late and still working. Eva started working on papers in the Expositur and the parents sat down in another room drinking some coffee. The arrests were haphazard in a way, they took some and let the rest live on with their fears and anxiety. This night they came in and brought out some including Karl and Lins. The men in black uniforms came and took them, mother and father.

*

'They just took some, to scare us I think, mother and father but they never looked into the room where I was sitting.'

'So ingeniously diabolic' Emmy says.

*

The three children were left behind, holding on, and they managed it for a month. Living as quietly as we could, often sleeping with friends, walking around, going to cafés, living a low life, trying not to draw any attention. Talking and talking about how to carry on, could we join the underground movement, escape or live on? And of course discussing about what could have happened to our parents.

But the day came when they were rounded up as well. They moved us to a square and on the way the Nazis beat those who did try to talk or moved strangely. Paulus walked slowly over to some men working along the street and managed to mix in but we sisters were forced forward when the trucks came.

*

'It was then Suse carried out her crazy plan. Well – I say plan, but it was quite impulsive I think, when it came to it.' Eva shakes her head at the images crowding her head. 'You know, we'd heard so many stories, stories about Westerbork, the camp in Friesland built by the Dutch themselves.'

Emmy frowns as she listens – dear God, what had happened to people, to everyone, during that terrible time? Eva continues:

'I heard it was not the worst, but what really did anyone know? And we had also heard about deportation to the east. That was worse. None of us were afraid to die or had got accustomed to the thought but Papa often told me that he was afraid that he wouldn't be able to accomplish anything more. He was also afraid of the reaction of others to him dying, of all the fuzz; he didn't want others to get hurt. He was afraid someone else in his family would die. We all were! Of course we were! We were all still so upset about Granny being taken before.' Her voice gets shrill, and Emmy moves closer, offering subconscious comfort.

'We were put in a long line with hundreds of others in front of trucks that looked as if their last load had been cattle. We had heard about these cattle trucks. We could see how people up front were being driven onto them. We were standing in the far corner, quiet, utterly silent, humiliated, scared, lost. We tried not to look over the crowd to see our brother.' Now she gives a huge sigh. 'It was then, all of a sudden, that Suse bolted from the line without warning – and she just walked away! There was not that many soldiers; perhaps they did not notice her.'

Emmy gasps. This is all too terrible to hear. It is as if she is there, back with them in that awful place.

'I didn't see her do it,' Eva continued, 'I mean we tried to be close to each other but there were so much people. If I had done, I might have tried something too, and maybe I wouldn't be here now. Paulus had already escaped. It wasn't until later that I heard about his bravery, and what he went through. He was with the resistance in Belgium and France and was starving and his feet froze, it was a miracle he made it to Spain and then to Palestine. But perhaps you heard that?'

*

Sitting alone with Helmut, telling him all this at last, is bringing it all back for Emmy. 'I nodded,' she says. 'I couldn't do much more than hold her hand as gently as I could, though Eva sometimes didn't even want to be touched.'

Helmut is listening intently. His mother continues. 'I was so upset I couldn't utter a word... I was murmuring and aha-ing and nodding.'

*

Eva continued her story.

'I went on the bed of one of those awful trucks to Westerbork and Suse was not to be seen. I hoped she had made it. I didn't know if Mama and Papa were in Westerbork, or what had happened to them. They may have been killed for all that I knew at the time...' All the others might have for what I knew at the time.

*

Westerbork was strange. Eva almost immediately met people she knew: here were most of the many Jews of Amsterdam, now in barracks. To her surprise, it was an organised place – there were even shops.

She had heard about this place; it had been built by the Dutch, and at that time, the prisoners were allowed to make many decisions about their day-to-day lives. There were even free-time activities. She was assigned to a barracks, squeezed in with many others. One couldn't really have any privacy, but men and women's rooms were placed opposite each other. There were working hours. They were allowed to receive and send post. Things weren't terrible, even though the privies smelled of sewage.

As soon as people arrived they were stricken with worries over transportation trains. Newcomers were arriving at the camp all the time now that Amsterdam, Europe's most Jewish city, was being cleansed of Jews. As people arrived, an equal number had to leave the camp. Very quickly, the knowledge of these transportation trains to the east began to gnaw at everyone – the uncertainty and of this life in limbo began to take its toll. Who was going to go next? Each day fear was etched on the faces of those who had learned that they would have to move on to a greater degree of uncertainty.

Then one evening, I walked into my barracks and found to my amazement that Lins was sitting there. She clapped her hands and cried when she saw me; we fell into each other's arms. Everybody around us hissed, trying to hush us – this was past the start of nightly silence.

'Where are Paulus and Susan?' Lins tried to whisper, but she couldn't help it, her voice came out loud, urgent. 'Where are my babies, my angels?'

It was time to prepare for bed. In the queue for the evening wash we were able to exchange some words.

'I think Paulus and Suse made it,' I spoke as quietly as I could into my mother's ear. 'I think,' I said, 'I do not know really, but Paul managed to mix in with bystanders when we were supposed to go to the trucks and Suse must have walked away just as we were about to enter the trucks. I didn't see it, but others told me she walked away. I do not know though, if any of them made it away alive.'

'We can only hope. They may have better hopes than us,' Lins said. 'So Gott will.'

Mother felt faint with relief at the thought that at least two of her children might be safe. 'Are you religious now?'

'No, not yet, not yet.'

Lins was shivering and could hardly hold the soap. Soon the lights went out and a voice called again for silence. It was all black and one could hear a child needing help to go to for a pee and then there was a sour, damp smell. We lay in our bunks full of memories and fantasies, their own fears and anxiety.

It's All Coming Back

*

'I remember, I tried to stretch my hand out but couldn't reach Mama's bed, but I knew she was there. I recognized the sounds that she was making, the snoring, and the coughing. That was enough for me to fall asleep that night.' Eva was reliving it all as she spoke.

'In the morning I met Papa. Of course, he had a lot on his mind. He walked around and spoke to many people, calming them, and tried to create some hope as far as that was possible.'

*

The guards felt that a doctor like him could do the most good as an ambulance man and his protests fell on deaf ears. He wanted to be a therapist, helping people. He tried to understand and then to explain to people why they were having the reactions that they were suffering – when he realised that I was there too, he wanted her to do the same. Of course, he wasn't allowed to this during working hours.

Bergen-Belsen 1944

'This is said to be an intermediary camp,' Karl said to a guard at Westerbork one day. 'What is next?'

Of course he knew it was pointless asking questions. He was sure that these men had been led into a kind of mass-psychosis, where their worst properties came to the surface. Properties that everyone knows very well and which we all or many of us have, but which are suppressed by socialisation, that are held down by more positive feelings and attributes, those making us fit for a normal society.

'If you behave,' the soldier sneered, 'All of your family can be on the next train. That'd be fun, wouldn't it, to go away? Nice for you.'

One cold day in February 1944 the three of them finally stood there in front of the train. It was bitterly cold outdoors in the open, rural Friesian landscape and they tried to warm one another by brisk rubbing of backs and hand clapping and hugging when the guards weren't watching.

They stood in front of a train; not like a passenger train that one might imagine, but old agricultural cars smelling of cattle; like stables only with machine guns on the roofs.

They had been crying all night.

If the destination was eastern Germany or Poland they thought it would mean certain death. If it was Bergen-Belsen there might be a respite.

Many stood there on that cold winter day in the watery sun, shivering. Most of them looked frightened, some utterly passive. Their emotions had taken a break or entirely vanished forever. This was indeed the worst time in their lives. This far, anyway. They were all pale and extremely tense.

This was where the next world started.

There had been cruelty in Westerbork, oh yes, but the most menacing of the German guards with their yells as sharp as knives were seldom there. But they were next to the train now, shouting, with dogs, guns and batons. Eva needed to go to a toilet or just behind some bushes but it wasn't allowed.

'Stand still or the dog will get you! You aren't going that far. And if you wet yourself I will give the dog the order to attack you!'

'Not that far,' she repeated quietly, and her need to pee vanished. 'Maybe Belsen...' A faint positive hum could be heard in the crowd as the word was passed on – 'not that far!' – but the guards shouting soon hushed the murmur.

They were shoved into the cars and had to stand, packed close, very densely. Now, crowded in like that, the stable smell disappeared and instead they got the smell of the generic soap and the mothballs and sweat, urine and bad breath. Not because of unbrushed teeth and ungargled throats, no: the odour was the result of fear.

Some who had received parcels at Westerbork smelled of perfume. They had splashed it all over themselves, as they were not allowed to bring anything of the sort with them, just a blanket and some clothes. Some had books, pens and paper. Most of the personal things brought with them were gone.

No one really owned anything anymore.

They all heard the murmur about Belsen and that took away the worst anxiety and fear. This was probably not a train going that far east and the war seemed to be near its end. There was after all a spark of hope in the dark wagon...

After about six months in Bergen-Belsen, the family didn't keep that close a track of time anymore.

Karl was bent, thin, and almost haggard. They were used to seeing forlorn people, in despair, dried up, dead or half-dead.

Together with others with an academic background, with rabbis and the richer Jews, Karl was working in the shoe command. All the shoes that have been collected from all Jews in all of greater Germany were coming by train to this camp. It was dirty work; they started by cutting the soles from the leather uppers. They were two hundred men and they began at six in the morning and finished at six or eight at night. Often the men tried to combine work with giving lectures to each other. The rabbis spoke most of the time, and Karl, who did not believe in all that, was still happy that there was some kind of mental activity to keep spirits up a little.

The guards shouted out their orders. 'Germany needs leather, cut like this with the knife! Some have hurt themselves with the knife; I guess you are not that stupid? Long strips! Now cut!'

When the sole had been taken off it was to be cut into small square rubber bits and all the buckles were taken off and the leather had to be cut in half-centimetre wide strips. The slightest mistake meant a new outburst from a guard.

He himself talked most of the time with an ex-colleague of his, who remarkably enough had also come to Belsen.

In the evenings, the family were free to do things with each other and others: Karl was even analysing a student who needed it and who wanted to be a psychoanalyst himself.

Sometimes he talked to all his fellow prisoners in the command about psychoanalysis, though not of narcissism or stupidity – he didn't dare to take it that far.

Karl was also trying to helping others in any small way he could, whenever an occasion arose. It kept his spirits up. It was a exercise for his intellect and a compensation for the wretchedness that he could do nothing about; the reduction of all them there to an object that only can obey instructions, yelling and shouting and roaring, no matter how conflicting it was. It was interesting to analyse here. In this environment there were new perspectives of personality appearing that no one has ever seen before. Eva didn't have the same possibilities of course. She and her mother stayed together a lot and they talked and talked.

Karl had a tough job in the shoe command, they all had a very tough time, and the soup was getting more and more watery and the bread slices harder and harder and smaller and smaller – now more often, there was nothing at mealtimes at all. People began hoarding a little food if they could. When Karl's yearning to smoke became too strong he exchanged a lump of bread for some cigarettes.

*

The lack of food made us all very tired by the afternoon but we had to keep up the same hard-to-maintain speed in all our jobs, never mind fatigue or illness, or if there was a lecture going on, or if your closest friend just died.

Of course, we all began to get thinner, but when you look at your own face you don't see the changes. But with Papa it was different. I remember one day when we were sitting a little away from him, watching him, the way that wives and daughters do at times, like monkeys grooming their loved ones: Mama and I watched his face, his body and his gestures.

Karl didn't look well; nobody did in Belsen. Rickets, diabetes, dehydration, sclerosis; the deficiency of our diet meant that these diseases were beginning to take us all over. He moved slowly, his pale face bleaker and his eyes, which had always been so alive, were now sunken. The gaze that previously could create such a presence had become indecisive, flickering and unfocused. His nose looked even more pointed.

He looked so tired.

Mama and I discussed it quietly, occasionally merely by exchanging a meaningful glance, a hum, a whisper.

We were interrupted by somebody whispering to me. It was a woman sitting next to me at the table. A newcomer, as you could see by her still full-bodied frame.

'Do you believe your father could help me?' The woman pulled slightly at my worn grey shirt. 'My daughter cries constantly, all day. Cries and throws things and wets herself.'

'How old is she?' I tried to avoid showing to anyone that I was talking to this woman, turning in a different direction, hardly moving my mouth and rattling with the cutlery when I slurped the brownish-grey soup. I caught a single barleycorn with my spoon and gave to the woman.

'She's nine; I have heard that your father knows about these things?'

'Does she speak?' I wondered if Papa still was able to give any advice, if he had any more help for people not just worried about their own situation – the hunger, terror, deprivation and weakness, and the threat of further deportation, further transports.

You know, we as analysts were out of our minds because of other people's reaction, Eva said.

'I'll see what I can do,' I murmured, 'What *he* can do.'

'God bless you, or whoever we should believe in.'

I left the table, washed my plate and walked quickly to the work barracks; quickly in order not to have the guards yell at me. I saw a striped goldfinch sitting in a bush. The bird turned its head; it seemed to be watching me. I had only seen this funny looking bird once before, in the Stockholm archipelago of all places, with you. I tilted my head the same way, as if we had something to share, a trust. Then the guards yelled that I had to move it. I rushed as usual to the kitchen garden where my work command was.

*

That night a small, skittish little girl sat down next to Karl. 'Mummy told me to sit down here,' she said.

'Your mother is here too, that's good: I think she's worried about you.' The girl doesn't answer. Karl looked at her for a long while. 'Do you like your mother?'

'She scolds me when I wet myself,' she spoke slowly with long intervals during which she studied Papa's nose. 'I am not allowed to suck my thumb and she nags at me all the time. You have a very long nose.'

Karl smiled and held his hand over his nose and was about to continue when he noticed how the girl, earlier so shy, put her head under his arm and appealed to him with a glance, opened her mouth to say something but closed it again and then opened it.

'By the way, she isn't my mother,' she said suddenly. Papa now held his arm around the little girl – he was no longer just an analyst, he was a grown-up holding an abandoned child. Roles were shifted in the camp. Simple consolation in the moment was sometimes more important than finding out the causes of whatever problems there were, even though Papa, more than anyone, knew that if you don't understand the causes you can't give lasting help. But lasting help was perhaps not what was needed here. I watched him and he said to the child. 'Come back tomorrow and we will talk some more. Now – eat what there is.

'I want to,' she said. They couldn't speak more.

I looked across the room, watching Papa. I nodded to the girl's mother and smiled.

*

Emmy holds Helmut's gaze with her heavily lidded eyes. "The next part was so painful for her to tell. She sounded so lost, so helpless. I could hear her heart breaking all over again

*

Eva shifted restlessly and her face was ashen.

"I met a man in the camp you know." Emmy bit her lip, nodded, and willed the poor girl to be able to carry on with this terrible tale.

*

We learnt a thousand tricks in order to meet. I was in love. Anton was so kind and strong and once or twice we had been able to hide together in one of the barracks. I was always worried for him. And now he was gone.

It was Mama who told me when she came out from dinner; she had taken her time washing the dishes. ' Eva, they have taken Anton! Somebody just told me!" She cried, "Perhaps because he was seeing you…' She tried to whisper but it was difficult; what she had to say was so emotional. We squatted down so as not to be seen, but almost at once a guard came by, struck the butt of his rifle against the floor and told us to get up.

'You are Eva?' he snapped. '*Komm mit.*'

In an open space between two barracks Anton was standing with four guards around him. Two guards held me tight a couple of metres away. When I called out for him I got a rifle butt in my side. And then… Oh I can't bare it! Then… They yanked down Anton's trousers, and one of them grabbed his scrota; he had a knife in his hand. I closed my eyes, I couldn't watch! First I heard Anton's scream and then there was a crunching sound. They were beating him savagely. When I looked up I could see blood on the ground and Anton hanging between the guards. Castrated and beaten… and then they took him away. I felt hollow, hollow and so full at the same time. Full of horror, shame, guilt. And yet empty of everything. It was just too much.

Eva covers her face and does not look when she says 'What I felt? It is so much it cannot be told. Sorry. At night I wanted to run out of the barrack, out towards the

watchtower, out to be seen by the guards, out to be shot...
Mama held me tight, otherwise I would have done it.

*

Emmy squeezes her eyes closed, so that all Helmut can see is the eyelids and the smearing of her make up, the tears gathering in the corners. She is so upset by her own story, and suddenly looks so broken as she sits clutching the arms of the chair. She shakes her head, unable to speak any more, and Helmut reaches out silently and takes her small hand in his own.

After a long while, they stir, and he speaks.

'Let me tell you now about how I realized all this, and what I did,' Helmut says, and Emmy opens her eyes slowly. He begins.

Somewhere in Sweden 1944

Well: you know me and a bunch of other guys from Stockholm were quartered in old barns in the wilderness by the Norwegian border. I was drafted, again. This damn war never ended! We wanted to be home with wives and kids, our girlfriends and buddies – we wanted to earn money, go jazz dancing and to the movies.

But here we sat, most of the time just waiting. Playing poker, talking of girls and music, and going for short walks in this new place, talking to farmers and feeling bored.

We were ordered to march to and fro in different fields or on dirt roads – it was so bloody monotonous.

One of the boys did a sketch of me. He said he had never seen anybody so unsoldier-like as I, with this big stout frame squeezed into a small grey uniform. It may be true! And it was all damn secret, 'somewhere in Sweden,' army mail, all of that. The slogans of the day all over all the platforms, on buses and coaches and in the streets were: '*En svensk tiger*' - A Swede is silent. (This could also be read as a Swedish Tiger – it was illustrated by a yellow tiger with blue stripes) and '*Spionen lägger pussel*' - The spy puts small pieces of the jig-saw puzzle together. These ideas were hammered into the civilian population and hammered still harder into the minds of the soldiers. Sometimes we patrolled the border. Most of the time nothing happened there either. If somebody came, it was important to be able to distinguish between refugees, people who might be active in the resistance, and spies.

One day something more exciting happened.

We were awoken by a bang and flashes in a clear sky. We leapt up quickly – or at least as quickly as possible! We had practised so many times, and knew exactly what to do when things were really happening. And yet it was difficult to line up. At first we didn't understand exactly what had happened but it gradually became clearer: a German plane has entered Swedish airspace, warning shots had been fired from the Swedish side and the airplane has made an emergency landing on the our side of the border. The pilot had made it out unscathed and he was coming unsteadily towards our camp.

I was the only one who knew German really well, so I was called to interpret. The pilot wanted to go home – he had just made a navigation error, he explained. The officers sent a cable to Stockholm: what to do? Stockholm was also wrong-footed. They wanted to get rid of him fast; otherwise it might be seen as meddling in the war, as an aggressive Swedish act. But they couldn't extradite him without getting something in return and they didn't know what that could be.

There were no plans for this.

Time passed: hours, days, a week. He was held in some kind of improvised detention, no cell, I tried to get his confidence; the German loved the landscape, the pine trees, the boulders, the heather and the scrub. We saw a jay, elk, some deer and hares; these ordinary things thrilled him, it was so different from the marshes near his home in Germany. He spoke about his life. The officers let us carry on talking, but they checked with the Swedish Secret Service if they had anything on me. There turned out to be some old gossip in the files, probably because of my contacts with those who helped refugees; but I was no spy, so he was left to me. He wanted to get home to his wife and children. He was ignorant when it comes to politics, so he said. He was worried that Germany would be occupied and that his family would be in danger. I suggested that he should stay in Sweden until the war ended, but the staff had other ideas.

The last autumn of the war flew by. We picked mushrooms and lingon berries and went to dances with the local girls. The German was not allowed to join us of course, but I filled him in on all the details.

One day I was asked to go to the captain.

'Soon your work with this pilot will over,' he said. 'We are going to try to exchange the prisoner for some Jews with Swedish connections. Stockholm is finding names.'

'I have two names,' I replied immediately. 'My uncle Karl and his wife Lins, my father's sister.'

'What's that?' The captain said put on his round glasses and looked straight at me. 'Are you saying that you want personal advantages?! Watch it! That kind of thing isn't done.' The captain was well known for his sympathy towards Germany. But then his expression suddenly changed. 'But what the hell! Who knows? I'll write the names here anyhow. What were their names, did you say?'

I was so tense that I could not sleep at all that night. The war would soon be over, I knew; at least, it would be over for those that had survived. I was soon off duty and back in Stockholm.

I was very tense and agitated when I came down Hamngatan and criss-crossed over the street down toward the Sidenkompaniet silk and clothes shop. I made it just in time, jumping between two number 7 trams as they came towards each other, my movements precise and perfectly timed. One of the new cable buses passed straight behind me, and luckily I heard it just in time; probably because of the flapping sound that's made when the wire is stretched against the wall. The weather was lovely, and the birds sang in the Kungsträdgården Park. Birds have a lot to do at that time late in the year, those moving late and those staying on. The church bell chimed two. I gave a salute with my hat when I saw some Jewish businessmen who were heading for the nearby synagogue. It was good to be seen in case something unpleasant should happen to me later in the day, whatever that might be, I thought. The war had really, decisively turned, but it still went on and on, and my relatives were probably still in the camp. That's what I thought at the time based on the limited information I had. I indeed laid a jig-saw puzzle, based on censored or non-censored letters I had gotten from relatives. I kicked at some cobble stones lying in the street as I walked past the Opera House and down towards the bay of the Baltic sea stretching right into the centre of the town facing the big Castle next to the outlet from the lake on the other side of the old town.

There were many swans by the rapids leading from the lake into the sea in late autumn, even swans flying.

My thoughts were interrupted by a number 2 tram clanking past me and a car chugging by with that wartime odour of the producer gas that was produced by wood in a funny looking reactor hanging after the cars. We did indeed handle rationing as best we could. Then I saw the swastika flag flapping from a house. That was where I was going, to the German legation. The swans were taking a flight over the sea and that singing sound of the wings met me by the embankment.

I didn't know how many of Karl and Lins' family were detained in Belsen then, and I knew that Bergen-Belsen was some kind of work or concentration camp; I had heard that much. Whatever it was, I understood their lives were at risk.

I had walked to the legation fast, but now I was suddenly hesitating, standing in front of the doorbell under that leering swastika. *You are about to enter the enemy's den.* Finally I pushed the button. Then I found myself standing in front of their German uniforms and just wanted to get away, *get away!*

However, I kept my composure, and was invited into an office by a man who had clicked his heels together and took my hand.

I delivered my message in Swedish and English; I was careful not to speak German. I presented my story; I had been caring for a German pilot who had been shot and I said that he could be traded for Karl and Lins' family. When they asked how many of my relatives there were in Belsen I became unsure of myself – my eyes were probably flickering. I swallowed, blinked, and said "Two." I didn't know. There could be five.

Feeling the sweat prickling in my armpits, I suddenly changed my answer to five, and at once changed it back again to two. Who knows what their reaction would be if I said simply, *too many*?

'*Das war ja ein Vorschlag,*' the German embassy man laughed and noted the names. '*Bitte, dieses ist nicht etwas für die Zeitungen.*'

'Natürlich, I will not tell the papers,' I replied in German after all, and quickly backed out of the legation. The swans had landed by the statue of Charles XII and a ferry to the archipelago hooted to announce its departure.'

*

He finishes there, and his mother goes to get some more tea.

'I am glad you cared so much for them,' she says when she returns, 'But then, I know you've always liked Karl.'

'It wasn't just that!' he replies emphatically, slightly offended. 'It was my duty.'

Emmy sighs and nods, acknowledging the truth of what he says.

'If it had only helped… if it had only helped.'

They sit quietly for a moment, the silence heavy in the air between them, thick with their separate memories. Then Emmy clasps her hands together, and steels herself for the last part of her tale.

'Let me finish Eva's story.'

Helmut nods, and she lets out a deep breath as she continues.

Bergen-Belsen 1945

In mid January, sparkling winter weather had come to the rural North German landscape. The sun shone down on Eva and Lins amidst all the grey, all the dead and grey. Dead and dying people are indeed grey. No other colour can describe it when you have seen it up close.

The January sun had been up for a long time'. Eva says, 'and it created a feeling of hope amidst all the wretchedness. Snow could be used to make water; water was needed for all those that were ill. We knew, everybody in the camp knew, that Germany's enemies were coming ever closer; I mean it wasn't told but we heard the rumours from the newcomers and we could hear noise, war noise very far away. It gave us some hope, but it also meant that still more Jews arrived at Bergen-Belsen almost every day, and so there were smaller portions of food for all. No one remembered when they last finished a 'meal' without feeling the pangs of hunger. Well, I had a job in the tobacco and vegetable garden and could cope a little better than most, as I could sneak away some vegetables to eat.

Papa wanted to help everyone in the camp with psychiatric problems – but of course, everyone had those now, and he did not even have time to eat what little food he was allowed. There was a real famine then, and every day many were dying of the typhoid and diphtheria which had begun to spread through the camp. Most people were starving, dehydrated and no longer had the capacity to make even the slightest effort.

Others had been deported east but now people were starting to come back from the eastern camps. We didn't realise why.

Meanwhile, the three of us could be together more, and had more opportunity to support others. My work in the garden was by then time mainly keeping record of the diminishing stocks, but sometimes I could hide some vegetables for my parents. It helped to keep the scurvy away at least. Others who weren't so lucky lost their teeth, itched all over, and developed open wounds.

The crematorium, situated in a separate barrack, couldn't cope.

There were dead bodies all around us.

We were used to the smell, all the appalling smells of the camp – our senses were almost entirely dulled. Though we had become accustomed to most things that can be imagined and more, and there was a biting cold that slowed down the process of rotting, the pervasive foulness in the place was unbearable. The guards were getting even more indifferent to people's suffering, and we realised too that there was fewer of them. Our guess was that the men were needed for to fight now – that the Germans needed every soldier they could muster to make one last fight. The ones left behind had become meaner. Each morning everybody was lined up for a count in the designated place, even in January when it was icy and the snow fell heavily. We had to stand in straight, military lines, sometimes for an hour, sometimes for several hours, without being allowed to move, without being allowed to go to the latrine.

Mama and I were sitting in the barrack for the lunch break and were watching Karl who had also come from his work for 'lunch'. He was almost crawling; his body ached everywhere. His face, already so thin, now was only skin and bones. He tried to listen to a fellow prisoner who was speaking about how he felt about the unthinkable, incomprehensible death that was pervading the camp. Karl responded calmly, sitting at the table, but Mama noticed him starting to shake and splutter; she was so worried about him. And of course, she was consumed with anxiety about her younger children, those who hadn't been brought to the camp. She spent hours imagining what had happened to them.

The winds were perhaps not quite as icy as the year before and the one before that – those were the worst for a generation – but it felt much worse now when we were in a much more critical condition, our thin clothes ragged, our bodies so very thin. Mama began to talk about old times, the way people do when they are going to die. She was worried by the image of death while Karl tried to analyse the situation, to have a clear mind. He tried to comfort her by saying that the war would soon be over.

And then the time came when we had soup for 'dinner' but Papa couldn't eat any. We tried to put it in his mouth but he literally couldn't manage to open his mouth. He was too starved, too dehydrated; all energy had just left him.

'Don't be sorry when my death day comes,' he said, 'Do something nice, that I would have liked to do with you. If you have the possibility.'

'We're going to make it,' Lins whispered to Karl. 'We're going to make it through to the end.'

Mama held him as they went to bed. She turned to the other side in the hard bunk and scraped off some lice about to crawl into her clothes. She stretched her hand out to me, lying in the bunk above. She couldn't reach me but we felt each other's presence.'

*

Emmy stopped suddenly.

"When Eva came to that part of the story, I realized what time it was. I had planned dinner, but realized that that wasn't going to be possible. I told her I would give her something take with her. I told her, 'I hope you have a safe and easy journey.' I mentioned something about taking care to avoid rowdy or impolite men when she was travelling – it was just the usual warning I would give any young girl. But Eva flinched as I was saying it. She had pulled her legs up under her body, sitting on the trunk but still as upright as if she was at school.

'Exactly,' she replied. 'Those lewd glances, those looks that tell me they want to rape me.' She had stiffened and now looked both straight ahead and yet deep into the past. Her head was probably full of so many images but she managed to keep calm despite all the memories, all the pain that must have been deep within her and which she obviously tried by all means to suppress.

'My child, forgive me; you have to leave. Remember: we are alive,' I said, and I held her, pulled her up from the trunk and took a couple of dance steps with her still in my arms. '*You and I are alive.*'

*

When Emmy has finished there is no need for more conversation for a long while. The rest of the evening is all silent, and Helmut hugs his mother before going to bed. He has never done that before.

The next morning he goes out and strolls around Hampstead and a little further afield, revisiting old haunts, and trying to remember how all the buildings now in ruins, looked before. The area next to Emmy's flat in Allingham Court and all the way up to Hampstead Town Hall had been heavily bombed. He swore when he saw the ruined houses, some only piles of brick, some had a gable and nothing more: *oh how he hates the war.* So he goes downhill instead toward the city centre. When he makes it to the West End, he buys some books at Foyle's for Anne-Marie. He himself reads a lot; Churchill, Neville Shute, Ernest Hemingway. She is more for detective stories and poetry.

The last week before Anne-Marie is due to arrive he is in a thoughtful mood. The last few days it has rained. London weather. The rain keeps the smog out, which he is grateful for, but there's a smell of coal and fumes hanging over the city, that the rain can't wash away. So he smokes a lot to make his own atmosphere, mainly Player's medium navy cut with the sailor on the package, a sailor reminding him sharply of Copenhagen, strangely enough.

London, last week of March, 1946

Finally Anne-Marie arrives in London.

She couldn't go to England directly from Norway after all, those were the strange rules immediately after the war; so she had travel first to Gothenburg, and then take the boat to Tilbury and then a train to Liverpool Street Station, right in the heart of sooty London.

She peers through the window of the compartment, trying to see Helmut; she expects him to be standing on the platform, waiting eagerly with a big bunch of flowers. But he is nowhere to be seen and she has problems opening the door – it opens from the outside, she suddenly realises, and she has to lower the window with a broad leather strap first.

It takes some time.

When she looks up again she is face to face with a stranger, an imposing little woman waiting to embrace her, and who does, in fact, then start to kiss her on both cheeks, through the window! And she holds her for a long time.

Once she has managed to extricate herself, a flushed Anne-Marie just gazes at this fascinating round figure with all her makeup and jewellery and speaking old-fashioned Swedish. For a moment, she can't think who it can be: Helmut's sister? But then she sees two more, younger women standing back a little – and with Helmut! – and she realises that, of course, what was she thinking? this must be Emmy. And indeed, her soon to be mother-in-law and two sisters-to-be Käthe and Ilse, along with Ilse's four-year old daughter Glenys, have all come to meet her at the railway station.

'Käthe and Emmy have rounder figures like female versions of her Aga, though not (not yet at least) as solidly fat as he is." Ilse is slender, more like herself.

It takes some time and a lot of everyone speaking at the same time before they all are settled in the, as she thinks, *typical London taxi* with seats facing both ways. Emmy reaches out to Glenys and holds her with her small hands but the child is shy with this new person here, and only wants to sit with her mother. Even if the little girl doesn't want to got to Emmy at that moment, Anne-Marie is so glad there is a grandmother here that notices and loves her grandchildren, who really cares about them. It isn't like that in her family now, even if Sven sometimes does bestir spend time with her nieces and nephews, showing them things, teaching them. But it's not the same as this. And she has no mother at all any more.

Ilse and Anne-Marie have clicked immediately; it's a kind of love at first sight. Their conversation has already become close and intimate while they're still in the taxi, as if they have known each other for years. They become friends, sisters at once. They share a cheerful blitheness, a kind of mercurial, volatile quality and awareness of their own attractiveness; they recognise in each other the same attitude to life and a shared sense of humour.

By the time the taxi has arrived at its destination Anne-Marie has fallen almost more in love with Helmut's family than with him.

Hampstead, London 29 March 1946

They are now concentrating on the wedding so there is too little time to talk of all what has happened since they last saw each other. He has learnt so much about family that he does not know when and how to convey to her, if it is interesting to her. But he thinks it should be. The day before the wedding, the thermometer shows that it's 65 degrees outside. Anne-Marie realizes she has to recalculate and normally she would consult an encyclopaedia but instead she asks Aga and it turns out to be 18 degrees on the Celsius scale. Warm for the end of March, and she is satisfied as she looks at the flowers in the small green stretches of land. Daffodils and Scylla. These won't appear in Sweden for a good while yet.

Is she prepared? She has her white dress, and now she sees that there are some flowers that can easily be picked. Ilse's four-year-old daughter Glenys is going to be bridesmaid. It'll be a small wedding; Anne-Marie has explained this to her father in her last letter to him. She had had no hope that he would come, but now she realizes that he really won't, and she discovers that she's a little sad about that. He's probably fully occupied with his third wife, she assumes. She sent him a photo of Aga, and all he said in reply was that he looked like he just came from wandering in the desert.

But her brother Björn will be there. Her brother Björn, who she's always been so close to. He and his wife arrive the evening before the wedding, and the two couples sit talking late into the night. They talk about everything, even of Bjorn's first wife, something that could have been a forbidden subject, but after all she was one of Anne-Marie's best friends. He had left both her and the Communist Party all at once before the war, and gone to England to work for Swedish Radio.

'I remember,' Anne-Marie said, 'How it was when the war broke out - this is about you Björn. I had just been enrolled at the Gothenburg School of Economics: I had passed the threshold to come in. I had time to stroll around in the city, smoking all the time, meeting boys and just generally having fun. No one would have believed that I, would have been able to sit still long enough to study.

'Mind you it took you some time though,' Björn says, 'a pension in France, a year at a school for domestic sciences, a summer and more sailing the Baltic.' Björn smiled, puffing on his cigarette though its holder.

'I was one of the few girls studying economics, and I was proud as I walked through the city. I couldn't get enough of all the parks and the canals; I sat for hours at the Garden Society, in the palm house. Mind you, I looked at all the notices that were pinned to the board at school, keeping an eye out for parties and other activities.'

'I'm sure you did,' Aga said with a smile.

'Well I like to sing and dance and exercise! I was targeted on taking my Master of Economics but I thought I wouldn't like to be the hardest working of all, and I wasn't,' she laughs. 'I didn't want to be a grey clerk; I wanted to live a life as well. I caught a tram one evening, let me tell you, and found myself in the middle of some picketing Communists... oh how I hated that the Communists who had agreed with Hitler that Germany should split Eastern Europe between the two!'

'You mean between Russia and Nazi-Germany,' Helmut intervened.

Yes, I hated those forceful dictatorships with their simplified ideologies!' Anne-Marie finishes off her cigarette.

'That was why I left the whole thing,' Björn said. 'That was when I did leave. I will probably write a book about that some day.'

'Yes you were such a committed communist; I remember when you were working as a full-time agent for the Communist Youth League, and what you wrote in the Communist daily *Norrskensflamman*. I read most of it even if our father did not want me to.'

'I confess!' Björn laughs with his hands up in the air.

'I felt so sorry for you when you were jailed in Stockholm for handing out leaflets for the socialist cause at the army barracks: but Dad was almost impressed by that.'

Björn just smiles at his young sister with his hat in hand.

'I remember when you told me you were joining, I was so small, it was Christmas and we were in a big cupboard in our big house in Umeå. Do you remember?' Anne-Marie says while getting a new cigarette out of the pack.

'Yeah!' Björn sat back in his chair, cheerful. 'And you took the cigar I was secretly smoking and panicked and thought the whole house would be set on fire! And I joked and cried *Revolution!* ... you were so small.'

'But I didn't tell them then. You had no contact for years, you and Dad, at least none that I was aware of? Or did you have contact somehow; perhaps through mamma Siri?'

'Well yes and no, we never met in person for years at least. But go on with your story now.'

'OK, well... I had been invited to a party at the house of a new friend of mine from school. He was a boy from Gothenburg who wanted all the new schoolmates to be good friends. He was living out in Långedrag by the sea among the luxurious villas, and I was dressed up with a small white hat and long thin gloves. You have to look swell when you go and call on the upper classes! The boy was rather handsome and there was another one as well who gave me long glances; in fact, he was almost irritating. Out in Långedrag the wind caught me, I was thinly dressed and the wind went straight through me, but it was fresh and invigorating, and I stood still for some time and let myself be filled up by the sea. It was a fantastic party with food served in the kitchen, talking to new acquaintances, singing, poetry reading, dancing, loads of wine.'

'And many men obviously,' Helmut giggles and she makes a gesture somewhere halfway between slapping and caressing.

*

'Well, late in the evening we walked down to the sea to listen to the soft waves breaking, to look at the lights mirroring themselves in the water, at the lighthouses and lanterns.

Some could afford a taxi back to town, but I stayed with a smaller group that kept on partying all night and were still there the next day, with a bit of a hangover but mainly merry – we had a picnic breakfast on the terrace where one could catch a glimpse of the North Sea far away. In the air we could feel a wind coming in, a warm wind but with cold threads sliding through it. Wine, chicken, white bread and an old radio. Fooling around, yelling.

The wireless was on but no one listened to Zarah Leander or to the news. But all by a sudden I heard your voice, Björn, from the radio. I tried to hush the others but they didn't have the slightest intention of being quiet. I picked up the radio and slipped into the house. At the far end of the larder I plugged the radio back in and sat with it in my arms like a child. I saw your faultless vest, your tie and cufflinks, in fact I didn't listen to the commentary at all, something on art or literature, but all of a sudden there was a crackling noise in the middle of a sentence and another voice broke in. I remember getting upset; this was no way to treat my brother. Why did they interrupt you in the middle of it? I got mad and could not hear what they were saying. When I had calmed down enough to listen again, the extra news had almost finished. 'When we have more news on the offensive we will come back. Let's repeat: German and Russian troops have today attacked Poland,' the voice said. Then there was another voice in the main programme, signing of your programme. There was to be war after all. I pounded my fists against the floor. Then I rushed to the terrace and cried out as loud as I could in the wind that Germany and Russia had attacked Poland... and then we sat and waited for more news in the drawing room, all ears sharp and eager to listen.'

Hampstead and Belsize Park, London 30 March 1946

The wedding is going to take place close to where they are; in West Hampstead, just up Haverstock Hill. This has been Aga's and his mother's decision and Anne-Marie accepts it all. The sun is already shining early in the morning and the temperature reaches almost summer levels before noon.

She puts on her white dress and he a black suit – nothing extraordinary – and they take the 15-minute walk to the venue quickly after the wedding breakfast, being watched and commented on by passers by. When they arrive at the town hall they find Björn all dressed-up in a light smoking jacket and top hat. He's going to be one of the witnesses and Harry is the other; Harry is Helmut's friend of over ten years, from when they were studying at Oxford, a very Jewish and very English lawyer. It was because of this friendship that Harry met his wife, Helmut's cousin Trudy. Everyone is well dressed but casual but not too formal. They have all understood that the idea is to have something small and informal, not at all like Käthe's wedding six years ago; that was properly Jewish.

This time there's no religion, no broken glass, and no blessings. Now that Sigmund has gone, Jewishness is not such a strong influence on the lives of Helmut's family, despite what happened to the Jews in the war just past. At least, not in a religious sense. They want to be just human and humanistic and to assimilate. They have always been the assimilating kind. But they are constantly reminded of their Jewishness, it creeps up on them, with all the news from the camps still coming in; it makes one think about what it means that you and the people you love are Jewish.

Helmut is not even a Zionist. He believes the Polish Bund, the Jewish left, has had a good idea about making Emmy's town of birth, Reichenbach in Silesia, into a safe haven for Polish Jews. But now Israel is being built in Palestine. He doesn't mind but believes this is not the way to get rid of anti-Semitism.

But! Today it is informal and non-confessional and no time to discuss politics. Even if he does let himself remember that Anne-Marie is a little Jewish herself, if only a very small part.

The ceremony itself is over in a wink and they step out with the bridesmaid first. Then they all move on to Hans and Emmy's flat where Emmy who often fixes parties for others has fixed a party in her home. They have moved the furniture and put up some rented narrow tables with loads of cakes and sandwiches and wine and some extra chairs for everyone. Harry takes some photographs when Helmut carries Anne-Marie through the big window. Very illustrative, Emmy and her mother Flora give away Helmut from one side to the other where Anne-Marie is, or accept Anne-Marie coming into their house. One could see it either way. There are no big speeches, just everyone sitting down and talking and eating and then more talking and eating. Björn has a job to do in the afternoon but he's back a couple of hours later and they're still sitting and eating.

He first carefully knocks a glass against another, but has to make more noise to be heard above all the babbling.

'My sister,' he begins, 'my sister and my brother-in-law! I am so happy for you, having found each other across the borders. Political and religious and national borders, or at least different kind of heritage. Let your marriage symbolize that we are not going to have any more wars, that these are new times!'

'Let's cross our fingers,' Emmy comments loudly, but Björn continues as if he hasn't heard.

'I am the only one here from my side of your new family and I don't know if I can be a representative for them – God knows I have often been considered a black or rather red sheep in that flock! – and so I speak mainly for myself. I am happy when I see you happy. Anne-Marie has always been the one who kept in touch with me, despite our age difference. Now it is love, and peace, and what else do you want? There's no glass to walk on, even though you, as I have, are marrying a Jew... which our great grandfather also was, and most of you are dressed in black...' Now the murmur was so loud that he stopped for a while and then just said 'Mazeltov!' in a short break in the noise and raised his glass in a toast for the happy two.

End of speeches.

Instead everybody started to talk politics even though they weren't supposed to. But it's the matter closest to everybody's heart; about the British leaving Lebanon and the UN starting its work here in London. The now opposition leader Winston Churchill has just delivered his iron curtain speech in the U.S. and Harry cites it: 'From Stettin in the Baltic to Trieste in the Adriatic an 'Iron Curtain' has descended across the continent. Behind that line lie all the capitals of the ancient states of Central and Eastern Europe. Warsaw, Berlin, Prague, Vienna, Budapest, Belgrade, Bucharest and Sofia.' 'He's right. I didn't vote for him but he's bloody right, not just right wing. It is hard for us, with our leftist past to see this development.'

'Indeed,' Björn agrees, 'we can expect to see the Russians expanding. You know, I was working with these people; I know what they can do. But they don't want any new wars either.'

'Are you sure?' Anne-Marie asks.

'But it was Churchill who gave all those lands to them in Yalta! He should have been stronger *then*,' Emmy says. 'He knew very well that this was going to happen. And this Atlee Labour government is too soft on the Russians. I vote Liberal, that's for sure.'

'I don't believe Stalin is so crazy that he'll risk anything... mind you millions of Russians died in the war,' Helmut chips in.

'He couldn't care less,' Anne-Marie adds. 'I'm glad you vote Liberal Emmy, we don't want any of these totalitarian ideas.'

'Yes indeed,' Emmy nods, and takes Anne-Marie's hand across the table, 'But we don't know what Churchill, Roosevelt and Stalin really agreed to. I think there was much more to it than has been officially announced. It is good to keep our eyes open and not just swallow everything we're told.'

Now Emmy's mother Flora intervenes. 'I need to go to bed and rest; I hope an old lady is excused. Politics is of course relevant but more the happiness of the young. I am so glad for you Helmut, and that you Anne-Marie are joining our family. And for the children that will come, so that we old ones can be replaced when we go.' Everyone smiles – no one can help but love this sweet and generous lady.

Emmy kisses her mother goodnight and then turns to her new daughter-in-law. 'There is coffee now, Swedish black coffee, and Swedish cookies; at least I learned something from all my years in Stockholm. For you Anne-Marie, and I am sure everyone else will want some too.'

As the time passes, some leave and some arrive and the storytelling really gets going, and the night seems never to end. The newly married couple are going to be travelling the next day, and they think this is a precious moment when things have to be said. *And indeed they won't see their English family for another nine years.*

Emmy is the most active. She is really in her element, and her way of telling stories, often with a little extra spice so that you can't be sure for certain what to believe, even though this has all become the truth in her mind. She might embellish, she knows, but it's *important* that everyone understands what she's saying, and if she has to add a little to be sure that that happens, well then...

She sits there, round and glittering, deep down in an armchair, the only one not smoking, and they all listen, mesmerised by those deep, deep set round brown eyes. The discussion has gone from war to peace and back to war.

'I am quite sure they haven't made peace soundly this time either,' she says. 'It will come back on us, remember my words. I shouldn't say this on a day like today, I know; but I'm worried.'

'No, no,' Helmut says, 'But you have to consider how everything now stands, at the end of this war, don't you? It's different.'

'Hmm... It's possible... but I think Mr Churchill and Mr Roosevelt did a bad deal. Mind you, Roosevelt was ill,' his mother muses.

'Losing so much to the Russians is hard, and what will happen now in the Middle East, where we fought so hard?' Harry adds.

'I know you did,' Helmut lights a cigarette and pours some port; a drink tray has arrived with the coffee and cookies, 'and the eastern and central Europeans won't accept Communism so easily. They were after all free between the wars.' Across Europe, families are sitting and having this same debate.

Every now and then Harry announces that he's going home, but each new argument gives him energy. He wipes his glasses and takes a sherry. 'The problem has been the peace in Versailles after WWI, he says. It was good these countries were liberated from the empires, but it will be new revanchism all over. I hear Germans are moving from Poland now into new Germany. How will that be perceived by the other Germans?'

'I don't know why they started the first war it in the first place' Helmut rubs his eyes and then takes off his jacket and adjusts his braces; all to still have energy enough for a long night, 'And it's *that* war that brought the last war and may affect the future as well.'

They now hear Flora who hasn't quite gone to bed yet: 'it is really Bismarck's fault, isn't it? Tell them about when you went to Königsberg, Emmy!'

'Should I?' Emmy asks, and her bracelets and her eyes are glittering and the others understand from her chuckling smile that she really wants to.

'So' she says, after a moment, nodding her consent to the unspoken request from her audience for her to go on. 'I'll tell this true story for you, Anne-Marie, so that you can learn something important about your new husband's father...

Königsberg 1917

I had travelled alone by train all day from Berlin and was getting closer to the war by the minute, the real war; war itself. I had not travelled this far alone before, not without friends, not without Sigmund, not without little Helmut and Käthe. Women did not travel alone, and mothers did not leave their children, not even those with nannies.

In Berlin you noticed the war when you looked at people in the streets: there weren't many men around and the women were working much more than normal. But now I was approaching reality, the uncompromising reality. The reality of men, the Kaiser's reality, and the misery we all had entered into after all the bombastic war rhetoric.

I was heading for the miserable war in the trenches, something the newspapers were not writing so much about, but of which I had gathered a lot from gossip and tittle-tattle, the talk of women whose men were there, and from the men who had returned, often without limbs. From this I understood this much: that it was something awful, dirty and stagnant. On the Western Front everything had been in a deadlock forever and ever. They lay there in their trenches and stormed across No Man's Land after long intervals, only to be shot at and quickly retire or, rather, sneak back again. The fronts were not moving much at all in the west. But on the Eastern Front, where I was going, the war was surging to and fro, which also lead to more suffering, more soldiers shot to pieces, more widows and more orphans. I tried to look bold but I had never seen as many blank faces and noses blown red as on this journey. The only other people on the train with me, it seemed, were troops.

The war had been going on for three years and all one knew was that everything was much more forlorn than anybody could have imagined. Not even the Emperor could have known how it was all going to be. I had left little Helmut, only three years old and Käthe, not yet two, yelling in my mother's arms. Flora is a fine grandmother and she could handle it; she could not get enough of the two children. Because I knew I had to go. I had to go to him.

And so here I was sitting in an old freight train that had benches hastily installed. There were windows enough for me to see burnt woods as the train passed muddy fields, where parapets were witnesses to the battles that had taken place, or which were placed there to prepare for battles that were yet to come. The front, the Eastern Front, was at that time much further east, in Latvia. Still, the enemy had been able to shoot far inside our German lines.

I didn't know a great deal about the realities of war out at the front, just about my husband defending the emperor against the Tsar. He had been out there in all those Baltic and Eastern Prussian places with their unfamiliar names, for such a long time, and so far away from the children and me. I couldn't imagine Sigmund taking part in the job of stopping the Russian hoards from entering *das Vaterland*... I didn't care any longer who would win this, as I felt then, perpetual war. I only wanted peace. Sigmund, as well as his family in Heilbronn cared so much about Germany's destiny – he was more German than I was. Sigmund wanted to defend the Kaiser. I wanted him back, and I was so worried.

He had been happy to go to war. Everybody was, to start with. There is a cheerful picture somewhere of him and his brother in their uniforms, and their old parents from Heilbronn sitting holding a sign declaring: 'War supplies.' It was supposed to be funny.

I wasn't afraid of the war either, just worried to be alone, alone with the children.

Oh yes I must tell you – I went on this journey because I got a telegram. A terrible telegram.' She frowns, and a shadow falls across her face. 'At that time, I didn't understand that much about politics. What I knew was that I cared about Sigmund. I was his in a snap, the first time I met him.'

Instead of continuing her story, Emmy suddenly starts to talk about her life before the war. The people listening are patient. They know that she will return to her subject.

'Even though I'd been living in Berlin since I was 15, I was a family girl. I had always been good, always been obedient, and I was a virgin when I met Sigmund at my friend Erna's wedding in Heilbronn; yes, believe it or not! Erna, who was marrying Sigmund's brother Josef, had promised that the wedding would be marvellous and wanted me to come, and she had told me that there would be a handsome brother there as well.

It all happened very quickly: he was so gallant, so taken by me, he said, bowled over, and I felt the same – and we got married fast. He wanted it to be fashionable and the wedding dinner was even held in the Hotel Kaiserhof: the best – to me, it was like a dream. You know,' Emmy stopped for a moment, her eyes focused in the middle distance in a way that told her audience that she wasn't seeing anything in this room at all, 'That same hotel was a Nazi headquarters later: how things change.

After the wedding dinner, yes, on our wedding night, we went by train southward for our honeymoon, and he was going to show me what a marriage was all about!

I was so naïve and innocent, it took quite a while before I understood the point and the rosy red dream could continue.' Emmy pauses again, and this time her eyes are wet with tears.

'I woke up from the dream when our first child died; he was born with hydrocephalus and he didn't have a chance of surviving; he was nine months old when we lost him. That's a long time to hold a child, sit by him, hope against hope. But I always knew that there was no hope, not really.' Every woman in the room winces in despair on hearing this, even those who already knew. Every man who is a father clears his throat, turns away. Emmy lets out the deepest sigh. 'Not one day goes by that I don't think of him... That was when I learned to understand the realities of life the hard way. But didn't give up, and Helmut was born after a terrible delivery. He weighed over five kilos, and I didn't think it would work out well that time either, but it all finally turned out fine. You really became the blessing of our marriage and for me. That's true Helmut!' She laughs in her particularly warm and disarming way, and he seems just embarrassed but Anne-Marie holds his arm and looks lovingly at him.

'Where was I?' Emmy shakes her head and her eyes stare back again into the past. 'Oh yes... I was on the train...'

'I didn't tell you how I looked. I didn't even remember myself until I saw my image mirrored in the window. At first I didn't recognize myself; I had cut my hair short and was wearing hardly any makeup at all. My fellow passengers were soldiers just like Sigmund, most of them. Many looked at me from top to bottom, but I think my new looks stopped some of it.

I didn't know what state Sigmund was in, and I was sick with worry; all that the telegram had made clear was that it was very serious – they had said nothing about what kind of injury he might have suffered. Maybe I was about to become a widow as so many others had, at only twenty-six? The telegram made me shudder every time I thought about it.

The train was rumbling through Northern Poland and East Prussia, alongside long rows of horses with scrubby carts, on roads as muddy as the fields. The horses of Poland... God only knows how much horsemeat we had eaten because of the war.

When I finally reached Königsberg the sun was setting. The towers with all their embellishments could be seen as silhouettes against the red and blue sky. They are probably gone by now. At the station I was met by hoards of soldiers closing in on me, looking me up and down, propositioning me, crude and loud but strangely I wasn't scared. I didn't know what to feel and what to take in. Most of all I felt sorry for them – these starved, dirty and wretched men who only wanted to feel like their old selves again for a moment, even if it was the worst of what they had been. I was beginning to realise that war does that to people,

Late at night, feeling hungry and unclean myself by now of course, I found a hotel. It was called a hotel: but as I stood and watched for a moment I saw women and soldiers running in and out, slamming doors, yelling, singing and crying. I saw that the night clerk charged by the hour and that there was no food available. It was in fact a brothel, of course, but I didn't care anymore. War was already working its effect on me too. I took a room, and the sheets were stained, and there were cockroaches everywhere, but I just blanked it all out and settled my head deep into the pillow, which was cleaner than the rest, and got a few hours' sleep.

In the morning I asked for the field hospital and was shown the way; I left the so-called hotel expectant, afraid, exhausted and shaky but at the same time focused and full of resolve. Soon, I found it; an old grammar school that had been turned into a hospital. A man dressed in white sat by an old desk at the entrance.

'Well, you see,' he said after having looked for a considerable time in a makeshift card register in an old shoe box... or was it a box for cartridges? 'The information given to me is that Sigmund, your *Feldwebel*, your sergeant, cannot receive any visitors. He is too badly wounded and ill after the operation, he can't see daylight and mustn't be exposed to noise. He has been ordered *total rest*. You can come back another day.'

'Another day?' I asked, incredulous. 'I am here *now*. My children – OUR children – will need me soon; I have to be back in Berlin very soon. I am here to see my husband.' Here I paused – I noticed the way he was gazing at me as if he was seeing through me. I suddenly felt cold creeping up my spine. 'The way you talk, would it be... would it be the last time?' And suddenly I was angry. I am only a little woman, but sometimes I can make myself tall. This was one of those times. 'I don't want the next time I see him to be his funeral! I am *not* going to be a widow; I believe I can give him strength.' I glared at the man in white. 'You, you are young and I imagine all the girls love you. Have you met a woman who has made you happy? You could get anyone.' For a moment his eyes flickered and I could tell he was thinking of someone. I let my voice soften. 'In that case, you know what a healing power love is. Good sir - let me in.'

'Do you want to meet the doctor instead?' the young man stuttered, as he tried to keep his face calm and not look me in the eyes. 'That may be possible. If you wait here he might come by, maybe in an hour, when he has done his round?' He looked hopefully past my right ear.

'*Ach!*' – I'd had enough. I ignored that young man and headed straight up the school stairs, which all Königsberg's boys had run up and down until only a year or so before. I remember, my heels echoed against the marble floors. On the wooden sign outside one door an old ornate German text said 'Teachers' and the text on the next, 'Headmaster'. On the second door, somebody had put up a cardboard sign, written by hand: 'Private, doctors only'. I opened that one without hesitating.

'*Guten tag,*' I said as a man with a small beard and a white coat approached me. He waved his hand, trying to shoo me away, but of course I didn't turn. Instead I stopped and tilted my head and with a very brief smile looked at him as gently as I could manage: 'I am here to see my husband.'

'Does he work here?' the doctor asked. 'This is a staff room.'

When told him Sigmund's name he went quiet and still, and looked steadily at me. 'Sit down. Would you like a glass of water?'

'Do I need it?' I asked as I tried to hold back the tears. The doctor shrugged, but his face said, *oh yes, you will need it*. As I sipped, he explained the situation to me.

'He was found in a trench; the back of his head was smashed. I mean, it was really badly damaged – when the mud and the blood were cleaned away a large round hole was left. Luckily – incredibly – no bullets had actually gone through the brain.' He kept talking, as I let the tears well in my eyes. 'We don't know as yet if he is going to survive or not. We are doing our best, the very best of our ability. But... the brain may still be damaged. So, if you really insist on seeing him, please don't have your expectations too high; it really may all end at any moment. And, I am sorry but you should not see him today.'

But I just told him I had to. My voice sounded to me as if it was coming from somewhere else far away – cold, and hard, and certain. After only a moment, he told me that on no account was I to put the lights on, or to excite him; and to talk only very quietly. I nodded.

I was then shown into a classroom where it was dark; the blinds were down. I could hardly make out all the beds inside but I could hear sobs, mumbles and groans. The smell of camphor, of ether and iodine were very strong and mixed with the those of sweat, blood and filth. The doctor lead me to a bed where a bearded man lay with his head bandaged so thoroughly that hardly any skin could be seen.

At first I thought that this could not be Sigmund. But the doctor pointed at a sign with his name. It must, then, be true. Kneeling by the bed, I took my husband's hand and held it tight.

After a long moment, he stirred. 'Emmy, is that you? What are you doing here?' he whispered very weakly from behind the bandage. 'I think life is over now...' I tried to hush him, soothe him, but then, half-understanding what was happening, he started to babble.

'Where is Helmut, the little man? Where are our children? Did you leave them in Berlin? You can't do that, they need you.' Suddenly in the weak light, I saw his eyes clearly, those very decisive, appealing, brown eyes. This, more than what he was saying, told me that this was certainly my man.

'Sigmund, listen to me: you will live, I know you will. We need you, all three of us do. I'm here now to help you, and soon you'll be able to come home. Helmut and Käthe are with Mother, Mother and Father are helping me, and so are your parents. Even your brothers are, from a distance, from Heilbronn: everybody who has not been called to service. Please, help me to help you and come home soon. I won't let them send you back to the front. Not that...'

'We'll see,' he said with such great weariness that one could see that it hurt all over. 'Listen now. I only know this: we cannot keep on living in this bloody country. You and the kids our children must live somewhere where there aren't any wars. Somewhere else. Denmark, Switzerland, Sweden. This damn war will never end... Go home now.' His eyes slid shut, but he was breathing steadily.

Of course, I didn't go home. I came back for several days to sit with him, to help them nurse him. To talk to him and remind him of our life together, of the children, his brothers, of all that he would still be able to do.

But finally I had no choice, and I left for Berlin again and a lonely life without him. After a long time, he came home with a metal plate fixed to the top of his head and continued his long convalescence with us in Berlin. He couldn't work and in the world outside our window there was total chaos and revolution. Perhaps you have forgotten...'

*

Emmy stirs and shakes herself, her eyes refocusing. 'That's enough!' she exclaims and waves her hand. 'We should all go to bed and leave these happy two to their own company.'

But Anne-Marie puts her hand on Emmy's arm and begs her to continue. 'We're going to have plenty of time together on our honeymoon and for the rest of our lives! But we're going to be in different countries, us and you – we're probably not going to see you all so often. So please: go on.'

'Oh we will see each other a lot now, we must, I love you dear' Emmy laughs and takes a grip on Anne-Marie's hand.

It's All Coming Back

And meet your family, your father and all. I will probably love him as I love you.' You can hear Hans snort and Björn sort of jumping in his chair. But Emmy ignores that and continues with her story.

Berlin 1919

'Sigmund was standing in front of the mirror in the hallway of our apartment in Trautenaustraße trying to comb his hair so that the metal plate on his skull couldn't be seen. The plate itself was under the skin that they had sewn surprisingly carefully at the war hospital so that it wouldn't show, but there was a spot where hardly any hair grew. Otherwise it had healed well and his hair had grown back strong and even, except on that spot.

He had been in hospital for a year, but now he had been back home for a long time too. He was feeling healthy, he said, but he still wasn't capable of working all day. He was still convalescent, and on top of that, no one wanted to buy his products. There was no purchasing power because of the eternal, the inconceivably long and miserable war. No one had any money to buy clothes, which is what he had always used to sell. People walked around in rags, even though it was cold in Berlin at the end of November.

He and his friends had been so sure about everything when they headed for the Eastern Front to stop the Russians. Then everything became so grey and boring, he told me – marching forward, building trenches, retreating, building new trenches... waiting for hours, for days, in a freezing trench, then forward again, and then new trenches, sporadic shots, and too often, men being wounded.

That was how it was for so long, until out of nowhere one day, that confounded Russian bullet crashed into his skull. It happened in Mitau, not far from Riga. The last thing he remembered, before the bang and before it all went black, was seeing some of his enemies buried in the mud and clay in the trench, their heads sunk, stiff and bloody. It was so unreal he said. He hadn't seen deaths that close before, and he had no idea it would look so calm.

Well, Sigmund tried to work a little in Berlin anyhow, though he wasn't really allowed by the doctors; he did some investigating into the possibility of selling cigars from the brothers factory in Berlin. He could sell that in his and brother Fritz shop in central Berlin but also other retailers would be good. Something to smoke is always needed, even when times are bad – maybe even then most of all; the comfort of tobacco and liquor is what people want. He had received some fine samples, and he had picked some shops and some wholesale firms.

One morning I remember, he was standing in the hallway ready to get his hat and coat, but first he had to open one of the cigar boxes and see that they met his expectation. I can picture him now, lifting a long cigar, smelling it from one end to the other... Helmut, you were five then, you were running around his legs. Do you remember any of this? You were heading for the hallway. Sigmund stopped checking the samples and yelled at you! 'Watch out for the rifle! Don't touch!' and then he called for me – 'Emmy will you come?!' You had found the rifle standing covered in a corner under some coats, yes you did indeed, you took it and held it to your shoulder, you could hardly lift it but marched a couple of steps anyway. Sigmund dropped the cigars, snatched the rifle from you and gave you a box on the ear.'

Helmut was watching her keenly as she spoke – glancing at him, Anne-Marie couldn't tell if he remembered this scene or not.

"'*Mein Kind, mein kleines Kind!*'" Emmy sighed. "He was immediately sorry for what he had done. The rifle had to be loaded all the time as the revolution could come to our part of Berlin, Wilmersdorf, at any time. Wilmersdorf was newly built then and not far from Kurfürstendamm. That side of Tiergarten was rather posh, and we liked it there even if it was not so near to the more pompous old centre of town where Sigmund was working. Mind you, we heard screaming, shouting, from the city, from Kurfürstendamm and, in the other direction, from Mitte. It could so easily come to Wilmersdorf too, one did not know.

Sometimes we could hear cannons rumbling, the loud retorts of shots being fired. It was revolution in Berlin. No one knew if the seamen from the marines in Kiel and the Spartacists would win or not. The seamen had deserted from the weakening German war machine and marched to the capital, and the Spartacists – the socialists of the left, people who wanted the revolution of the masses – they had taken advantage of the situation to try to seize power. Their leaders, Karl Liebknecht and Rosa Luxemburg, wanted to be the new rulers of Germany - they wanted it to be run the way Russia was going to be.

Sigmund gathered up the cigars and put the rifle in a cupboard, and locked it carefully. He decided to wait until later to do his sales round; he didn't expect to have much luck in any case. My God, I was uneasy. I held Helmut, and Sigmund sat down next to me and Käthe came to her father's knee. We sat with our arms around our two small children, in the new flat in Trautenaustrasse in what had become black Berlin. Black houses everywhere from all the fighting. Then the maid came in, very upset and dark herself with soot.

'I think they are coming soon!' she cried. 'You must defend us sir!' She had been out buying supplies and seen soldiers marching on the streets, even here, in this outskirt of the city.

On the eastern front where Sigmund had been at war there was peace now with the Soviet Union; we had to get used to calling it that, this new state that had succeed Russia. On the Western Front the trench war, the damn trench war, was also over but instead they had got this grotesque revolution.

Sigmund had joined the Social Democrats, and felt secure with their middle of the road politics and their sense of responsibility.' Here she cocked an eye at Anne-Marie. 'Do you know all this, all that happened in Berlin?' she asked. Anne-Marie shook her head, lost for words for once. 'Tell me please,' she said quietly. And do please keep on explaining what I might not know.' Emmy nodded.

'He had had an offer from them, the Social Democrats, to take part in defending the city. There was the more militant Garde-Kavallerie-Schützendivision, but also more defence guards legalized by the Social Democratic town rulers, and he joined the defence. He was given the gun, and the task of patrolling an allotted area of the city, Trautenaustraße up to Kaiserallee, over to Nikolsburger Platz, all the way to Hohenzollern.

Now he sighed, put his coat on and took the rifle from the closet and slung it over his shoulder. It would be cold to march around in the streets, winter was going to be hard that year, and he knew it. But he tried to cheer up.

'Rosa Luxemburg, Karl Liebknecht, you have no chance!' – he tried to cheer us too. 'We are safe here!' he assured us, and tried to sound merry.

'Come back soon, Sigmund.' I urged him. 'Be careful. Put enough clothes on! It's cold tonight.'

*

'"Can I come?" you asked, Helmut.' Now Aga smiled, and his new wife with him. But Emmy's face was grave.

'I had to hold you, Helmut, and comfort you so that Sigmund could leave. He paced up and down the street for two hours. It was empty, deserted, he told me when he got back, and he saw neither soldiers nor Spartacists. Eventually he returned to the flat. War would not catch up with him again. It was then he said the words that would decide our destiny. "*Verdammtes Land*!" he spat out, "We cannot live here! I can't, shoot, I am not the man with a gun, you know? And yet our children need protection! *Verdammtes Land*, I damn this land!"

That was when we decided to move on, and we choose Sweden... or, first Copenhagen, but that's another story.' Emmy suddenly stands briskly. 'Now it is enough! It's time for bed! Thank you everyone for coming.'

And everybody says good night and there is a lot of cheek kissing.

It is still close to the war and nobody knows when they will meet again and Helmut and Anne-Marie are going on already the next day. Käthe's husband Henry who stayed on with the last, whistles '*We'll meet again, don't know where, don't know when*' as he goes.

'Oh yes, I have heard and I almost remember the feelings at the beginning of the 20s,' Helmut says.

'We thought it could never get worse than this damn war and all the prey it took, you know?' Emmy nods at Anne-Marie. 'War and warmongering took its toll. Poverty and diseases after the war took their own victims. But then, in the 20s, there was a growing feeling that something quite different; something *new* had to be built from the ruins. So some took to the streets to demand change, and that also meant new victims. Others sat at home wringing their hands until their knuckles turned white. Others were just calm; quiet and self-composed.

'And they got their medals for bravery,' Anne-Marie snorted. 'Sven's brother got the Iron Cross for his contribution as a Swedish volunteer in the German army.'

'Oh yes,' Emmy sighs. 'The Iron Cross was also given to Sigmund after his head was crushed to pieces.'

'And Sven got a medal from Mannerheim for what he did in Finland,' Anne –Marie adds. 'What are those medals worth after the war, other than a proof of disagreement and controversies among peoples and men?'

'And some politicians in those days started talking about *the people*; they wanted the best *for the people*; we have to fight like *people*; we must protect our *people*. *Das Volk*,' Harry said. ' The *people*, including you and me and at the same time pretending that you are part of something greater, maybe more important. That people somehow are all meant for one cause. That is dangerous, I tell you, this vague notion of something joint also gave birth to more radical ideas, right wing and left-wing. German misery was at its worst. Politicians' demands for a new society were growing, coming from different sides. Some wanted revolution and some wanted revenge. Those in the middle were standing on the sidewalk when the processions of demonstrators marched by. And such processions were coming more and more often…'

'Some protested against the first war after they had seen the wretchedness. Karl became a committed pacifist,' Helmut adds.

'Well it is up to posterity to decipher and understand it all,' Trudy adds. Have you now read what my brother Gerald wrote about Sachsenhausen and how it felt to be whipped? That is when it comes close, when you feel it in your skin, that has to be told as well as all this reasoning.'

"Indeed', Helmuth says thoughtfully, 'so much unnecessary suffering. We have been through horrible times and those of us are left who perhaps should have done more. So much has vanished over time: thoughts, feelings, and impressions – and yet the desire to understand how all this is connected is on the rise. And is our understanding of it all any help?'

'No time for more lamentation tonight, we are happy today, aren't we,' Anne-Marie says and pulls her husband's arm.

'Indeed, it is a new beginning,' says Emmy and the party slowly dissolves.

London 1 April 1946

The next morning the new couple wake up with all they heard last night swirling around in their minds, and with the happiness of waking together and of being married. Each one's picture of the other is gradually getting clearer and they're still not irritated by anything they see.

They are married, but they really know only parts of each other; but what do you need to know when the whole world is starting anew and they are putting all that is past behind them? They're not bound by conventions; their love for each other is what governs them, and that is a very strong force.

They have decided to change their plans and go for a short honeymoon to Copenhagen. They have changed their tickets, and they're going to leave England today with a new British service called BEA from Croydon, not on the 9th of April as they had originally planned. Croydon used to be London's major airfield before the war; it had been a military airfield during the war but had only in February been handed back to civilian use, the new updating of Heathrow airport is still in it's opening phase.

So the next day they go down there by rail. She has much more luggage than he has; she has not been home since the beginning of the year, and now here is another trip. So they've also had to use the laundry services at Finchley Road a lot. With so much to carry, they take a taxi to Victoria station and then the train to Croydon and another taxi to the airfield. There they find a very small aeroplane with double wings only suited for 15 passengers or so. When they climb in, Helmut taps on the exterior of the plane. 'Is this plywood?' he asks Anne-Marie doubtfully. The stewardess, right behind them, answers, "Indeed! But it has proven to be a very stable means of construction, these planes have served well during the war and before that: a very reliable plane.'

They are offered two seats a little apart, near the rear of the machine. Between them is a place that is surrounded by a small railing, it looks like a hatchway in the floor.

'Don't stand there please!' the stewardess instructs them cheerfully. They ask why and she says that this particular aircraft has been used in the war and they have not had time to remodel it. 'This used to be a bomb hatch,' she explains in a much more formal tone.

Anne-Marie grows very pale imagining that the pilot might open the hatch by accident and Helmut has to walk around it to give her a hug. But it can only a short one – they have to sit tight and put on the safety belts and look for the life vests. As soon as they are up in the air Anne-Marie has to run to the toilet, which is very small and located at the other end of the plane. But the ride is smooth and that evening they arrive at Kastrup airport and takes a cab straight into Copenhagen.

III.
Swedish spring

Arvidsjaur, in the north of Sweden spring 1946

Anne-Marie's father Sven is out on business in the wilderness as he so often is. They go slowly, jolting along Långträsket; another one of those lakes that are widening the river flow, making the rapid streaming water run slower. Peace has come after the long and wretched war in which Sweden was not directly involved but which came so close to hitting this very district of the most northern part of the country.

The British or the Russians could have opened several new fronts in the north.

The Germans tried to reach Russia over the narrow strip of land north of Sweden and there they had one of the hardest battles of the war. The Germans were severely constricted. But they didn't attack Sweden, not then, or earlier.

Sven had followed the events each day. He saw that the Germans could not get supplies to their Arctic troops. The transport lines were too long and transport corridors too few, with neutral Sweden as a wedge in the midst of all the territories occupied or contested by Germany. The Germans could have tried to get another corridor through Sweden up here.

Sven knows this is no longer anything to worry about, he knows peace has come and that the war is over. But he is still very concerned about Russia and Stalin. He believes that their control of all Eastern and Central Europe is very worrying. He knows exactly what Stalin and his gang are up against. They want to rule the world. He will ally with anybody who opposes that. If he still has the power, that is. His heart is aching more and more often, but his energy and eagerness has not diminished.

The river knows no war; it does not distinguish things in that way. It only knows it is time to get going. It is still frozen, and the ice is glittering, warmed by the very first pre-spring sun. Maybe it is only temporarily warmer... on the other hand; the cold wartime winters may be over now. It won't be long before the water will cut through the ice walls. The same scenery year after year; it is always as exciting.

Water, like fire, is something that people can look at for very long time.

Sven sees a hole in the ice, would like to swim and be able to feel the clear fresh water with its bracing force and murmuring, purling noise. Cold to make the skin, the whole body, contract, and you have to fight it, fight for survival. He shivers thinking of it, feels his body tense. Sauna, bathing, and swimming in the ice is needed to rouse his body, it is so much stiffer nowadays. He wants to be strong, he knows he is superior when it comes to swimming in cold water, but it isn't weather for that yet. Spring is far away even if today it is zero degrees centigrade. One of those rare sunny March days where the forest is getting somewhat more scattered and the hills are rising, where you feel that soon higher mountains will appear, mountains where the treeline will be passed.

He is a man of cold lakes. The warm sea is for weak ones; it is nothing to him. He remembers how he met Laura by the cold waters of Lago Maggiore. Nothing can be undone and yet he wonders about that choice. Why do his thoughts go that way? It is so long ago, another life.

Now he is here with Paulie, his grandchild, his and Laura's grandchild. Such a long time ago. Laura and Siri. Both his two wives are gone now, dead; they left him one after the other, each in their own way. He curls up and the shadows from the pine trees fall over him. He purses his small mouth and pinches his eyes. Life has been mean to him. He sees flashes when closing his eyes. He never understood why he was so hurt by it, by them. A cold shower or swim would do well against these damn sensations of weakness. He is so pathetic and unsettled at times. He hits his cheeks hard enough to wake him from all those thoughts of these women, and yet carefully so the others in the car do not notice his inner pangs. He has hopes for himself on the personal level however, newly married as he is. The children do not like it of course but he does not care. The children do not care about him and he does not care about them. But he likes *their* kids; they are promising. They are lovely, fine. He would like to be able to stop and calm himself by looking at the river, step out of the car and just stand there holding the boy and telling him about nature. There are probably both grayling and char; that would be something. But it's not possible, there's no time, he knows he has to be useful, do some darned good. They are going to the next session; there are always new court deliberations in this sparsely populated part of Sweden.

He is restless, unsettled, rushed. He wants to finish the week's work to be able to go for a longer trip. He had looked in the mirror this morning when he was about to comb the wisps of hair on each side of the crown of his head, he had looked into his own small somewhat beady eyes and had noticed his big, sleek, pendulous cheeks and he felt tired and lonely. He wanted to be stronger and be able to work more, go for more trips, help his clients. His eyes were flickering and his head was down and he wondered about the meaning of life. The new woman in his life was fantastic but would things stay that way? Had he got anything left to fight for when politics had not gone his way? He buttoned his waistcoat over his now-too-big belly, stropped the razor and shaved carefully in spite of this being a day off. He enjoyed splashing the stinging lotion on his cheeks; as if he were giving himself a thrashing. After all he is the one who can alter things, he knows very well how to get this end of the country moving, if only people didn't let themselves be fooled into backwardness and dependency on subsidies.

You have to be strong. He has to work even if everything is going wrong politically. Well, he always wanted to go against the flow, always wanted to show that he is solid in his convictions, in his ability to defy the ruling powers and fight for what he believes is right. It is so grey now, no lights, no strong colours, and no eagerness. During the porridge at breakfast at the hotel he had a sudden wink of alertness when he was reading the local paper, yesterday's paper up in these far away parts, and saw that the government had new problems with the municipal elections this autumn.

He perked up even more when Paulie arrived at the hotel to come along with him.

He imagines the sound from the river and the lake, the purling, the gurgling, from below, a sign that water has started to move down there by the boulders, a signal to the fish to start moving, to start living again.

If he could only stand by the lakeshore, looking into the clear water.

But now he is in the old Volvo. The car is growling and the sandy snow is crunching under the wheels. It is somewhat slushy in the sun. The producer gas has been disconnected and now petrol is being used again and the change-over is not so easy for old cars. But this motor is spinning. They scare one or two skinny, stray reindeer, those having chosen solitude or those who were left when the herd went down to the coast for better winter food and are now just waiting for the others to return. They pass a homemade, horse-driven cart with tractor wheels and a woman driving in Sami dress and a kerchief.

He has driven these ninety kilometres between Arjeplog and Arvidsjaur before, as he has almost all the roads in the northern part of the country. This time with the boy and the public prosecutor for this area. The three of them form a travelling party. They are going to the same place; another time he might have said no to the prosecutor but this time he is in one of his generous, positive, happy moods. 'Come with me,' he said and smiled his best smile, when he saw the police in the dining room in the morning. 'We do not need to solve the case now, we have to let those jurors in their innocence believe that they make the verdict.'

The smell inside the car is of damp wool and petrol. He has been telling the boy stories about the river, about mountain lakes, about ice nets and herring fishing by the coast. The boy has told of how he has gone fishing with his other granddad. The prosecutor is quiet, has been so since he entered the car, pressed in on the other side, next to the window. The boy and Sven are comfortable, as comfortable as Sven can be with his long legs and body and the prosecutor sticks to his corner.

It's All Coming Back

He belongs there, Sven feels. He has nothing to say to the prosecutor at present. It is important to keep information to himself and not reveal it until they are sitting there on opposite sides at the session. Then the case will be about water, about the desire to stop and change the flow of water in order to get electricity into houses. That seems reasonable and intelligent but they do it without caring how they ruin the farm villages and Sami camps. Here the water still flows unregulated, undisturbed, grand. The prosecutor deserves only an occasional, furtive look. Sven controls him, making sure that he sits quiet and still in his corner. He has talked with the boy enough for now. The subjects are done with. He hates petty talk commenting on nature. At the hotel it was different; there they talked about homework and the boy's marks at school, about the lad's future and what they will do by the coast when Paulie joins him there.

The boy is ten now, so nice, alert as a mountain creek, so happy, and he knows so much. He reads more than any of Sven's own children did, more than Sven himself did at that age. There is no sign of early puberty, just a wild lust to discover the world with his curious blue eyes. He must be going to a higher level at school and this sparse area is no good for that. Paulie had a letter from his mother, from Margit, who wants the boy to come to Lund in southern Sweden, to meet her new husband and live there. Sven would gladly have given Paulie a room in his big house and helped him in his studies but the boy's grandparents, Margit's parents, have also said that he is going to Lund. Well, his other granddad has not said anything to Sven, he is a committed communist and local politician and Sven cannot talk to him. But he likes the grandmother; she is serious and honest in a way, simple. It was she who asked if Sven could accompany Paulie down to Lund, as Sven was going that way anyhow. And yes, he will. No staying for long with Sven in Umeå, not now in any case. London is obviously out of the question even if Björn, Paulie's father lives there now. Strange. Sven believes Björn should take more responsibility; he has always been so damn irresponsible. At least he is done with all the communist fuss for Moscow and those constant trips to the Soviet Union.

No, the three grandparents have taken full responsibility. Sven has his clear views on what would be best for the boy and he had wanted Paulie to stay in Umeå, which had been close to Arvidsjaur and all, but he accepts the decision and says nothing.

A lorry laden with milk overtakes them. A minute ago it had stopped by a milk stand and loaded up the big metal bottles and now the lorry overtakes them again. That milkman doesn't usually drive that fast, either; he only speeds up when their car is in sight. Sven's irritation increases when they are overtaken again, which the boy notices. Paulie wants to be friends with granddad and wants him to be calm and so he keeps on talking, talks of what he will do in Arjeplog while the session is on: go watching cars and Sami people, go to a café and maybe have a bun with marzipan.

The milk lorry does the same procedure again by the next milk stand, brakes suddenly in front of their car and then on and off with the heavy milk bottles. Strong these men may be, but they seem to have problems with traffic codes. You can hear the bottles clanking on the lorry when they accelerate again. Sven feels under his waistcoat for the gun in its holster, then feels the watch in the waistcoat and his wallet in his inner pocket. Those three should always be in their respective places. He pulls out a shining two-crown coin, polishes it carefully and gives it to the boy.

'Granddad, Granddad, why does one have to remarry? Why is everybody remarrying in our family?'

Sven hushes him. The milk lorry overtakes again, slows down again. Same procedure. The chauffeur in Sven's car has great trouble in adjusting his speed. Sven shouts.

'Where did he come from? ! Overtake the bastard again!' he cries, and grabs the chauffeur's shoulder. The man now notices how the lorry again slows down after having overtaken and he throws out the indicator to overtake, but the lorry drives slowly now, probably looking for the next stand. Gravel is thrown up behind it and the chauffeur has to keep a distance. This goes on for a couple of kilometres. The chauffeur hoots and starts to talk to himself.

'He just sort of suddenly comes up like that and blocks the whole road. Who does he think he is? I have got the solicitor and the prosecutor in my car. You can't drive any old way you want! You just can't! I'll report him to the milk company, so I will.'

Sven feels under his waistband for the gun in its holster, it is there for all eventualities. You never know, as a lawyer you may get enemies and you have to be prepared, not that he usually uses it other than for practising. But you never know. Except that time in Tampere, of course, at the end of the first war. He takes the gun and slowly winds down the window and leans out. Aims carefully at the lid of one of the milk bottles as if it were a game, but he pulls it back and winds up the window again, when the prosecutor starts moaning about the cold. None of the others has noticed the gun, small and handy as it is. Then he decides, cocks the gun fast and winds down the window again, leans out, aims and fires. The others react when they hear a dong like a church bell though sharper and faster when the milk bottle is hit. The lorry slides and almost goes into the ditch and the driver chooses to pull over and let them pass. Sven makes a gallant gesture with his hat towards the lorry. The prosecutor is quiet in his corner. So is the boy.

'A sudden shot,' says the chauffeur and does not brake, 'Damn good.' It is quiet for a long time in the car.

'Granddad, it's terribly fine that I'm to go with you to the south of Sweden. Can we meet my cousins along the way? And Aunt Anne-Marie?

'*Terribly*? That is a word meaning awful, worrying, monstrous. You should say *extremely*. Of course we can meet Harriet and your cousins, but Anne-Marie, she is on her way to England to get married. They kept it a secret from me, the bastards, but it is good that she is finally getting married, after eleven engagements. I have seen a photograph of the man, finally. He looks very Jewish.' Sven smiles, his eyes peering, the prosecutor still squeezed in the corner. The chauffeur changes down to second gear to overtake a tractor-cart. They hear the wheels spinning against the snow. Far to the right, the wrong side and close to the ditch, but he manages. It is a complicated manoeuvre. He changes down to first gear and is ready to use the hand-break to be able to stop in a hurry. He presses the accelerator and the wheels spin even more. The car makes a light slide with the rear tires, which he counters and drives on. Then he accelerates and puts it into higher gear.

After a couple of kilometres the car starts coughing. The exhaust pipe gives off a shot. Everyone listens but there's nothing more. The trip goes on. A couple of kilometres further on the snow is deeper and the road is all white. The car keeps sliding on in what is now rather deep snow. The day has clouded up and soon it begins snowing, wet spring snow. Sven winds down the window again and puts out his hand to get snow on it. He takes some and puts it on the boy's cheek and the boy turns away. At the same time the car coughs again, more this time, then slides and stops. The chauffeur presses the start button but to no avail. He gets out, pulls out the crankshaft and starts cranking. The motor coughs a little, but that is all. He lifts the side lids, inspects the ignition system and takes out the spark plugs, puts them back and tries again. No way. There are no cars in sight and the driver starts walking down the road in the wet snow. A kilometre or so back they passed some houses and that's where he's headed. It is a long wait in the car for Sven and Paulie and the prosecutor.

The prosecutor sticks to his corner while Sven and Paulie get out. They move their hands back and forth, embracing themselves to keep warm, and they run up and down for a while. Then they get back into the car, but now into the front. Paulie sits behind the wheel and pretends he is driving. After a half-hour the chauffeur comes back sitting on top of a tractor. They have to tow the car to a nearby farm where it might be fixed.

'But, what do I see, welcome, solicitor!' the farm owner says as they open the door. He wipes his hands. A swarthy man with a black eye. 'We met in session last year. Yes, I paid the fine. But he was a mean one, he was. I sued him, I did. Sit down, sit down, and welcome! I have planned to start a car workshop here for quite some time. I will fix it, and don't you worry! Agdur, do we have reindeer and cloudberry sauce left? We have got fine visitors. The solicitor, I am astonished! And chocolate for the boy to drink, can you fix that?'

Sven takes off his hat, peers at them and smiles. His cheeks feel pinched and he thinks he will explode from the inside. He takes a deep breath and holds on to the table, dizzy for a moment. This is quickly noticed by the others in the room – he waves them off as best he can. 'The angina, my heart... *shit*... maybe I can lie down on the sofa? Do you have a pillow? That's it.' He finds his tablets in his pocket and throws them into his mouth. 'Bloody hell that heart isn't just for fun.' He cocks his eye at the farmer. 'Yeah, indeed, I recognize you. But your eye wasn't black. Is that also something worth suing for?'

'Well, it was a bit wild.' The farmer grins sheepishly. 'My fault too. Never mind.'

Sven carries on regardless. 'I recognize you all right. That black hair, and that sweater, easily recognizable. Don't you ever wear other clothes?'

'Agdur makes these, do you want one sir?' the man asks eagerly. 'Or maybe for the boy?'

'Subpoena?' the prosecutor suddenly interjects, having begun to thaw in the warmth indoors. 'That was against Lindström, wasn't it? About some dam. Isn't that coming to session tomorrow? Your name is Sundgren, then.' The house-owner nods.

'You need a barrister,' Sven says rapidly from the sofa. 'I'll be there tomorrow.' While they speak, Agdur has brought flatbread, big round soft ones, some dried meat, a big bowl with the yellow cloudberries and she starts whipping milk for the chocolate. The boy sits down by the very big table and begins to read the mail-order catalogue that's lying next to the obligatory bowl with sugar lumps. Sugar for the dram and the coffee and maybe for the sour berries. He counts the places around the table. More than around king Arthur's round table, he reckons. He counts to 18. Not all of those are free. His granddad on the sofa takes three places and Sundgren one, and there is also a cat on one, and three children with big eyes in a corner.

'I'll go out and fix the car,' Sundgren says, 'My brother will help me.'

'I'll come too,' says the chauffeur. After a while the door opens again and a couple of men enter, taking their caps and mittens off, and sit themselves at the table. They are as swarthy as Sundgren. One of them has bruises up his cheek. Agdur asks what they want.

'Our intention was to talk a bit about the dam. We think it is unnecessary to go to court,' one of them says. 'We may have a proposition,' the other says after a brief whispered discussion. 'We are planning a small power turbine for a sawmill. We started that project.'

'Don't be so hasty,' the first one says. 'Prosecutor, can you make a note of what we say? If you do we may put forward our proposal. We intend to propose, our plan is to suggest, well, to let the water, or let some water, past our dam and he can pay for what he gets.'

'Wait a second!' Sven interrupts. 'That was no proposal, was it? I am Sundgren's lawyer. You have to do better than that. We are going to court tomorrow. We have time to wait. Sundgren has no reason to pay. Let us wait for him.'

'No, no, we do not want to go to court! Doesn't look good, does it? Maybe we can let some go by for free, enough for Sundgren, maybe, if he states exactly what he needs… maybe.'

'That sounds more like it,' Sven says gravely. 'We may call it a deal later. Don't change your minds now. Yes, that is all that we have to agree. Wait, I will write an agreement and you sign. Get Sundgren as well, he's outside.'

It is all done.

'What do you say, prosecutor?' Sven asks. 'You get one case less tomorrow. What do I get for that? There is a need for lawyers to help you at times, don't you all forget. I don't make as much money. But it is worth it.'

Later in the day they set off with new spark plugs; the old ones had been ruined by the producer gas made of wood that until recently was the car's fuel. In the trunk Sven has put two round wooden pine casks, one containing salted char and the other cloudberries.

Now they are jogged to sleep in the dark as the big Volvo rocks its way through forests and over open land. Sundgren also wanted to give Sven a gutted black grouse cock but he managed to say no to that.

Umeå, in the north of Sweden March 1946

Some days later Sven is back home, at work in the town by the river outlet. He is back home and with his new woman. He is not a man for reflection. He likes to get things done, to act in the moment. If he does think about the past, or of what would be correct in every situation, he just gets confused or filled with retrospective ideas, even angst. He doesn't want that. He doesn't know what it is that has made him think back now. Perhaps it is the new political situation. War is over and he has been on the losing side. Winter is still prevailing; or rather new snow has come on top of what had already almost thawed away. This winter had a slow start, but since then it has restarted again and again.

He looks out from their new flat at the square, snow is coming in big chunks. He is reminded of his childhood when his father spanked him twice for all pranks, both as his teacher at school and when he came home, as all fathers would. He remembers other boys filling his shirt with snow and filling his face. He thinks about his exams and his student life. But he passes that quickly.

When he met Laura and the first time with her. They were happy then. His businesses with boats and with sandwich machines, first so successful, but then after a while his creditors haunted him. He was even charged, and had to flee to save his legal honour. They went by train to Berlin, him Laura and little Björn, and from there he went on without them. He was in Cuba for some months, picking sugarcane under an assumed name, he had decided that a year would be enough to stop all persecutions, but he came back sooner. He first went to another lady and Laura's parents were pushing for a divorce, but he came back to her and they fled together on from his Stockholm foes, to the north of the country. And then he was accused of hitting a colleague in the street.

Accused. Oh yes, he gave him some, but they didn't know the whole history, did they?

Then Laura took too much medicine and left him with all the children.

Then Siri, that strange but good woman came in and took care of the children and he worked like hell and at the same time fought against exploiters and liberals. Oh yes.

And now Siri has left him as well. She really did before she died.

And the Germans, who he had supported all the way, had no control over their country in the end. He was there in '43 and it was chaos, and no one wanted to meet with him. He who had been their closest ally. He had been a Nazi all-right; he remembered when he had been almost alone fighting for the cause and when many supported him a decade ago. They had tried to establish something new; he does not understand why everything went so bad. He has to blame Hitler. Indeed he puts a lot of blame on this corporal.

Now he has to start anew. His darling Anne-Marie is doing it, and he will too. She has had so many nice fiancées, and yet she has finally chosen this one: but what the heck, she does what she does.

It has been a hell of a life.

And the angina.

But now he feels strong. He takes some coffee and a small aquavit. He has time to go skiing; he leaves the house and puts on the skis. It soon becomes overcast, but he fights on even if his heart hurts at first as it is getting colder; he feels his own limitations already after a couple of kilometres. He doesn't have his old breath. A silk tail flies out of the reeds when he passes a small lake and Sven stops, leans on his sticks and watches the bird flying over the lake. It turns out to be a whole flock. The shy birds fly in great curves over the reeds and then they find a bush full of last year's hips where they settle down, far from all huffing people. He stands for a while, hanging over the sticks with his elongated frame and sees several small birds flying in and out of the bush. There is one he has never seen before, striped in black, white and red like a semaphore or as if it were trying to show its political colours. The goldfinch looks at him before flying up and diving down out of sight again. The pain relaxes and he fights on in the trail, a bit wet over the ice. 'Free the trail, let me pass,' he hears somebody calling him when he is struggling, breathing deep. Free trail. Nobody should ask him for that. He picks up speed again, even if it is hard and his cheeks are getting red. He increases the distance from the younger skier behind and then goes in to a side trail to rest.

Paulie has stayed on with him in the town for a long time, though Sven promised they would soon go south. Sven will pass Lund and leave the boy with his parents. The reason for the delay is the German. There is a German in Umeå, one who happened to come here when the war ended, an airman, another one of these existences that the war left here and there without functioning lines of connection or escape routes. The newspaper heard a rumour of him and they think there have been secret espionage flights. Sven helps him keep away from attention, from peoples' talk and from possible interrogations from the authorities. They have long overnight talks about possibilities, difficulties, hardships and chances. They stay put in Stöcksjö, in the summerhouse of Lisa, the woman Sven is now married to. Sometimes they use another cottage that he is able to borrow from a friend. The German complains about the primitive conditions, bad insulation and cold privies. Worst of all is the privy placed high above the river on the steep slope with the great drop - it blows in so darned cold from below. But what are his alternatives? Sven doesn't know if the German should have been arrested and the German himself does not know what he did, why he was flying over the north of Sweden. He didn't have enough fuel and had to go down in Sweden.

Sven should have gone south long ago. He promised the boy's grandmother and mother. Now even Björn has sent a cable from England to ask what's up. Is Björn coming to complain? What right has he got? Sven gets irritated and pokes the ice with his stick. Maybe he will stay longer and the boy will have to go alone or with someone else. Paulie is starting school right after Easter down there in Lund and should be there by then. But Sven has the tickets in his inner pocket. First class for him and second for the boy. Their departure is planned for Monday. Sven coughs. She, his new wife, complains that he does not follow the doctor's orders, but what the heck! The sun is now high over the reeds. He sets out again over the ice, fast with long, steady strokes.

IV.
Honeymoon

Copenhagen, beginning of April 1946
Day 1

They find the hotel they have booked is in Vesterbro, not one of the poshest parts of the city but very central, and although the hotel hasn't got the highest of standards, it's perfectly acceptable. They find it clean and quiet, with flowers on the table and what they like most, very nice bolsters and Danish-German style big and soft eiderdown duvets. They accept the room and finally they have time for each other. When they are alone in the room Anne-Marie immediately creeps down between the sheets and duvets. However tired they are from the journey they have wanted so long for each other, for being together on their own, it was hard for them to be alone as much as they wanted in England.

The next day they wake early but go out late – they almost miss their first Danish breakfast, like the ones they have been anticipating, and this hotel has a remarkable breakfast with Danish pastries of different kinds of course, Danish rye bread and several sorts of herring and home-made jams and all you may wish for. Then they just walk around the whole day and sit down when they feel like it, eat when they are hungry and just do nothing except be together, really.

After a long sunny day they are simply happy and the elm trees in Kongens Nytorv are covered in their first grey-green shimmer: a slight silver veil in the low evening sun. Behind them is Nyhavn's noise – laughing and talking – and slanting across the harbour canal comes a wind from Öresund, a breeze from the sea bringing the sharpness of salt to the lips. Evening has arrived, and in the square the lights are lit, warm red gaslights, making it feel warmer. Now, at the beginning of spring, it can be really properly warm when the sun has shone in the daytime, and yet it can be so icy cold at night.

It isn't very cold now, but they already have their hats and coats on at six. Many happy people pass. Copenhagen lives, the city is revived.

Less than a year ago, German troops were patrolling this square and many Danes had to sneak around street corners. The German quarters had been across the square in Hotel d'Angleterre. Somewhere, however Danish pride prevailed, illustrated by the King on his daily ride through the city.

Many people have already put that behind them; have thrown off the war like the elm trees throw off their leaves in the autumn. Forgotten. Now spring is beginning, the long-awaited first war-less spring. It isn't like England, where the daffodils already give a yellow gleam to parks and gardens. Here it is just a hunch, a sprinkle of spring, a weak but hopeful spring.

And yet the spring of 1946 already feels more intense than it has for many years. Anne-Marie is walking hand in hand with her husband, her man – not *a* man, *her* man. She has changed her name, assumed a new identity; she is now part of Helmut's family. It will be quite another life; it already is, yes, she has thrown herself off, without caution, without caring in the least about having contact with the ground, without the slightest need for control. Every second she is full of him, has to touch him, look at him, twist around him. She isn't controlling like she's always been before. She can close her eyes at times, pinch her eyelids to reset herself, just to be able to open them anew and make sure it is all true, that she finally has found him. She has hoped so many times, thought that she had found the right one, imagined things about that man and life with him; done that with each one that she had been in love with. But love had always become boring and formal after a while, and demanding. This is not at all like that. She still feels warm when she touches him, she quivers, her eyes are only set on Helmut and she doesn't care less what others might think. They have created a bubble around themselves, a love bubble where they see only each other, and where it feels like life had started anew.

They walk slowly now, across the square. Sheltered from the sea winds, they walk across the eastern side of Kongens

Nytorv towards 'Det Kongelige,' the Royal, as the theatre is called and towards the Magasin du Nord. They zigzag between pedestrians, trams, bikers, and cabs. They are heading towards Ströget, a long narrow pedestrian street that goes through the centre, between cosy shops and smaller houses up to the quarter where they are staying. Then, suddenly, he moves swiftly away, away into an alley between the houses hosting the opera on one side and the theatre on the other side in the houses of Det Kongelige, Denmark's national theatre. He breathes more heavily, harder. His eyes look harder, and in fact he looks scared, something she hasn't expected at all. His self-assuredness was one of the first things that struck her when they first met. She has paid attention to his big, round body of course, but he carries himself so confidently – he is so assured. She has been seduced by his big, hairy hands, which hold her so safely. Now Anne-Marie sees a new side of Aga.

So far, every time she has discovered something new about him she has been pleased. She loves his relatives in England; it is all so simple and clear to be with them. It feels as if they have known each other for ages, and yet they only met a week ago. Now he takes her hand and holds it firmly.

They are heading for the hotel beyond Ströget and Rådhuspladsen after a dinner of oysters and Chablis. She is excited after having drunk and eaten well and then enjoying the decadent and richly physical Nyhavn with its sailors, tattoo shops and half-naked women. They have just given way to a tram and he has stretched out his arm to take her hand and walk on towards Ströget, when a policeman comes strutting in front of the main entrance to the opera, heading towards them. And he reacts so intensely, all of a sudden becoming someone else, someone other than the noisy, alive, dashing, big man she had known for five months. Though they have seen so little of one another they already read each other like a book. She knows he can be melancholic, like her father, like all men. That he wants to be alone at times.

But now, standing with him in this Copenhagen alleyway, this time she can see his fear, his deep apprehension, sparked by the appearance of this Danish policeman. Has he committed some grave crime? Could that be it? As a businessman, she suspects, he has probably been careless with taxes and employment rules. She wouldn't put that past him, certainly. He can be anarchistic to a degree at times. But surely that shouldn't cause such unmistakeable fear of the police in a foreign land?

They stand close by the wall of the opera house under a blue mosaic on a roof that is also the floor of a gangway above the street between the buildings. She holds her body close to his. He holds her shoulders: firm, but absent. She looks up, wrapped in the scent of his body, and pushes her small, decisive nose against his neck. She has let out her long, light blonde hair and it falls over her high cheekbones, hangs like a Venetian blind in front of her intense blue eyes. She hears his heart pounding. 'What's this?' she asks him. 'Whatever is this? Tell me! I'm really getting worried! Is there something you haven't told me? Is it the policemen who are scaring you? Tell me, now.'

Helmut slowly shakes his head. 'No. Nothing. I just needed to hold you a while. I don't feel too well, it was the oysters probably, it's too early in the year for them.' And then he sets off again. Anne-Marie wants to ask more, but it's tough trying to keep pace with him as he walks decisively towards the hotel in a manner she hasn't seen before either. *Must ask him again later. Have to know.* Suddenly a chasm opens up – has she chosen the wrong man again? That *can't* be. His mother and his sisters in England had helped her to understand some things. Aga has had a lot of women before her. This big sturdy man is perhaps not somebody people expect to be a ladies' man, at first. But when you have seen the depth of his brown eyes or had a chance to experience his complete and compelling focus there is no way back. It is not possible to resist when he holds her firmly and looks at her in that determined way. He didn't have to ask, she gave in to him at once. Even so, she also understands that he has probably been shyer, more uncertain in front of her than in front of other women. Perhaps because she is more important; she wants to believe that. She doesn't really know from him what he has done before, even though he sometimes mentions other women. But there is so much he hasn't revealed – like what he did during the war. Maybe something heroic... or something rash.

They move faster on the paved walkway; they bump into Danes muttering about Swedes. Helmut answers one in German, another in Danish, a third in Swedish. Now he shows that assuredness again, the manner that has made it possible for him to walk in anywhere, even when he isn't invited.

But then, he doesn't know everything about my family and me... I don't know if he'll understand, if I can understand myself... if I can make it all right.

Her thoughts end there: now it is only about getting the key ready fast and then rushing up to the room.

If I can't understand I can't tell. Or, maybe I will understand through telling. She sits down on the only chair in front of the washbasin and tries to read the detective novel she has brought along. He has fallen asleep after a visit to the toilet in the corridor. He makes hardly any whining sounds as he is sleeping, and that surprises her: she has already got used to them. She eventually and cautiously gets into bed, just on the edge, and lies for a long time, still reading. And after she becomes tired of the book, just looking at the wall and at the window with its blind.

Day 2

In the morning she sits restlessly on the small chair and puts her pocket mirror on the windowsill. She braids her hair. The different parts shall not be too uneven when they are to be braided, the one over the other. She opens the small silver medallion she wears close to her heart and looks at her mother, her mother who stands there by a birch tree in a traditional regional costume, with her hair in a nice braid, finer than hers. The mother who she never had the chance to know, who is a mere feeling, a feeling of a bond, a sorrow and also an idol, a picture of an earlier life. Breaking out of her reverie, Anne-Marie returns to her own braid, but when the hair tumbles out of her grip once again, she gives in and puts it all in a bun on the back of her head just to take it down again and start anew. Outside, Copenhagen has woken up to a new day. She sees the sun shining, watches the early morning commerce on Vesterbro. Walking softly past their luggage, she opens the window and takes a deep breath and takes in all Vesterbro's morning scents. She can feel that the street has been sluiced overnight, the shopkeepers have thrown out the rinsing water, making it stream down the gutter, but one can feel, too, that smell of impurity that has been rinsed away but still somehow lingers.

A small vegetable stall by the crossing has opened and some bottles change hands on a street corner, a couple of women with too much make-up adjust their stocking seams as some sailors pass. The small tavern opposite has already received their first sleazy beer guests, the ones that probably haven't gone to bed. She sits down on a trunk and drinks in the sounds, the smells, and remembers yesterday with a smile. Soon they will go down to breakfast, or at least she will. He has been running to and from the toilet at night, and she knows he needs his sweet sleep. Now he moves and gropes after her over the bed and grunts. He half rises when he notices she isn't there. When he sees her, he smiles. 'Thank you for yesterday. Don't you want to come back to bed?' He pretends she is there already and that he is caressing her.

'No! You are contagious! No way, what a honeymoon... Let me braid my hair.

'But, I want to braid in, to be interwoven with you, with your dreams. What's on your mind?' Helmut asks, now lying on his elbow looking at her.

'And I with your memories,' she replies, meeting his eyes. 'I want to know more about what you did in Copenhagen. I mean – during the war,' she wants to be clear, and her tone isn't as warm as it was before.

He quickly withdraws, curls up on his side of the bed, his bones folded under him, and closes his eyes. Doesn't want to see. *That question.* He holds his nose as if he was bleeding, remembering the blows hitting his face and his body, all that he had tried to forget and never ever wanted to talk about. He only lies like that for a short moment; for him it is like an eternity passing. *Never, never again.*

'Aga,' Anne-Marie sooths, 'You shouldn't hide: I want us to share everything now, I want to know everything about you. Please, don't be so selfish; there will be a thousand opportunities for what you want now, once you get a little more healthy, less contagious.' He opens his eyes and sees her now grey-blue eyes glimmer as the light from the small window finds its way into the room and mirrors itself in the simple roof lamp, in the glass of the small painting and in those eyes. He feels a desire to rub his head against her soft hair. To be close, and blow into her ear. To forget.

He whispers in a low voice that grows stronger and stronger, 'No problem, there is no problem. I feel fine. Come.' And she comes to him, responds to all his hints and suddenly forgets his sickness and all of her hesitation. She begins slowly humming and caresses his head.

And they start telling stories about each other and about families picking up where Emmy ended a couple of days ago.

All those old stories of the past are haunting them, chasing them, taking their attention away from love itself. They are supposed to be in the most intensive phase of a new relationship, but they also have to know. He about her folks, she about his. And he, who never hesitates to tell a tale, likes to see other reactions, wants to amuse, he develops the lives of the past in such a way that they become as alive as you or me. Exaggerates, points out details, smells, tastes, lust. You can see it in his face when he is just waiting for the pun to be understood. She has to work a bit harder to make her stories so alive, but she takes her queue from him and her tales become fuller and fuller. The art of storytelling is soon their common excellence. Making love and telling stories is their life, in the shabby hotel, on sightseeing boats along all the canals and harbour ways, in cafes and restaurants. Not always decent, never hesitant. She still likes his dominating manners, as if he owns the world and knows exactly how to get where he wants to get, but she has begun to see the first glimpse of the man underneath, a bit more uncertain and afraid and unwilling to show all his faults. She also has this openness: people who have never met them before think that they know all about them after a quarter of an hour, but they have their closed cupboards, their secret integrity like everybody else, it's just well hidden behind smiles and stories.

In this they are alike.

And now that the door of the lock is opening and the water is gushing in, one story leading to another, one revelation leading to the next question, and they still carry on.

After a while they decide to take it chronologically. It doesn't make sense otherwise. This means that the whole twentieth century history is running in with modernization, trenches and the lot. Wars and small periods of peace and quiet, a big picture and the small one. Still broad tales, still not touching on the really difficult stuff, the stories that have touched them themselves, the ones that are not being told for puns, but which are thought-provoking and call for consideration and perhaps compassion. And they don't want to have compassion, not even from each other. They are neither of them experts by any means on showing other inner feelings than their love for one another how ever extrovert they may be.

So later they go to a movie, which means that they don't have a chance to tell each other stories for an hour or so. They watch The Ziegfeld Follies, which could have given him a chance to talk for a while about the refugee Jews now so prevalent in American filmmaking, or about how they in the film didn't show real love… or about beauty and attraction and Lena Horne and Esther Williams, and she could chip in too, about Red Skelton and Gene Kelly. They would agree mainly about Lena Horne, how her voice, looks and behaviour makes her superior to the others. They will have this debate afterwards of course, but during the film they can sit quietly and reflect, after all the film has no real story to be preoccupied by, they can just sit and let the musical rinse their ears and eyes, even though he meddles with her ears at times and sneaks his arm in under hers and touches, barely softly touches her breasts or her blouse rather, and she pushes him off to be for herself a slight moment, next to him but not intertwined. They talk about friends, trying to find out if there are any who they both go on well with. She has gotten very close to a Norwegian girl with whom she spent the sanatorium days with, talking about everything, and she has her old childhood friend from Umeå and Harriet's nanny or helper: they don't spark much interest in him. He has the other Helmut, and he also had a friend who is now a doctor and very much engaged with radical politics, especially to do with health, working towards creating a new social order. She likes the work he talks about with family planning. But these are not such close friends, so maybe that is nothing either. And there are all the old girlfriends and boyfriends of course. Maybe not of considerable interest.

'I've got you, that's enough,' he says smiling.

'But I just got some new friends!' she smiles back. 'They are called Ilse and Emmy. Those are my friends and yours too I gather?'

'Ilse, definitely. A mother is perhaps not a friend.'

'She is my friend now, and that will be swell.'

Day 3

This is how it is to be married.

Anne-Marie sips some tea which Helmut, her Aga, her husband, has brought for her. First he has had stomach problems after a dinner in Nyhavn in a, they realize now, not so clean place. They have been careful to avoid the whitefish roe, they know it may contain tapeworm, but hadn't realized the oysters had been washed in used water. And, after he has got better she first gets red cheeks and has a temperature and then she too has to run to the small toilet in the corridor. So instead of breakfast it is tea this morning.

He is much better and has been down to the breakfast room and comes back up with tea. He also has bought a newspaper for her. He really cares for her. They are supposed to be back on April 9th after only a short honeymoon in Copenhagen, but now it will be longer. He is so worried about her tuberculosis.

Is this a honeymoon? she wonders. Sitting in a small hotel room with one chair and the toilet and bath in the corridor? Maybe *this* is what love is, to care for each other when sick, to exchange diseases, to have someone to be miserable with, testing love far away from paradise. And they also have time for hugging, just looking at each other, holding hands and discovering each other, making love carefully and softly - they do that despite the sickness.

They decide that they should stay indoors today and only go out for short errands; it's good that he also has bought some books. 'Look at this!' – he shows her the book he is reading, a small volume full of aphorisms. 'Listen to this!' He snorts with laughter and holds a page in front of her: 'We all have our faults, except the German, there are few faults in his land, at least of those he would understand.'

She doesn't look as if she understands, but smiles. 'Aren't *you* German?' she asks, and he just shakes his head... she quickly changes the subject.

'Do we dare to go out today, do you think, a small excursion, a minor exploration?'

He looks at her carefully; she is so bloody foolhardy and bold. He loves her daring; all the women he has known have been so inhibited one way or another. Anne-Marie is not that kind of woman. She really lets herself go and if there is something that has occurred to her she makes it happen, she goes through with it fully.

He wants her to see a doctor first. They ask the hotel staff, and it's arranged for one to come there. He prescribes rest with only short tours for the next few days, and he also gives her a prescription for some pills. And then, despite all that trouble, they decide to go out after all.

Once away from the hotel, they find that she can't go into a restaurant with all its strong smells. He goes into one at the beginning of Ströget and has a bitter drink to ease his stomach.

While she waits outside, she looks at amber in the window of a shop across the street. She would like him to buy her a ring or a necklace, just like that, without asking first, but that isn't his style, she has to point it out or buy it herself. However, he is a master when it comes to other things like serving tea when she is still in bed. She feels the cold wind from Rådhuspladsen, the City Hall Square they just passed, and pulls her coat tightly around her. And then there he is beside her in a minute, warming her with his big body in a bear hug and holding her close as they walk on. They sing and hum and just look at people and at each other.

After a short walk they see a small place called La Glace on the street above Ströget where they have ice cream and coffee. He looks so happy when he has a giant ice cream bomb and a cup of chocolate with whipped cream. He is pleased just looking at it. She has to make do with a cup of tea, some dry biscuits and a tiny blackcurrant sherbet; she believes her stomach can deal with that. It has to. She is already so tired of boiled water, juice, white bread with nothing on and grated apple, while the other guests at the hotel are having all the delicious Danish food and Danish beer. But she feels better now, not least for him being happy; she loves it when his big body is laughing and when he courts her. He is larger than life and totally unpretentious and nothing like those gentlemen she knew before.

They pass the station on their way back and extend their tickets for a couple of days. When they return to the hotel room they are not quite OK, they notice. Their stomachs sound a bit out of the ordinary. They read, she continues with the aphorisms, he reads about the war. And subsequently, his father-in-law is occupying Aga's mind. It seems that neither Anne-Marie nor her sister or brother have told him everything. They have been rhapsodic about some things in their past, quick to brush over other, difficult, subjects and have said that he must make up his own mind. He will of course; he has gathered that Anne-Marie's father, Sven, is it seems rather far to the right, and was even during the war, but he doesn't know quite how far. Does he want to? Why care about that, anyway? He has married Anne-Marie, no one else.

Day 4

'Aga, do we dare to go to the beach today? The doctor said a small trip would probably be OK,' she asks the next morning. Helmut inspects Anne-Marie carefully: it is perhaps not good for the illness, but what the heck, she wants it and what she wants is good for her, he thinks. So they go to the beach. They take the train from Copenhagen Central to Greve and goes straight down to the sea.

'I want to have a swim!' she cries, and, shrugging her jacket off, runs towards the sea, the cold windy sea. 'You know,' she calls over her shoulder, 'I'm an excellent swimmer! I exercised practically every day, before this damn disease!' She stops at the edge of the waves with a shy smile, and Helmut just looks at her quietly. He really believes she will go in, but she doesn't. She will never ever stop surprising him. Instead they walk on, inhaling the sea air, basking in it, looking, searching in flotsam and jetsam thrown up on the beach, peering through the mess of seaweed, reeds and wood for things to examine, to talk about, maybe to save. Anne-Marie holds a smooth stone, shining with vibrant colours that she thinks might look fine on a windowsill before reluctantly throwing it away and grabbing a new one. They are wary of metal and walk in wide circles around anything that could be duds, mines or other charges. They can hear a foghorn from across the water where there are heavy fogbanks only a couple of hundred metres out. Helmut cups his hand and tries sounding like a foghorn – a couple of seagulls veer away, startled. Some crows are chasing each other across the beach. Helmut looks for small creatures. At this time of year things often come in from the salt sea into Öresund.

She sits down on a wooden rack by a tuft of reed. He looks out at the fog, remembering nights during years recently past, how they had passed mines and traps out there. Turning, he goes up to her and holds her tightly. She stretches her arms out as one does when yawning, a gesture somehow both sensual and loving. 'Darling, I have to tell you about Copenhagen during the war,' he says whispering into her ear.

'Tell me what you wish. I will tell you all I know. We must get that kind of thing over with. We cannot fool each other or keep anything back. It is only you and I. You are like an open book; I can see what's in your mind and what you feel before you tell me. Nothing can be hidden any more.' She moves up even closer, taking his hand. He suddenly squeezes her hand hard and stares frowning into the tufts of reed. She follows his gaze, his body's language. A stubbornly staring and very frightened gaze. Now she sees what he has already seen. She stiffens and searches for both his hands, holds him tight.

In the reeds there is a round, large, black, metal thing with several round ribs like antennas. A weak metallic ticking, threaded through the eternal cries of the seagulls, carries on the wind.

He sees several gulls around what he believes must be a mine, and then he points up into the sky; a bird of prey is circling over them. Helmut has to concentrate his eyes in the mist. Two gulls are on top of the mine, the one trying to impress the other by walking around, pecking at it, trampling. The other stretches its neck up, raises its head, and opens its beak. Helmut carefully takes Anne-Marie's hand in his and then they slowly rise as if they are only one body. Cautiously, slowly and quiet they sneak backwards without letting the birds out of sight. They have to get far away, and quickly, but without frightening the birds. If the creatures take off, it would be all right. The problem is that the next landing on the mine might be more sudden, and if the bird of prey swoops down from the sky, that would be worse. Of course, the mine might be a dud and completely safe - but it might also go off. Especially if one of the birds press down on those jutting antennae. The love play of the gulls is deadly dangerous.

Helmut pulls back again and points to a pole standing by a sand hill. Another hawk is also sitting there, the same colour as the sand and with a pattern that's hardly distinguishable from the reed straws. If that hawk attacks the gulls the risk would increase considerably. Now they don't sneak or step lightly, they run over the soft sand, no more slipping and sliding, but flying.

Helmut falls over and right down after a couple of hundred metres, his head driving into the sand, and the smell of rotten seaweed and the salty grains hits him, mixing with a smell of blood. He pulls himself up at once, clutching his bleeding nose, and quickly calculates how far away they are from the mine. Anne-Marie has stopped a bit further ahead. They have run quite a distance. They are no longer able to distinguish their position amongst sand dunes, reed tufts and stones, and the mist doesn't make it any easier. He decides they are sufficiently far away, so he walks towards the water's edge to wash his nose, to rinse his mouth with the icy water to get rid of all the grains of sand he can feel on the inside of his cheeks and between his teeth.

The water of the Baltic is saltier here by Öresund, icy and salty. Anne-Marie is still standing a little further away and she suddenly notices that some people are coming from the other direction, happily chasing each other, throwing sand. They are heading straight towards the mine. Anne-Marie has been focusing on Helmut in order to see how badly off he is, but now she has to concern herself with the people walking towards them. She raises her arms to show them that they shouldn't pass, but they think she is trying to stop them getting close to Helmut.

'A mine! Birds! Risk of explosion!' The garbled words come tumbling out in her urgency.

Anne-Marie shows with her hands that they have to walk in a circle, a big circle. They shake their heads but she is tremendously relieved when they do in fact walk up closer to the houses above the shore. Very quickly, though, they are running around again.

Helmut slowly approaches Anne-Marie; she doesn't make the slightest effort to move from her spot. She welcomes him with her hands stretched out and immediately begins examining his nose. They sit down on a rock and she searches for her handbag. 'My bag...' she says agitatedly after a moment. 'It's still there, by the mine.'

'Calm down' Helmut is soothing, 'I'll fetch it.'

He gets a proper hug as he leaves, one to be on the safe side. He shrugs her off, brushes his clothes and walks slowly down towards the water again. He's realised that he has blood on his hands that has to be washed away. When he's done, he carries on, along the water's edge. Now he isn't very careful. He marches on, imagining the meeting he will have with her father, the encounter that will finally take place. He stares into the waves, he goes through small bays, goes around sand dunes and small, natural pools, past leisure boats and over narrow footbridges, and all those things they have hardly seen when running. He walks too far, has to turn around again. Finally he sees a broken-up mine in the reeds. It is empty of its contents, looking like the backside of a sphere. Some sea gulls sit on top. It's a harmless backdrop.

He walks over to the other side and there is her purse.

He looks in her bag and finds a handkerchief, which he uses to staunch his still-bleeding nose. Then he runs with it over the deep sand. From far away, he sees Anne-Marie. She's sitting on the stone where he left her, kicking sand with her head down as if she has been crying.

'I was so worried! Where have you been for so long?!'

He sits down beside her and holds her firmly, very firmly. In this part of the beach, just here, the ground is flat. They can hear gulls and ships and even the water gurgling where it reaches the shore. The sun can barely be seen through the now thin haze. But it gives some warmth.

'You hate intervals, pauses, times apart, but they are needed. We will have to wait for each other at times and we have to live with that, manage it: you'll have to manage.' He hears how trite it sounds, almost goading; so he buts his head into her belly by the navel, over and over again till they bubble with laughter. She wants to hug, maybe make love, even if it is far too cold and means getting sand in their clothes. She rises and stands behind him, very close, tries to caress his head; to rest her own against the back of his neck – wrapping her arms around his chest, she presses herself into him. He hums and sighs, but soon turns to her, and they tumble about in the sand for a long while, the sun heats them, and finally they reach what they are both seeking. Then they have to walk around half naked and shuddering and gather up their discarded clothes to be dusted free of sand. The wind has increased despite the sun, and the clothes fly away and aren't so easily collected. When she has picked up her bra, panties and corset, underskirt, sweater and jacket, and they are all back correctly on her body, she sits down again and lights a cigarette, hugging herself to keep warm. He is almost out of the sand by some grass, which he combs in the hunt for small creatures; always an interest of his.

'I'll tell you about dad and the war. I'll tell you now,' she says full of energy. 'Or rather, about before the war. If you want to hear it, that is.'

'Are you feeling well then?'

'Never been better.'

'OK, I'll listen,' he agrees. But then, immediately – 'Look the fog is coming in, rapidly!'

'You're not listening! You don't want to know! You keep on about my father, you want to know everything, you've said so, so many times, but now you're more interested in the fog and your old memories of it!' There is sand in her hair and she shakes it out. 'I'll start when we were south of here on Rügen in 1936.'

'You were in Germany after me?' he asks, surprised.

'Yes I was. You know, it was also the Baltic coast and he was interested in natural history, like you.'

Rügen 1936

'Grouse!' Sven shouted, standing straight, his hand gesturing out over the low marshes and up towards the chalk cliffs sloping into the Baltic. He was wearing a bathrobe, standing in the middle of one of Rügen's sand- and grass meadows behind the swimming pier: he spoke as if he wanted to convince himself, but very loudly, if anybody wanted to hear. They'd travelled to Germany, he and Anne-Marie, a summer tour, a kind of diversion although he also intended to do some serious business. It was all about making contacts, fraternizing with the right people; and he had brought her. His thin and remarkably pale long legs and his big flat sandaled feet were visible beneath the blue and white striped gown, its belt carefully fastened around his waist. The small tufts of hair by his ears were wet. He put on his small round metal glasses. The grouse had lifted off the shrub with a considerable commotion and an irritating clucking, and from the red-brown mass of heavy wings a larger brown fowl could be seen ascending. The grouse were no longer a possible prey when they were flying in a group. The brown marsh harrier cried out, a creaking sound; he was clearly annoyed at the lost meal. Then he flew with broad, calm, heavy wing beats out over the sandbanks, heading for a distant fishing boat.

There was a light morning mist over the Baltic. In the distance it was possible to make out the construction cranes by the coast where they had started the building of Prora, the giant resort which was supposed to be one of world's seven wonders. The day before they had been given a tour of it by Kraft und Freude, part of the new German Nazi labour movement. Three miles of resort is being built as one single extremely long house.

He had been for a morning swim; had swum several hundred metres in the still-cold springtime water. He swam straight out and felt the salt of the brackish water on his lips and in his mouth. He dived down until his vision blackened. He didn't know if it was to see if he dared to do it, or see if he had the ability to, or if it was to feel a little bit of death, to have no respect for boundaries, to have no sense of where he should stop.

She came running from the small boarding house where they had spent the night. 'I was worried when you didn't appear at breakfast!' she cried and flung her arms around him. He held her back, they didn't normally express that kind of intimacy.

'It's I who should be worried!' he replied, as he flexed his arms. 'When, in fact, did you come home last night?'

'I tapped on your door and when you didn't open I got worried,' she said. 'Then I saw you far off out at sea. I was very worried, do you understand that?'

'Oh, well you can think better out there,' he said ignoring her anxiety.

'My thoughts went to mother,' she said. There was a pause, just too long.

'Have you seen the harrier?' He pointed to what was now merely a small dot in front of the sun; it was coming through the mist just above the horizon to the east. 'The brown devil tried to snatch a couple of grouse,' he explained. 'Now that he's gone they are lying still and are scared to death; see, over there? They don't think anyone can see them. If I had had a gun we would have had a splendid breakfast. Are you cold?'

In the dining room in the boarding house a group of young men, all wearing the same brown shirts, were sitting eating breakfast. It was very orderly, the tables lined up, smelling of overly fried bacon and sausages. There was also dark bread, eggs and a very sour cottage cheese. Anne-Marie heard a lively tune in the background and recognized the *Horst Wessel Lied*.

*

Here Helmut intervened. 'How bloody awful, you were staying with some Nazis. Perhaps we should pause here and go back, it is getting colder.'

'Please, let me finish this part of the story about him. I'm starting softly you know. Please.'

And he sits down and lights a new cigarette and listens.

'Well they all looked up as we two Swedes entered…'

*

'You asked about mother,' he said when they were seated. 'I wrote a letter to Siri last night. Wrote that I am worried about you, though everything is as it should be. We have met wonderful people, but there may be one or more black sheep even in a group like this. A father is always concerned for his daughter.'

'You're writing letters to Mother Siri?' she asked, her eyes wide. 'Again? You sent one the day before yesterday from Trelleborg and one the day before from Omberg. Every day! She has left you! Why aren't you trying to break that habit of writing to her? I don't think it's any use to keep bothering her.'

'She's on my mind: it may be hard for you to understand,' he said and looked steadily at her with his small azure eyes, irritated and yet wanting to explain.

'You know, I would be happy if everything gets better again,' she replied earnestly. 'I like Mother Siri very, very much.'

There's another pause. They both look at the table.

'But the point I was making is that you don't seem so interested in this trip after all,' Sven says after a moment.

'I came along primarily because you asked me, because you didn't want to be alone. And for the Olympics of course.'

'I'm glad we came at the right moment. It'll be fun to support the Swedish boys, won't it? Maybe I can arrange for us to meet some of them.'

She watched him wearily. 'There *are* other things on my mind apart from boys,' she snapped.

He ignored that. 'I think our greatest hope is that sprinter, Lennart Strandberg – him and the football lads. That German Lutz Long will be exciting in the long jump. But that black American Jesse Owens has jumped over eight metres they say...' He stood up and paced out over the floor to show me the distance. 'Soon they will have beaten all the records. Won't it be fun?'

'Sure, Dad. You don't have to worry about me.'

'And nor you about me. Finish your meal now and then we have got to go and find Carlsson, and then go in and say good-bye.' He had finished his meal, ready to go in search of our chauffeur.

They were soon on their way. The motor of the old Volvo taxi was humming. Sven was sitting up front with his waistcoat and his jacket unbuttoned in the summer heat. She was in the backseat, studying German words in order to be able to complete her exams after the summer.

'Dad, do you want me to learn better English as well, now that you've met an Englishwoman?' she asked. He was drawn from his thoughts, not just by this sudden question, but also because the car had stopped when a flock of sheep slowly came up the road from a field alongside, and were soon spread all over the roadway.

'Autobahn,' Carlsson said and his face lit up. 'We are waiting for Autobahn to be finished.'

'Well until it's built, you still need to get rid of the sheep!' Sven was irritated. 'Sheep have their place as well, I suppose. But hoot at them then, do it!' He turned to her, 'English; I don't know. There would be some trips to England of course... How did you hear about her?'

'It is too bad for Mother Siri,' she said. 'She is a true mother.'

'You are grown-up and can manage without a mother, can't you?' her father snapped.

'I just hope that all will be well between you and Siri again. Can't you understand? I want a family to come home to! And I hope you'll be reconciled with Björn.'

Sven wriggled and sniffed, picked up a newspaper and began to read about Hitler's speech on the Spanish situation.

A big Alsatian had run up, barking at the sheep and at the car. Carlsson hooted and the animals gradually dispersed. Slowly, very slowly, the car started rolling again.

'Though I don't think this is much of a family these days,' she continued. 'Siri has moved out and you're dragging me along on this trip...'

'What do you mean 'dragging'? Aren't you happy to come along? There it is again! Aren't you happy to see all that's new? You've been going on about Germany and that you haven't seen much of it ever since your brothers were at boarding school here and I've been coming to visit. It was *you* who wanted to come along!' He lowered the newspaper and turned to look at her.

She didn't like her father examining and criticizing her. She actually didn't regret having come along, but she felt that she always had to be the mediator, the helper, be supportive. She did feel so sorry for him, for the whole family, when he and Siri split up. She was the one keeping in contact with Björn, something she also had to be secretive about. She was the one writing long letters to her brother Ivar who had moved to Argentina, and she was the one going with her father to Germany like a kid; a bloody kid.

Carlsson was very happy to have been accepted as their chauffeur for the trip. It was his chance, him, just a common cab driver from Umeå, getting to go to the Berlin Olympics and have so many new experiences. But he didn't want to be drawn into a family quarrel, to listen to the wrangling and to the stubborn silence. A military column was beginning to overtake him. Military vehicles had right of way and he had to show that he respected that.

'Shouldn't Germany be disarmed?' he muttered.

Sven frowned at him but said nothing as he bent over the newspaper again.

If only Björn was there, she thought. All father's reasoning would be blown away. But she was not like her brother. She wanted to be friends with her father even though he could be so very narrow-minded sometimes. But then, so was Björn. She carefully read what he wrote; she had to do that in secret.

'Dad, it was lovely yesterday!' she said, deliberately making her voice more cheerful. 'There are a lot of nice people in this country.'

Sven agreed 'With belief in the future, yes indeed.'

'But for me, their hatred towards the Jews is a big issue,' she said with sudden vehemence. 'Mother Laura was a Jew, wasn't she?'

Sven looked out silently over the broad fields, towards the new motorway being built in the far distance.

'And isn't it true that if one's mother is Jewish one is also Jewish?' she pressed on, 'Which means that they will hate me too, isn't that so? How can I agree with that? I'll never believe in what they stand for as long as this hatred towards the Jews exists.'

Sven shook himself like a dog trying to rid itself of water. 'So much talk about Jews! There is *so much else*, my young friend.' He turned to her. 'It is about Europe's future. A new world order. You are talking about different things. Your mother and I... Yes, I liked her, she was fantastic at first, but it wasn't that easy when business became difficult for me. She, as you know, left us.' There was a moment while they both considered this. 'And by the way, I don't think she would have counted as a Jew, and you definitely don't – what counts is if you have a Jewish grandparent. You don't. Henrik Schück, your mother's father, wouldn't be considered Jewish; he had a Jewish father but not a Jewish mother. And his wife wasn't Jewish.'

She huddled up, pulling her knees in tight under her body. She was furious.

'Have you figured that out?' she spat. 'Have you calculated who will suffer like the German Jews; not me but my grandfather and all my aunts?'

Sven wriggled again but didn't answer: he didn't want to hear another word.

'And what would you do if I fell in love with a Je...?' She stopped the words even as they tumbled from her mouth.

Sven lifted his newspaper again, and sat rigid, trying to let his anger abate. After that it was perfectly quiet in the cab all the way to Berlin.

Day 4 cont.

'You mean he was interested in Nazism?' Aga asks, now becoming quite perplexed and irritated.

'Let me try another story,' she says. 'You know the communist newspaper *Norrskensflamman*?'

Anne-Marie starts and Helmut listens.

'Yeah, your brother worked there.'

She nods.

'Was Sven there? Was he one of the attackers?' Helmut now has his eyes wide open.

'No. But he defended the attackers. Or one of them, a public prosecutor by the name of Ebbe Hallberg.'

'That was a good scalp for a northern barrister, wasn't it?'

'Sure, and I'm not saying this because he thought the attackers were smart. I'll tell you the whole story,' she says frankly and he sits down in the sand, makes it comfortable by pushing it up against his sides so it becomes like a chair.

Umeå and Luleå 1941

Sven was sitting at home in the big house in Umeå, working. Two grandchildren were watching him from the door to the hallway. They stood there, blonde with their eyes wide open, sullenly staring, hand in hand, as if they were about to rush in for some prank. They stood there for a long while, just looking at him.

Sven wanted to have his grandchildren in his house and was always positive when asked; sometimes he even asked the parents himself if the children would like to come to him.

He wanted to see them grow up into responsible adults. He taught them manners and took them out into town; with one in each hand he walked along the main street, into the shop with reindeer meat and game, and taught them everything about salting and preservation. Now they just stood there in the doorway, peeping, and this made it hard for him to work. Soon he would be off by train to Luleå – he was to see his brother there for dinner and then the next morning go to the trial. Erik and he are going to talk about the political situation; they always do when they meet. They haven't always had the same views but these days they did.

He was just about to call the maid when he looked at Paulie and got a bright idea. Yes, damn, of course, Paulie's father Björn worked at the communist newspaper in Luleå; let's see how was it now? Somebody had put a petrol bomb by the newspaper building, which Björn discovered and called the police. It didn't go off. It must have been a couple of years ago. Sven smiled at the children and they ran away. He scribbled down his notes, packed his things, found and patted the children and left in a hurry for the train, asking Siri to take care of the children.

*

'I saw some of this but the rest is as I was told,' Anne-Marie concludes and Helmut nods in his sand chair. 'Sven was going via the post office with some letters and money orders, for Björn's former wife, for some political friends and organizations, a bid for a painting Siri recommended and some more. He made it just in time for the train.

*

The next day he took part in the trial in the Luleå local court.

'I know this is not the only assault on Norrskensflamman; not the only time someone has tried to burn this house; you see my son Björn who worked at the paper discovered a petrol bomb two years ago. 1939 it was, yes it was, so the explosion and the fire this time were not necessarily connected - many people tried to set fires in that yard,' he said and looked a little smug making his point but trying to keep himself from looking as if he was sneering. Several of the public moved in their benches and looked at the tall bald man. Some knew about his political sympathies, some have even been to the meetings that he and his brother and Holger Möllman arranged at the beginning of the thirties; but they didn't all know that he was so closely related to Björn, the communist journalist, the activist, the agent, he who had now left the party and the paper. They remembered Björn from the parades on 1st May, always at the front with his nice black suit and waistcoat, sometimes with a pram, alongside the Swedish communist leadership. Sven and Björn were equally bald but Sven was much taller, more self-contained.

The people in Luleå heard of Sven mainly as a barrister who got the most renowned cases, maybe also the most difficult ones and as someone who defended small people against those higher up.

'Damn, he isn't afraid of being associated with communists,' one could hear one of the listeners say. 'I thought he was the one supporting us.'

The courtroom was full.

Sven was sitting next to his client, the public prosecutor, Ebbe Hallberg. Hallberg was sitting straight and proper with his short hair with its grey stains. He looked scared. He had fought for a long time against this newspaper and its insurgent tendencies and incitement of the populace. He did not like his barrister claiming that he really should be declared as not responsible for his actions, that he should be brought to Stockholm to the Långholmen jail and to be investigated in a mental hospital there.

Sven knew he has to go for this; it was the only chance to save Hallberg from a harsh punishment. He tried to look at this case as one of many even if he agreed with the attackers that communism was the biggest threat to Sweden. He believed that the communist propaganda that the paper was diffusing was awful, and it was continuing to spread it. He didn't go in for this type of direct action himself, attacking a newspaper was beyond his limits. All the councillors were relieved that the trial was only about indemnity for destroying the print machines and not the fact that five people had died as a result of the attack. What Sven said about the petrol bomb and other attempts to set fire to the building was said to avoid the case being one of manslaughter.

It was on 3 March 1940 that five men had entered the printing works and set a bomb to detonate and destroy the printers. The entire building with its editorial office and dwellings caught fire; some of those living there were able to come out through the windows and climb down a rope improvised from sheets tied together, but five people died. Sven did succeed in getting Hallberg declared unfit as a citizen.

Day 4 cont.

'And what was so terrible about that then?'

'Perhaps it wasn't quite clear from what I said.' She brushed away some ants that were crawling up her legs. 'Dad was of the same opinion as the attackers. I am trying to say he was Brown. It's not anything more than that,' she keeps staring at her shins. 'He was a little Brown in his political colouring, he had his own political party in the town council and cooperated with other friends of Germany or people who were tired of the conservatives; it was called The National Socialistic Bloc. Let me explain – '

'I don't know. I don't want to.' Helmut, who has been gazing at the sea turns and looks straight at Anne-Marie. For a long while he sits there quietly. It's even windier now, and she ties her kerchief around her neck. Yet it's as if she is undressed, as if she has given all her secrets away.

'No, I don't want to hear,' he repeats, and then he stands. 'I don't want to hear all these things that you should have told me a long time ago. For Christ's sake, Anne-Marie, your damn family probably have room for even more family secrets! Your darned fine family with more skeletons in the cupboard!'

'Take it easy,' Anne-Marie says, trying to soothe. 'There is more, yes, there is more to know about my father. But you know, many were Brown at the time. Is that so strange, even if you and I don't believe in those values? Didn't believe in them, even then?' He doesn't reply, and she goes quiet and kicks hard, very hard into the sand, bites her lip, and pulls out a cigarette. But then she continues while waving with her unlit cigarette:

'Though nobody knew that much then. I know you don't want to hear that. It's been tough for me to tell you this much. You think you will like him, you said. You will never understand him, definitely not all of him. Satan.' She sobs. 'I want to have you both! Mainly you.' She stands up and tries to wrap her arms around his big body, still with her cigarette in her grip. But he shakes her off quietly. He walks away from her, fast, walking off along the beach, away, far, far away from her. She can't call him back; her shouting will drown in the wind. She sits for a long time but he doesn't turn. She sees him grow smaller and smaller, getting further away from her. Soon he can't be seen at all because of all the tufts of reed. She sits alone, very lonely, smoking, thinking, sniffling, abandoned, and freezing. She sits there for what seems an eternity, for so very long before he slowly loafs back and asks if she is cold and gives her his jacket. Her entire body is really shivering when they slowly walk back to Greve station without a word.

Sitting opposite her on the train, Helmut's mind is full of his father-in-law. The man who is turning out to be, to honestly be, some kind of Nazi. At first he is so deeply shocked by this revelation that he can't think: his mind goes blank. After a while he calms down and mainly feels sorry for her, for her to have this legacy, to be connected to her father, the old Nazi. Guilt by association. Helmut hates this, to be connected to someone's views just because you know or are related to the person. *Everyone in his or her own right*, that is common sense, he believes. Still, he knows it is not easy for her.

The illness gives room for nakedness. Nothing is hidden any longer, even the deepest secret; nothing can be hidden from someone once you've suffered the indignity and pain of a severe stomach ache in front of them. This creates a new type of openness. They have the chance to tell each other everything in between visits to the toilet and periods of sleep, to tell all the things for which there has been too little time on the few occasions they had together before the wedding and in the letters they exchanged. They had thought they knew everything about each other.

Now they both know that there is more and they both demand to know it all, small and big, to see if there is any more in the closet that needs airing, to be viewed and maybe stored anew, carefully sorted and arranged.

Day 5

They have a lot of time for each other, Helmut for Anne-Marie, Anne-Marie for Aga. What they do in Copenhagen has less importance, they are mainly occupied with each other, in that first stage of love, when they just want to touch, taste, look into each other's eyes and recognize all the nooks and crannies of each other's bodies - love increases by the day. The sickness is weaker now but returns over and over again, despite charcoal tablets and keeping only to certain foods. But it means nothing when it comes to their love.

They have to get out to the spring sun again the next day. They just have to. They feel they have to do this in shorter excursions until they are strong enough. In the morning at the hotel he is as he used to be. He nods and says some kind words to the waitress, watching her legs while he cuts the marmalade toast into small squares, sliding them into his mouth one by one, and drinking only silver tea.

Anne-Marie notices his glances at others but doesn't care as long as he cares for her, is with her, holds her, only her. He looks closer at her when he hears her coughing, it's getting more and more severe; she almost loses her breath there at the breakfast table. He hurries to get hot enough water for her and pours some warm milk in and some honey.

'I don't believe it is the TB,' she gasps after a while. 'That's a worse and more constant ailment than this. The doctor said it can't come back, but I don't know really. I have got a slight cold plus the stomach thing. No, it must not return!' she almost shouts, really angry. 'That bloody disease spoiled so much!'

'I was also hospitalized during the war too,' he tells her, his face troubled.

'Mmm... I spent a full year in Österåsen sanatorium up in the north, did I tell you that?' she asks, her mind clearly back there in the past. 'It was mainly boring but we had some fun there too.' She seems suddenly calmer.

'My hospital was no fun,' he tries.

'We had a lot of fun! Have you heard of Österåsen? A giant yellow building in the forest with a magnificent view of one of the rivers up north. Tuberculosis had afflicted so many, it was a plague for the poor mainly, but it suddenly hit little me. No one really understood how. Maybe an animal infected me or perhaps a friend. I had it for so many years whatever the doctors said, but now I think, I hope, that it's gone. Mind you there were some girls… and men… there who I learnt to know and we did a lot of pranks and danced and had loads of fun, but we were supposed to lie still in our berths most of the day.'

He looks at her and puts his hand on her forehead, opens up her mouth and holds her tongue down with her teaspoon. 'Say *Aaaah*.'

She tries to eat his hand instead of saying *aah* and he has to withdraw the spoon. 'Don't you see?' she snaps suddenly, 'It *might* be TB again, and then you don't go out, you lie still for years… You can't have babies! You get passive. Do you want to live with a vegetable?'

'You are not so bloody badly off, and if it really is TB, we'll soon know. And Anne-Marie, I am going to live with you whatever happens. Come on.' He holds her and gives her a cigarette.

She snatches her coat and hat, takes his and presses it down on his big head. They go out. He walks slowly this time, does not march on with big strides, getting worried when she is not as fast. That is how it usually is, but today he is looking at the world through more cautious eyes. She is glad about that, happy that they can walk close together, but in practice she rushes ahead and he trots after her. Normally he is like a sheep dog, quick, straight ahead, targeted and she on the other hand is more interested in investigating things, looking at shop windows, smelling restaurants like a bloodhound for which every trail offers up new possibilities.

He is walking here with his wife. That he would ever be married was something he had hardly believed in – when he was thirty a couple of years back he didn't believe it would happen. Ever. He had never before met a woman where the idea of a shared future was important to both of them. Now he is there and somehow it is perfectly natural. After all those times of departures, breakdowns, all those love affairs. It's not just her simple beauty. At times he finds himself watching her hair, her chin, those blue-grey eyes, that disarming laughter, her frankness, her body. As if they had always known each other. She is so natural, so open, so self-evident. Her face doesn't carry any secrets. She is present with all her feelings, directly showing her happiness, anger, sadness and disregard. She changes her appearance so fast and he can see what she wants or feels before she has said anything. He understood instantly when they met that they belonged together. Before her, it was simply sexual attraction that had caught him, had invaded him. He is a subscriber to *Vogue* and carefully pulls out Vargas' pictures of girls from each edition. He will have to cancel that now. He is obsessed with the female body. And so often the physical thing had been the only result. When previously that certain common understanding has been strong, the intimacy has been there. Oh yes, he has been in love many times, has written girl's names all over the place, has tried to write poems for them, been impatient and keen and hot. This time he feels inner warmth, an inner calm when watching her, touching her, feeling her presence.

Life has become self-evident to him; it has become self-evident that life is a common thing. Her life and his have become one and he likes it, he likes the mere thought of it, he who has had so many problems connecting with others, he who has always known best and walked his own path. Yes, there will be sacrifices and adaptations and fewer of the personal feelings and experiences of one's own. But that is what he wants now. It's just letting the common force in, and seeing that they both have the same understanding and readiness. Now all that exists is the future.

He had reacted strongly to all the talk about her brown-shirt father. It was the second time that he got really upset during these days in Copenhagen. The first was when he was reminded of his last visit to the city, when the war was on... He doesn't know if she could truly understand how it really was, if it's any use to try to explain to her. He understands no one else can really be part of his feelings; it's too personal. That he felt such primitive, basic pain. He is one of the many who sniffed the war, and hardly that. What right does he have to pity himself?

Yet, he can feel pain and anger returning. Thousands of others, millions of others, have suffered so immensely, so much, much more. But still his wounds are there, although he has tried not to dwell on it. Now those memories are coming back, and he is alone with them. He should have realized this would happen when they decided to go to Copenhagen.

He can't let go of how it was the last time he went over Öresund, when he took the small boat overnight. Out there, in the war. He erases the images of yesterday's police and also of yesterday's stomach problems and even of her brown-shirt father. It should be them now, just them. They slowly walk along the road leading from the station up to the small lakes and to the next railroad station.

Disease, illness and sickness can pacify people, can divide them, but may also be a force that afterwards create new courage and can unite them, like the moment after a hard rain. The rain engages you completely and afterwards every blade of grass, every flower that has survived can be seen as a victory, and the air is clearer than ever.

Now she allows him to carefully fold his arm around her and they walk cautiously so as not to put stress on their poor stomachs. He puts his big coat over her shoulders but she throws it off. They now walk serenely and steadily like a couple of Ardennes horses. They don't even look at the patisseries with their Danish pastries and marzipan cakes that earlier engaged their attention so emphatically, with all their tastes and scents. Instead they take detours around them. This morning they don't want to sense the city, to drink the city, and they have to be very cautious when walking through the scents that are a part of this town; of bread, cigars, sea and petrol fumes. They sense the city's hesitating morning pulse after the early morning rush, which was something they just got an idea of from their hotel room. They have to make way for all bicycles. They still feel a void and uncertainty in their stomachs, both of them. She is still red-nosed; it is gleaming from all the feasting, all the travelling, and all the miserable nights lately. He brought his camera, his Rolleicord. His photography had been quite important during the war, and he remembers this very street corner.

In Vestre Farimagsgade they pass a burnt-out building. They saw London's ruins just a week ago. Each and every block had some burnt-out houses, houses that were now just piles of bricks and dust and the smell of soot and often of gas; houses where the cleaning up had merely started, and others where the job of rebuilding had already begun.

London had been severely hit five years ago. In his German homeland it must be much worse. He can hardly imagine it, even though he had read all the articles and seen all the pictures. Even the town of his childhood, Heilbronn, is completely destroyed.

This city that they walk through now is almost undamaged except here. 'The Shell building,' Aga says gesturing with his hands. 'This is where the Gestapo were, and the Nazi occupiers held many from the resistance in captivity here. They managed to catch quite a few of them at the end of the war.'

'Wasn't the Gestapo in Hotel d'Angleterre at Kongens Nytorv?'

'Yes, there were Germans there as well, but this was Gestapo HQ.'

She stops and watches him talking, his hands gesticulating – he will be a good storyteller for their kids some day.

'English bombers came in with their Mosquitoes, from Öresund. They had to start high up and then come down fast to avoid being attacked by the German air defence. And then they tried precision bombing, to pacify the Germans and allow the men from the resistance to get out. You probably read that story?'

Now she remembers; it's dead children that she pictures. 'Did children die here?' she asks quietly, her voice vibrating.

'They had of course done a good job of reconnaissance, with photography and the like. There were people here on the ground doing that kind of thing, people who helped the allies, helped them to do things right.'

'And yet it all went wrong,' Anne-Marie says.

He looks away. 'They bombed a school didn't they?' she continues. 'Didn't several children die? Reconnaissance you say? Damn useless reconnaissance, I say.'

'The survival of the resistance was important.'

'Yes, I read about it. It was an eye-opener to see the cruelty, the way it has been with the camps now. Now one really understands how people suffered.'

'It is not that simple. *Not that simple,*' he emphasises while lighting a new cigarette.

'Maybe the children died because of bad photography or bloody-minded fighters. Sometimes it is all so exact and at other times many innocent people die.' Anne-Marie kicks a rock lying on the pavement.

'It wasn't like that!' Aga insists again. He is paler now, and runs his fingers over the camera in his jacket pocket, trying to press it down. 'It didn't happen like that.'

She shakes her head slightly and walks on, a little in front of him and rather fast, away from his hesitations and explanations. He has to struggle to catch up. He comes alongside her and puts his arm around her waist.

'By the way,' she says when he tries to look at her close up. He wants to comfort her, and to see how she is feeling. 'By the way, I have to know why Danish police make you anxious.'

They are now by the small lakes. Some crows fly up and flap over them, croaking, and then slowly head off for the city centre. Aga doesn't reply. Instead he grinds the end of his cigarette into the pavement and picks up some gravel in the same movement, and then throws it into the lake; some ducks let out a scared cackle and swim off.

She looks at him inquisitively, but he doesn't care. They pass the lake, walk past a pavilion to the other side, up the boulevard to the sandwich restaurant. They stop outside.

'Are you ready to eat now? I'm starving – maybe I'm not sick any more.' He says, shivering with delight; the process of recovery after so much illness moves and excites him.

'Yes, let's. I want to eat too. I didn't cough all the way here, not once, did you notice?'

'We'll get our well-deserved lunch, and you tell me more about my father-in-law,' he says. 'I bloody well ought to get to know to whom I am married.' He has raised his voice and then turns around to see if anybody heard him, anybody but her. The restaurant is almost empty. The waiter comes with an ice bucket and an unopened bottle of Aalborg and gives them a glass each. He opens the bottle carefully, serves them both and puts the bottle back into the bucket.

'Very regal,' Anne-Marie says. 'We are only having a small one. You know it is only just past noon?'

'That is how we do it here at Davidsen's. You only pay for what you drink. Enjoy now.'

She lifts the glass to her mouth, tastes it with her lips and then drinks it down in one go.

'The germs will die: stomach bugs, tubercles and whatever else may be down there!' She pours a second. They order from the long, rolled sandwich menus. Only rye bread with scrambled eggs. Their stomachs won't manage any pâté, no jellied gravy, no small pickles, no herring, no salmon, no eel, no roast beef, and none of the assorted roes. Not yet. Not even meatballs with beetroot cream and shredded horseradish. But Aga feels when reading the long list that his sense of taste has returned, that he can imagine all the smells and flavours again. This has not been salmonella or any really dangerous stomach flu after all. Anne-Marie orders a couple of Tuborg beers.

'I'll tell you more about my father, but first you tell me of your earlier experience of Copenhagen,' she says and feels revived by the march to get here and by the aquavit, which she can feel is turning her cheeks redder.

'Well… you know – do you know? – that when we left Berlin, we actually first came to Copenhagen? My father thought business would be better here and not least the politics. But he got a good contract with Sweden for selling cigarettes there and so we only stayed in Copenhagen for a year or less when I was nine or so. And then when we lived in Stockholm, and a couple of years later my father didn't feel so well from his head? Or was it his heart already? I don't know… but anyway, we moved to Malmö for another year when I was in my early teens. As if Malmö was a healthier place to live. But it was close to here for touring across Öresund. Yes I know this town quote well, but it was indeed some time ago.'

'But, I thought you were here later? I know you were: you have to tell me.'

'I know, I will'. Het threw back another aquavit in one go, and she thought that he looked pale compared to her own red cheeks. 'It wasn't nice, but I will.' He drank down another, and then began.

Stockholm and Copenhagen 1943

He sat on the bed in the Saint Erik's hospital near the city centre of Stockholm with a letter in his hand, a letter from Emmy, from England. This was the first time he realized that Karl and Lins had been interned. They knew nothing then where he was, he could only imagine from the little he had read in the papers and heard on the radio. Now he pictured forced labour, screams, beatings. He had felt so sorry for himself up until that point, in a mental ward, as if he were insane or something. But what was that in comparison to what he was reading? He got up and threw the letter towards the window, wanting to get rid of it all. Why wasn't Karl allowed to be in Sweden? He was devastated. The letter had been sent from England via Portugal, opened by the British secret service, stamped with swastikas by Germans in independent Portugal and for certain opened there and finally opened by Swedish authorities and maybe also by the hospital. He guessed the letter would never have reached him if all those censors had understood the message. The Germans wanted no news on the camps to leak out. This damn message, it was really well concealed – Emmy was making the most of her talent for writing. *The Landauer family had left the capital for an outing and had gone camping.* It could only mean one thing. He remembered that he hated all that was German and the country he was born in, their ambitions to rule the world and their fight against all the ideals of democracy, liberty, openness and equality; all that he believed in. He looked out across the hospital park towards the city centre. He was not allowed to leave the building, and yet life was only a couple of hundred metres away.

'This is news to me!' Anne-Marie is exalted, 'Are you mentally ill?'

'No! I had a nervous breakdown... you know; it wasn't easy for me those days. I climbed on the walls and wanted help, but they took me in. I'm sorry I didn't tell you this earlier.'

She takes his arm across the table, 'Poor you, poor, poor you. I hope we can prevent that in the future.'

'I think *you* can,' he replies, and puts his hand on hers.

*

He picked up the letter again to be sure that he had understood it correctly. What irony. Emmy had had to wrap her information up very carefully. Nothing about Holland, no mention of concentration camps. She had written that Karl and Lins had gone to camp for a while, just them, and nothing about the children. She also wrote that she had sold his collection of stamps, which he got really mad about; those stamps were very valuable! He had hoped that the war would turn after Stalingrad and El Alamein, but the Germans were still sticking to it. It was not over yet and especially not for Karl, his favourite uncle.

He got up and began to put on his ordinary clothes. They wanted him to remain in hospital; he had been carefully warned not to leave. He didn't know if it was an involuntary commitment, maybe it was or would be... He knew what mental care could lead to, to one of the large asylums and definitively to passivity. He already sensed his dignity slipping away, and was really worried that he would just become limp, empty. He hated the thought; he knew, then, that it was that or that he would have to accept some angst. He was full of drugs, and he did feel a kind of a limp solitude or loneliness, he also felt some angst but he tried to hold it back and tried to think that there are things bigger than him.

It's All Coming Back

He felt urgently that he had to get out, away from that damn place, that he had to take part and take his share of the work against Germany. He dressed fast – and just walked out. He tried to look as normal as possible, as if he was on his daily tour of the place, tried to walk as naturally as possible out of the ward, out of the hospital, as if walking away from a closed psychiatric ward is the most natural thing to do. Some did look at him with surprise. An older man with stubble was sitting at a table drooling. He gave Helmut an encouraging look and a gesture, the thumbs-up; this is what he would like to do as well. 'Good luck in the sunshine.'

Helmut nodded and strode fast out to the street where he stepped straight onto a tram, an open summer carriage that had already started to leave the stop. He had to run to get it. It took him to Norrmalm, the centre. That was where his office was, and Norma, the café at the corner of Sveavägen and Kungsgatan where many of the asylum-seekers met, all those who had come for political reasons from the occupied countries and from Germany. Maybe he could learn something there about what to do, how to take part?

Before getting ill he used to go to Norma a couple of nights to meet free German minds and discuss politics. Most of those sitting there were social democrats from many states. He agreed with them: the Swedish premier Per Albin was trying to be accommodating to the Germans but what choice did he have? Those who wanted to do more had to fight it themselves, that was his conclusion.

So, the same night as he got out of hospital, Helmut went to Norma again. He sat alone at a table and looked out across the room. Finally he understood with whom he had to speak. In a corner, a silent, lonely man was sitting, and he went up to him and asked if he could help him in any way. Could he give him a cigar or maybe something else, something for Denmark? He had come to the right man. He was given a task and started planning.

Strangely enough the hospital didn't make an effort to get Helmut to return, and the next military draft was postponed, so he was able to plan in detail what to do in order to give some small aid to the anti-German cause. He did it for his relatives too, but in fact he knew nothing of their whereabouts. He managed to get a forged passport in the name of 'Jon Andersen,' and tried to build a story around the man in the passport, a man with a mixed Nordic background. He practised some mixed Danish and Norwegian, and checked his camera, not the Rolleicord; that was too big and conspicuous. He had borrowed a small Minox, ideal for taking pictures without being too visible. He had been tasked to meet at a Malmö restaurant and so he arrived there for breakfast dressed in a fisherman's sweater under a drab coat, a cap, and a carrying a briefcase containing today's Danish newspaper, a thermos flask with milk and the Rolleicord. The Minox was hidden in the coat lining.

It was dark when Helmut finally found himself sitting on the thwart of a small boat that was being rowed across Öresund; he tried to scout over the rail but was told to keep down. He saw Copenhagen's morning lights in the distance and sensed the smell of the brackish sea, of algae and tar. The most important thing was not to do anything that drew attention. He had robust shoes and tried to look like a labourer or fisherman. The boat sneaked in north of Langelinie where he quickly disembarked and trudged up the shore. The boat was already far out to sea again by the time he reached the road above. And then he walked decisively towards the city.

He took the pictures he had been asked to, lighting a cigarette and holding the camera in the same hand; a quick snapshot and then quickly on, the Minox back into the lining of the coat. He was careful and tried to blend into the crowd but still a policeman stopped him. He mumbled and pulled out his passport with suddenly numb fingers.

'Jon Andersen. 29 years. *Jae*,' the policeman said, talking in the Copenhagen dialect. 'Did you see anybody run past here?'

Helmut shook his head, trying to talk as little as possible. The policeman cried out something and I understood that he thought I was lying. I was taken to the police station where he interrogated me sitting by a desk.

'When did you come to Denmark and what way did you come?'

'I have been here for a while,' he answered in the Norwegian-Danish. The policeman asked again. He was silent.

'You can't remember? Really? Can't you?'

'Quite some time ago,' he replied.

'No, no,' the policeman said grimly and grabbed Helmut's hand as a wrestler would. 'If you want to talk we'll let you go. Otherwise... Think carefully. If you can't tell us, we *will* find out.' Helmut noted the policeman's muttered warning tone, as he was pushed into a cell. A couple of short jabs hit his arms; it did sting. He was whimpering as he was pressed onto a bunk.

'The best hotel the Danish state can offer, be our guest!' the policeman laughed.

There was a smell from the toilet: mould, disinfectant and old vomit. Helmut tried to concentrate on other things, like the Swedish movie that had been sold out for many months in Copenhagen, not because it was so good, but just because it was a way for the Copenhageners to show that they sided with the neutral Swedes on the other side of Öresund. And also because it meant that they wouldn't get more German propaganda movies.

He understood that he would be tested on his acting abilities. As he waited, he focused on building 'Jon Andersen' up with more substance. The big problem was that they had taken his briefcase, the camera and the coat. It was quite possible that they'd work out that he was there to take pictures for somebody else. His fervent hope was that they had just torn the film out of the case and thereby exposed it all.

He felt the side of his body where the heaviest blows had landed and tried to calm down by thinking of Karl and his family – reminding himself that they were far worse off. More and more stories of the concentration camps were filtering through now; that was why he had joined the resistance. That was why he was now Jon Andersen.

He concentrated: who *was* Jon Andersen? Norwegian mother, Danish father, had lived in different places, which was the reason for his strange dialect. He had studied and worked intermittently and even changed his last name a couple of times. Helmut tried to remember different places in Denmark, Norway and the Swedish west coast about which he would have to talk. It was all going to come down to the details, he was quite certain of that. And of course, he was going to have to explain why he had the cameras... he worked in a factory, and photography was his main hobby? Something like that would work, he hoped.

Fortunately, he didn't have to develop his story any more than that, because in the event, there was no intense interrogation. After a couple of hours he was free, with no further explanation, freed by another cop.

He was given back his coat, briefcase and Rolleicord, the latter with the film hanging out.

After he'd left the station, he took a long detour and tried not to go too close to Kongens Nytorv; he figured that he may have been followed, and didn't want to be too near to the German headquarters at Hotel d'Angleterre. So; a long detour trying to look ordinary, as if he was walking his normal route. He had to be in time for the rendezvous with the boat and the other people who were coming along. To do so, he had to walk up north of the city and he really had to sneak about for quite a long time, creep about, without making it obvious in any way. There might be some picture left in the Minox to send to the British. He arrived late to the rendezvous and lit a match to give the pre-arranged signal. A small boat came into shore and, after clambering in, he had to help row, the boat was filled with people, across to Malmö. Everyone was quiet until they parted there.

Day 5 cont.

She has watched him intensely, smoking cigarettes, eating carefully while he has spoken. 'Oh, dear, now it's all falling into place. Was that why you were so thrown when the police came? They beat you? It must have been very traumatic indeed! You had your touch of the war. I'm so glad they didn't find out who you really were. It was a foolhardy thing to do, do you know that?'

'Yeah,' he hesitates and goes on, 'maybe it was, and now I am marked by it, as you said I noticed when we saw the Danish police. You know, we're all marked by our memories, for animals it is more instinctive, but we reflect on our memories, which makes it worse.' His Uncle Karl comes to his mind, and he recalls how Karl taught him all about animal behaviour – and human behaviour. He has this small mark. He also figures that Anne-Marie was shaped by the fact that her mother died when she was very young. She had told him that of course, and he wonders how it must have affected her. So many are gone now. Many will have to manage without the older generation.

'Marked maybe, or protesting against them?' Anne-Marie says.

'Did you protest, then, against Sven's somewhat Brown ideas?' he replies instantly, changing the subject.

'Somewhat,' Anne-Marie says, embarrassed. 'Too little, too weakly.'

She is picking at her sandwich. She ordered one more as she felt her stomach would allow that, this one with scrambled egg as well, but also with a small piece of smoked eel. At first she carefully takes off the eel but then picks a very tiny piece and its saltiness is what her mouth wants and she takes more. She eats the eel in small pieces one after the other. 'You are so gentle,' she says, 'and kind to me. Your mother is so sweet, but also so tough, strong. I am so glad for having got to know your mother. She is one for hugging. She's *alive*. You know I hardly have anybody like that in my life now.'

'What do you mean, no one? You have me, your sister, your brothers, your father.'

She holds his hand over the table. 'Of course I have, well – you in any case. I just mean that your mother is like a mother to me. This must sound very banal, but she fills a room that is vacant... I had hoped that my father, that you two...'

'Your father? Who knows? I may be able to discuss things with him. You seem to have problems in your relationship with him.'

'He's hardly the hugging type, and he is a very complex man. It wasn't easy during the war, and since then I've hardly seen him. But I am a darling to him of course,' she smiles again.

'Tell me now then,' he answers rapidly, somewhat surly. 'I want to know what you mean. The war is over, you know. We have to build a new future. That bloody war can't eat us up for ever!' He pours another Aalborg an throws it down in one go.

'Well you've already got to know quite a lot. But I don't think you'll ever understand him. *I* hardly do. It is difficult, you know. Sometimes he wants to be so damn remarkable. He enjoys going into a small farmer's cottage and having everyone greet him and offer him aquavit and local bread, and he can help them and suggest how they can stop the authorities from interfering with their land. And they think he is good and the best.'

'That's fine, isn't it?'

'Well, yes, they know he helps them. And he likes making the liberal Governor angry, he hates liberals, and he likes to throw a party.'

'Yeah, what the heck, I will like some of that. But I want to know more about his views, his politics.'

Anne-Marie throws her hair back and looks into his eyes. 'Oh no, my father is a committed nationalist or patriot, one of those ultra-Swedes maybe... I don't bloody know how to characterize it... you must ask him when you meet him... He was a Conservative at first but after he was in Berlin for the trial after the Parliament fire – you know he was covering

it for a Swedish newspaper in fact, the only Swede actually.
– Well, he changed his views then I think, and ran for the National Socialist Bloc in 1934. A lot of military people in our town supported him of course, but his wife didn't. He was out in all the constituencies all day campaigning, and had first arranged for Siri to cast his ballot; he had it all prepared in a closed envelope. But he didn't trust her enough so he changed his made and went home and voted the ordinary way. He was right not to trust her in politics. You know, he got the highest percentage of the votes of any National Socialist in all Sweden, but perhaps it was because he was well known. He is the way he is...' she sighs in sudden irritation. 'But you haven't bloody married *him*! You know, these days I am ashamed of him and everything that he has been connected to. He has never been easy to cope with as a father. He wants the best... but I don't know any more.' She puts her head in her hands and he embraces her, lets her father be as he is. 'I am so happy you care,' she continues, ' that anybody cares to this degree, that you are here, that neither of us was in Germany during the war. How different it all could have been.

'Indeed it could. I hope he has given up that now.'

'I don't know; I sincerely don't know.'

'We'll see if I ever can make friends with him. You have given me a difficult one.'

'I choose you, if I have to choose.'

'I am glad of that, indeed I am.' He caresses her. 'But you have to understand me as well. I don't know that you ever will understand how I feel about the war and so...'

'What? What is there to understand?' She pulls back.

'You'll never understand, I guess!' Helmut raises his voice, 'That I should have been there, ought to have been there! That I should have done more!' He stands, suddenly, his dark eyes blazing as he looms over her. 'Why should I be here now?' He kicks the leg of the chair, his fists clenched. 'How would it be possible for you to ever understand? That sense of being useless, the injustice in the fact that I was lucky and made it when so many were killed, that damn feeling that I should have done more! Maybe my actions could have meant something for a human life, just one, if only I had been there, if only I had started to protest earlier, started resisting earlier! Damn it, Anne-Marie, how will we ever agree completely if it is impossible for you to understand?!' Slumping back into his seat, he pours another big glass of Aalborg and downs it again in one go.

Anne-Marie stares at him for a moment, and then rises and stands behind him, holds his body against hers, tries to make him let go of the glass.

'I think we're leaving,' she says, and calls to the waiter: 'Can I have the bill?'. She holds Helmut lovingly, tight, very tight, but he holds her off with one hand and keeps a firm grip on the glass with the other.

'Let's go,' she says. 'Can't you show me Copenhagen, as you saw it when you were a child? After all you lived here for a year? I wish I could have been there with you, been here.'

'Don't talk such nonsense!' he growls, and lets go of the glass, which falls to the floor and smashes. The waiter rushes over with a brush. Helmut laughs as if in a trance. 'You will understand,' he says, calmer now, 'That one cannot get away from that damn guilt, the worrying, the feeling of inadequacy.'

She nods. 'Do you remember anything from then?'

'From my childhood? I am happy you didn't see me then. Clumsy, inexperienced and lonely,' he says. 'I had nothing to dream of.' He sits brooding silently. She still holds him, persistently, as if he's trying to get away and she just wants to be close. But he finds her proximity claustrophobic somehow and shrugs himself free. She keeps picking at him, at his hand, searching with her fingers inside his shirtsleeve, up the hairy arms. They look at each other, loving and interrogating each other.

'I remember a big glass house,' he says, 'Probably in the botanical gardens. I used to go up there, instead of building a tree house, that was what the Danish kids did. I sometimes spent my time there, in the heat among the flowers.'

'Let's go there!' she exclaims, and pulls him up and towards the door, so that the waiter has to catch them with the bill.

It's All Coming Back

Outside, a spring rain greets them. Refreshingly cold and at the same time so hard that they realize they will get very wet if they walk. Rain and the sun shining between the clouds, the quickly changing weather by the sea in the spring. She puts her arm under his and blows in his ear. They run past the lakes and through the broad streets, laughing, pressed tightly together with Aga's coat over both their heads. The soon reach Botanisk Have and they run past the big iron gates and rapidly into the largest greenhouse. Aga climbs the narrow cast iron staircase all the way up, almost to the roof. 'I thought you had vertigo?' she says.

'Don't remind me!' He is standing lost in memory. 'This is where I hid. I recognize it after twenty years.' He looks down at her ruefully. 'I'm sorry I was angry at you earlier.'

She hears his apology, accepts it, as she climbs up to join him, but something else has caught her attention. 'Hid from what??' she asks.

'Who knows? Maybe I just wanted to hear the pattering on the roof. Listen,' he cups his hand over his ear and directs it upwards. 'Feel this humid air. You know, a man in the resistance told me there was a special refuge in a greenhouse somewhere, maybe that was here? Imagine sitting here watching the search lights circling outside.'

She turns her head round, round, as if following the lights. 'How exciting. Would you like to tell me more about it?' She holds him cautiously from behind, around his belly and kisses his cheek.

'No, not now, listen to me.' He turns away.

'Now you are a resisting me? You are so keen to talk about all sorts of things. Then you must tell me more about your childhood,' she sighs.

'I don't remember anything from Copenhagen, not really.' He leans against the railing and looks through the glass into the far distance. 'Look at the bumblebee down there,' he points. 'Those pretty colours and the easy movement from flower to flower, despite that heavy body that shouldn't be able to fly at all.'

Now he is close to Anne-Marie and she's surprised. She notices that he doesn't seem to be affected by his vertigo.

Sometimes he can be troubled at a height of a couple of metres, but here he can look several metres down at an insect. He never wants to go up any towers or hills to see the view. Now he is cool, extremely cool. He kisses her tenderly and she can see it directly in his eyes, feel it in his hands, that he has his intentions.

'Come,' he whispers and his hand is already up beneath her bra straps. She turns away.

'Not here.'

'Come.' He doesn't give in. It is not that she doesn't want to, not at all. All the stomach problems, all the coughing, that's over with and she has an intense longing for him. She kisses him again and tries to make him keep quiet but lets his hands carry on. He fiddles with the button in her blouse, a small metal button and he tears it off in his eagerness. It falls, slowly, all the way down. They stop and hold each other in a breathless moment. The button hits the floor, narrowly missing a bird that has come in to walk along the rows of palms and banana trees. The bird cries and tries to fly way at the sudden *clink!* and this attracts everyone's attention. The greenhouse had been empty when they entered but is now full of people who have come in to escape the rain, and are now turning around to see this display. But no one notices the reason for the bird's behaviour. Aga looks down over the rail. His vertigo has returned. He quickly moves to the middle of the small platform. Anne-Marie tidies her clothes and quickly descends, holding her hand up to hide her partly opened blouse. She expects questions about whether she has just fed her child but nobody asks. She quickly walks through the greenhouse with all its exotic plants, and Aga is one step behind. The sun has come out and it has become as warm and refreshed as only a spring day can be after a hard rain when nature does all its best to make things grow. She wipes a wooden bench, puts her coat on it and sits down. He sits beside her and carefully holds her hand. 'Be a bit more cautious, could you?' she says, 'Because I do like you so much.'

'I know. Do you want to go to the hotel?'

She grabs his hairy wrist again and fiddles inside his sleeve, her other hand on his shirt, over the buttons.

'Wait,' he whispers nuzzling his head into the back of her neck. He stands up and walks away a short while to calm down but still feels the same powerful yearning. He wants to and yet somehow he does not. They can spend all day in bed and at other places too, tasting each other. This time he decides to wait, to execute self-control for an hour or two at least. When he comes back after a couple of minutes she hasn't moved. He sits close to her and leans towards her, gently touching the locket around her neck. He opens it and looks at the photograph inside.

'Your mother. Please could you tell me what she was like? I've only seen this picture. Dark, intense eyes and that braid that she must have spent hours on.'

'I remember nothing.' Now it's her turn to become agitated. 'Don't you understand? I was just a year and a half old. I've told you that, haven't I?'

'But I still don't understand how she could leave you?'

'I don't know! Listen, I only know that the north was an exile for them.' She falls quiet and he doesn't know if he should continue asking or wait for her to say more if she feels she's able. The silence seems like an eternity to him.

'I don't know if they really had to go up there,' she continues. 'Dad is always keen on doing business, but when he was young, he was scammed, at least according to him. I think he believed that himself. But who knows? He had a company, he sold sailing yachts and then sandwich automats, where you could get sandwiches out of the wall after closing hours; very modern at the time, big businesses for a young man… and all of a sudden he went bankrupt. He was under subpoena and fled Stockholm in a headlong rush. The north was far off, a place where you don't meet your old clients or friends, where you're not confronted with stupid questions or mean looks. And it was a place where they thought nobody would sue you. It took a very long time before they could love the north. If they ever did. Mother Laura never did.'

This leaves Aga silent for a moment. Then he says: ' you don't hate the north, I have understood that much. But I know too little about your childhood up there. 'The north,' she says reflectively. 'Icicles, rosy cheeks and the terribly short summers. Some southerners can stand it. Dad didn't mind the weather; he goes skiing and swims in holes in the ice. I believe mother could never cope with the cold, and not with the loneliness, either. As you said, not even all the northerners stand it, and move south. She was used to academic life in Uppsala and Lund; you know that was quite different from little Umeå. She thought she had come to the Arctic, I guess. Mother Siri had quite a different view, I'm sure. She encouraged us to go out into the snow, making snow angels, skiing, hiking, and skating. I haven't told you very much about Mother Siri...'

'But leaving you, to be in such a wretched state that you leave behind small children, that is just such an unthinkable thing to do, it's unacceptable! It probably marked you for life; well, I don't mean you notice it now or anything...' Lonely orphans or children who have been abandoned – he would have liked to talk to uncle Karl about that: what to do, how to behave.

Her expression is frozen and then she purses her mouth. They both fall silent for half a minute or so. 'I don't follow you now. I don't think she left us on purpose, I believe that we children meant everything to her. I wasn't *abandoned*,' she says emphatically. 'And dad was there and my big sister and brothers and different aunties. I was fine and then Siri came, nice, gentle, understanding Siri. I don't have her any more either.' She begins to sob, and he's there immediately with his big handkerchief.

'I am so glad I have *your* mama now. She is so fantastic,' Anne-Marie gulps. 'Wild.' She bends her head to meet his eye. Her hair falls down over her face. Aga shakes his head.

'Your brother and your mother, the two who ended their own lives, he had a role in that hadn't he?'

'I'll tell you about Paul´s death and about Siri then, if you insist.'

'So many who died that way in your family,' he murmurs doubtfully. 'Yes do. Please explain to me why.'

'*Why* is not a question that can be answered. But I can tell you *how* it was for me.'

'You poor thing.'

'No, I honestly don't want your pity: just listen and behave,' she says when he tries again to hold very close.

Umeå 1933

Outside the red house by the river where Sven and Siri and Anne-Marie and her sister lived, the leaves were in their first turning, red and yellow, as beautiful as it can only be in the North of Sweden. Birch trees with indescribably coloured leaves, soon to leave life up in the trees and fall to the ground where they would return to the earth: a very short time of a yellower bright colouring, a life flaring in the hour of death. That night would be a turning point in more than one way. Turning the life of this family upside down. But it was still quiet; Siri was looking into her dressing-table mirror and was, perhaps, able to take some time to think about what she was really doing in this red house.

Siri's life with Sven had not turned out the way she had hoped; Anne-Marie later became sure of that. What had she hoped for then? It was now nine years since she moved in. The children trusted her at once, let her care for them, even let her caress them – this had been a home without a mother for too long, and she had become very close to them, especially the girls, but also to Paul. That's how it had begun and yet, what was had been so bright was no longer that way. Mamma Siri, we called her, we really meant it even though Mamma La, Laura, was constantly present especially for the older ones. Siri probably thought that some of the things she had been told about Laura could have been about her, as if the house and the children were handed over to her as a legacy to manage and care for. And Sven, he had really changed too. These days he was more melancholic and difficult when he was at home. The years had become longer and longer, time ran more slowly for her, though he was always out or working, to the point of exhaustion.

Siri combed her grizzled hair, corrected her collar and her black dress. She had come directly from her work at the college. At least she had been able to continue her job; the marriage to Sven hadn't changed that. To the children it seemed that she was happy in her employment, and in the fact that she could work with young people and help nurture them at schools and kindergartens. She had her ideas about how to raise children, going back all the way from her time as a teacher in Stockholm. Boys and girls need to be together when they are young, she believed, and be allowed to learn what they want, and not just be crammed full of facts and figures that they didn't get a chance to appreciate or understand.

In practice, however, it was different; she had only ever educated girls and young women. Björn, Ivar and Paul, her stepsons, had gone to boarding schools in Germany. Although, she never used the world stepchild, she hated it. She wanted to be so much more, and was so much more. She hadn't changed her ideas either, but she had left active politics; it was difficult for them both to be active when they had such different views. She had established a small garden at the school and she sat there often and late. She was most content when she could visit her family in Ångermanland County. Sven also liked the summer place in Dekarsön, they both liked it there: he could talk to the fishermen and catch salmon. He was in his element. The children always noticed that their father was different then, at the feasts eating fermented herring, he even sang, he was revived.

When Siri was home she gave the children a lot of freedom, but she was always there to help them when they needed it: with sports, with carpentry and sewing, painting and drawing.

It wasn't just the blasted politics that created a problem in the house, but also Sven's way of *living* his politics; he liked a debate but he could sometimes take it so very far.

Siri's father, who was a Christian Liberal MP and a writer, would probably have thrown his lot in with the small minority Liberal government they had then. They came to power balancing the big parties, but they could in fact hardly do anything. Sven wanted to have the

Conservative government back, but he said their leader was getting too old, and couldn't keep up the resistance against socialists and communists. The Conservatives were still his party then. Sven and Siri didn't politics much at home. Sven wanted to be like the new orceful, strident leaders who were suddenly coming to power all over the continent; she primarily worried over what it would all lead to. They really could have had a lot to talk about, the discussion could have been fierce: but it was better left, by then. They would only disagree, and besides, she didn't want to hear Sven's right wing excesses.

Democracy was not so successful in those days, it was true, but that was no reason to paint it all as black as Sven was doing. That the interest of class was dominating politics so much then was something she disliked as much as he did however: ideas and facts should be primary, they both believed, and they actually joined forces at home to nag about the flirtation between Agrarians and Social Democrats.

Björn was another political creature, who, like his father, put politics before other things in life, but from the totally opposite perspective. Sven was so negative towards Björn that he refused to talk to him. Siri never accepted that, never understood not talking to your own children, your own kin, whatever their ideas. And she didn't like way that Sven dealt with money when it came to his children either. He demanded to get every penny back of what he has lent to them, he didn't understand their financial situations. Politics really marked the children's' home as it did Siri's parents,' but in a totally different way. There, everybody took part in her father's public functions. In Anne-Marie's home, politics was always present, though they did not talk about that very often; politics ruled, everyone had different views and everybody beat about the bush.

This was a time just when their father darted about like mad, not just as a barrister but also going to and fro to Germany and the trial concerning the fire in the German Reichstag.

Anne-Marie was often out with friends or even boys. Siri was more liberal in those matters than Sven ever was; he was as hard as flint. Siri also liked Paul a great deal. The girls at her college sometimes asked about him and sometimes it seemed as if he had somebody dear: Sometimes Sven noticed that Siri and the children had their secrets, and he became stern and demanded to know what was being kept from him. But Siri had tricks to reassure him.

Paul became devastated when things didn't work out the way he had hoped; sometimes he was so light-hearted, chivalrous, and then suddenly so gloomy. However he always liked to play with his little sisters, and they had their eyes on his friends. Anne-Marie was doing her last year in girl's junior secondary, dreaming about boys, going to parties, drinking punch and trying to be a grown-up.

Siri combed her hair some more and picked the small mirror to make sure that it looked good from behind too. She put only a touch of red on her lips. She looked tight and reserved, but that was something she did not want to be perceived as at all. You should look proper even at home though. She heard Anne-Marie come in, they sometimes kept the same hours and that gave them a chance of being together. Siri liked that.

Anne-Marie settled in the big room with her homework, but was mainly gazing out through the window. Siri came and seated herself at the other end of the sofa and gradually they began one of those rare but important conversations, about boys, about life, about dreams of the future, all those things they couldn't talk to anybody else about. They could talk to people who were like-minded – Siri to her colleagues, Anne-Marie to her girlfriends – but it wasn't the same. It was cold outside, but the maid had made a fire, and it was nice just sitting in the cosy warmth. Later, when thinking of this moment, Anne-Marie remembered asking Siri about her history homework. Siri was knitting, and had some student work to attend to at the same time. So they sat, at opposite ends of the sofa, and felt a kinship. They belonged there, together.

But soon they heard someone in the hallway. The maid came into the room looking bewildered. 'An officer is outside and he doesn't want to say what it's about! He wants to talk to the barrister, he says, but I think he is not home?'

Siri stood up, her hands clasped hard in front of her. 'Show him in.'

The policeman entered. He looked very grave, gave a salute, took off his hat and held it stiffly by his side.

'Sit, please, by all means sit,' Siri said, her voice catching. 'What's this all about then?'

'Is this the barrister's wife I have the honour of talking to?' the policeman asked, still standing. 'And his daughter? Maybe the girl should not be present. I have some very unfortunate information.'

'She can stay,' Siri said decisively. 'Well?' her voice was urgent now, she looked wide-eyed at him, 'Tell me then, please, tell me!'

Anne-Marie was not able to even look at him. A thousand ideas passed through her head. It couldn't be Sven as the policeman had asked for him. She stood up as well and went over to the fireplace, jabbed in it with the poker. She didn't want to hear, she wanted to put her hands over her ears and run away, she wanted to hide, but she had to listen.

'It concerns the barrister's son, Paul,' the officer said. Anne-Marie banged the poker into the wall of the fireplace and the others turned, startled, to look at her. Paul, her friend, her very best brother, her very, very best brother.

'He had his exams as a naval cadet yesterday,' Siri said. 'We're expecting to hear from him, but he has not sent us a cable.' She looked at the officer, appealing to him. *What is he doing here? What does he want, intruding into our peace?*

After a second's hesitation, the policeman blurted out his tragic news. 'He has been found dead with a pistol in his hand. I am sorry.' He moved forward awkwardly and held Siri's hand.

Siri jerked it away and rushed over to hold Anne-Marie. She in turn broke loose and ran up the stairs and threw herself down on her bed. Siri felt as if her legs had no bones – she sat down, devastated and quiet. She couldn't say a word, and after a little while the policeman muttered something and left.

Anne-Marie didn't stay in her room for long. She rushed down to the hall, snatched up her coat and ran out. She walked around, dazed, for an hour or two before returning as if in a dream to the house. When she went in, Sven had come home. The three of them sat silently around the table for a very long time.

Suddenly, Anne-Marie swore – '*Damn, damn, bloody hell!* God no! No!' and for once, she was not asked by her father to stop.

Sven remained sitting there, quiet, still, long after the other two had gone to bed.

Night was coming down in Umeå. Another person in our family had died by their own hand. Sven probably sat and puzzled, tried to find the reason in history, in genetics – that was the sort of thing he believed in – he probably tried to remember what had happened in the past to lead to this degeneration of the people he loved. It must, he thought, come from Laura's family. Of all of his children, he had had the greatest expectations of Paul. He felt so sad, and forlorn, desolate: alone and miserable. Björn was lost to communism; Ivar had started his military career but wanted to go to Argentina to the Swedish settlement in Misiones; Harriet was ready for university... and now Paul wasn't here any more. He felt anguished at the thought that all his children would leave him soon. Anne-Marie crept down the stairs to fetch some water, but he didn't see her. She heard him moaning and talking to himself. He poured a brandy; but then poured an aquavit. He gulped the brandy and swept the aquavit down after it, and then he coughed, a very deep cough, and when that was over, he folded his tall body and crawled like a baby into the armchair. She guessed that he wanted to be alone in his misery so she tiptoed slowly and cautiously up the stairs with her glass.

When she was almost there she heard him open the windows and then she heard him again: a mixture between a cry and a roar.

Day 5 cont.

'Oh how lonely he must have felt, how lonely you all must have felt!' Helmut almost whispers, very still and silently. He is very touched by her story. 'But why did Paul do it?'

'He didn't dare show his father that he had failed the exams to be a naval officer.'

'But really, is that the real reason? Was there a girl or something?'

'Not that I know of. What I just told you is the best explanation I have. It's all so sad. You know, I met him when my sister and Sven and I went to Stockholm just a few weeks earlier to put Father onto the train for his work with the Reichstagsfeuer and all that.'

'You went to Stockholm just to follow him to the train?'

'Not really, but we did that too. Then we visited Paul at the naval school at Skeppsholmen and went out for a meal and he was so happy.'

'So it was Sven's demands on him that were so strong? Strange. He wasn't depressed before?'

Anne-Marie shakes her head as if his words are actually stinging her. 'No! That's enough! That's all I know. You sound like a shrink. Why is that?

'I am probably influenced by my Uncle Karl. You now my uncle was very learned in psychoanalysis, and he taught me a lot about it. I wanted to be like him.' He stopped, lost in thought, but after a moment he brightened again. 'We also went to the train going south at the Stockholm Central Station at that time! My family went to England, but I stayed on then. Emmy and my sisters left Stockholm for good in 1933.

'That could have been, yeah, I think I saw a group of people there, and a handsome young man. Was that you?'

'Perhaps! Was your father going on the 12.12 from Stockholm to Berlin?'

'Yes,' she smiles, 'But I don't remember the date now.'

Jon Kahn

'It was a terrible year that one,' Aga says as he takes off his coat and hangs it over Anne-Marie's shoulders. He wants to talk some more now, when they're both in the right mood. He feels the hard wooden bench against the inner side of his thighs just below his knees and against his buttocks but he has to fight it this time. She looks relaxed, cold and relaxed, so he continues.

'So much was changing in 1933, in the world, and obviously also for both our families. When you look at it now it becomes more obvious what happened. The great depression had been going on for years and new governments were formed trying to make it better or trying to gain from the situation. The latter was true for Germany where the Nazis were consolidating their power.' Helmut was getting into his stride, he loved to think out loud, explore his own thoughts, and he didn't mind too much if he was telling Anne-Marie anything that she already knew. 'In Sweden the Social Democrats had come to power in a coalition with the Agrarians, and in England a National Coalition Government reigned trying to stabilize the economy. In America, the New Deal, Roosevelt and Keynes would make a change, most people were certain of that. Well, we now know that it did. But it was also a blame game. Capitalists, old governments or even us Jews were collectively blamed for the economic chaos. It was a time to take sides and for those who could or had to move to decide where to live and who to support.'

'Indeed,' Anne-Marie replies, perhaps a little dryly. 'Sven was going to and fro Berlin and Leipzig more and more and becoming more and more impressed by this new strong Germany that was arising. He even tried to influence the case! I remember one day when he came home and immediately wanted us to sit down. He walked to and fro in front of us with his hands clasped behind his back and talked about how he had met Manfred van der Lubbe –you know, the man who was accused for the fire. He said he had given a clear analysis of van der Lubbe to the attorney. And he did take an aeroplane to Umeå, just to vote in the town council. He was becoming a bit of a megalomaniac then. But he was influenced by the spirit of the time I guess.'

'Others had to hide from those evil spirits,' Helmut says and now he is walking around her. 'Karl and his family had had to leave Frankfurt where he was heading the Frankfurt Psychoanalytischen Institut. First the Nazis took the Institute for Social Research, which he worked with – I mean they closed it down, and the leader went to Switzerland. Karl was left wing and a pacifist, he was Jewish and he looked into other people's brains. All things the Nazis hated. On 1 April 1933 they expelled of Jewish doctors. It was no surprise that they came to the Institute he had so successfully built with the help of Freud and others. They burnt all the books in the building and hoisted the swastika flag on top and he didn't really know what to do. Karl and family felt as if they were caught in a trap. He wanted to go to America where he had colleagues and friends and he asked my family in Stockholm for help and advice. I talked to some friends at the Karolinska Institute and Dr. Alfhild Tamm invited him to become an analyst there. I don't know if it was me who influenced that. Perhaps not. She wanted to establish an Institute for teaching psychoanalysis in Stockholm and wanted Karl as a lecturer. He came to Sweden as quick as he could and had nothing arranged really. But we took him under our wing. He was devastated of course, but Karl applied to stay in Sweden and lecture and also to practise as a psychoanalyst.'

'And the family, did he just leave them.'

'They were supposed to come after. Helmut pauses thoughtfully but continues after a short silence. 'But at the same time my father, Sigmund decided that London was going to be his prime office. Emmy wasn't so pleased. They had a small record shop as well which she managed, she had her dog, a dachshund called Brax, and she had built a good social life. But she agreed to the move, after they talked over for a while. London was exciting of course. Most of Sigmund's other brothers kept up the tobacco factory in Heilbronn.'

'You say the whole bunch was leaving? Sigmund, Emmy, Käthe, Ilse? What about Karl?'

'He left before as he couldn't get a proper answer from the Swedish authorities. I stayed on in Stockholm at the flat in Grevgatan. Somebody had to keep the office there, but I was determined to be a doctor like Karl some day. But first: business.'

'And girls and booze and more pretty girls,' she grins and twinkles.

'Indeed.'

'I remember now,' she says dreamily, holding his coat tightly around her body, 'There *was* a lot of activity in Stockholm Central Station. People were moving, a lot of people in the big hall heading for the trains both north and south. The sun was flooding in through the windows high up on the walls by the ceiling; the light was slanting low, it was the beginning of autumn. It had been an almost warm start to the season, but now the wind was picking up in that open part of the city, and the northern gusts were sweeping in. Many were muffled up for the first time this year; it was cold outside but warm in there, and some had their outdoor clothes hanging over their arms and struggled to carry those as well as their luggage.'

He looks carefully at her, impressed by her way of describing things. He shrugs a little and sits down and tries to cover them both now with his coat. 'To reach the southbound trains to Södertälje, Gothenburg, Småland, Skåne and The Continent you have to take the southern exit, past the restaurant and the model engine standing in a glass box next to where people were showing their train tickets or buying their platform tickets seeing friends, girl or boyfriends, kin and business relations off.'

'Yes. I adjusted my stocking seams in front of the counter. I was sixteen then and cared about my looks and the men around me. I don't know if I noticed the smell of oil and coal, the sheer presence of the train but it influenced me, I am sure of that. Made me want to rush into things. I was staring straight at a boy of around 20, rather big and stout, his hair combed backwards, a member of another group. He looked back unabashed.'

'Now you're making it up, aren't you?' he smiles and turns to her, they're sitting very close, and reaches for her ear with his mouth.

She doesn't answer him, just turns her head and they collide and she looks closely into his eyes. 'It could have been us.'

'Oh,' he answers, 'There are so many coincidences. Karl and his family went to Amsterdam, you know, he never got the positive answer from the Swedish authorities; they wouldn't let him practise as a psychoanalyst in Sweden, that was how it was. Not even the Royal Medical Board. He was allowed to give lectures but not do real psycho-analysis.'

You are repeating yourself,' she says smiling.

'Maybe I am but I couldn't then and still can't understand how they could be so stupid, so naïve, so *blue-eyed*, the Swedish authorities. They didn't welcome anything new; they probably didn't want a Jewish psychoanalyst. They didn't say that explicitly, just that Karl may not practise. Damn country! He chose Holland and we know what happened there. Yet still, I had chosen to stay. Emmy was standing in the big station hall. She was waiting for Sigmund and me but we were late. She couldn't wait any longer. She went with the children to the luggage counter to have the bags registered. Sigmund would have to register his when we arrived. *Why can't men ever be on time?* she probably thought. But of course we did get there in time. We had a business appointment and a business breakfast with some colleagues and you know it took time, a full Swedish breakfast and saying goodbye to old friends.

The rest of the family had their hands full, registering all the trunks and hat cases, and arrived on the platform just in time. Unnoticed, they had seen the men rush through the hall. We got to the platform first even though I had to buy a platform ticket. Now they had to follow us like ducklings. We knew by then that the Landauers were safe in Holland but also that they wouldn't return to Sweden again. We had talked to them over the phone.

'If the dentist is going to pull out all your teeth, ask him to save one so that you have something that aches!' Karl laughed to me during that telephone conversation. He laughed at his old Jewish joke and caught his breath at the same time and sounded almost like a steam whistle.

'The Royal Medical Board? I don't need it, never again, *nie mehr.*'

'Well, you'll be able to practise again soon,' I said to him. 'You'll look into all those Dutch brains, with or without peepholes, and you'll know which is the ego and which is the id without the Royal Medical Board intervening in what you may or may not do.'

'The Royal Medical Board has a castration complex!' he laughed, a little hysterically.'

'Your storytelling isn't bad either!' Anne-Marie laughs. The sun has now come out more clearly and shines on them. She shrugs off his coat and settles herself in the corner of the bench watching him.

'It's is not easy for me to understand your father's opinion at that time,' he says after a moment. He knows she'll follow his train of thought.

'I know,' she agrees. 'He started a newspaper later in 1933 and wrote that the people shouldn't be deceived by foreign capital and pointed to Sweden's need to be a strong nation.'

'It sounds good, but when you analyse that kind of talk you realize the right-wing ideas. *Foreign capitalism* was of course the Jews.'

'I don' know if he ever was an anti-Semite,' she says cautiously.

'I'm not so sure. I'll have to ask him. The most interesting bit is of course how he affected your mother and brother's suicides. I don't think that was the main reason, but it may have played it's part. Oh, hell, I won't judge him, not as yet.'

She looks at him, somehow appealing for him to stop this preoccupation with her father, and then she bends down and holds a flower as if she is going to pick it. She holds it for a while and looks down at the ground and then she looks up, a little guarded.

'I just don't believe it is possible to make other people commit suicide,' she says quietly. She's freezing again, holding her arms around her body. Aga sits silent now. She rubs her arms to keep warm, he peers into the sky, then he wraps his arm around her and they rise together slowly, very slowly and stroll through the park. He catches a ball that some boys have kicked too far and starts dribbling with it, towards and around her. She tackles him, gets the ball and kicks it back to the lads. They wander around for maybe another quarter of an hour. They're heading out and down towards the city centre when Anne-Marie stops, feel over her blouse and then quickly walks towards the greenhouse again.

'The button. I'm going to look for it.' He follows but more slowly, still strolling, kicking the grass, and looking around. Soon she's far ahead and stands waiting for him. He has to ask of course, she figures, and suddenly she has a feeling of overwhelming grief over her family's fate: she can feel her strength draining away from her. She takes a faulty step and then another before she can banish her distressing thoughts. In the distance she sees him close to a child and somehow this calms her down, the image of him as a father, a man who can talk to children, a different type to her father, quite different. *My new family won't be like my old one, she decides. I long to have a child with him.* She heads off again and runs into the greenhouse. She comes out, shaking her head and they sit down again holding each other.

'Your father can't have had an easy time with Björn,' he says.

'Why don't you look at it from Björn's perspective? You'll never understand our family. Father's view is that some people are villains, others are to be admired. I hope you'll belong to the last category. He's quick to judge people, and that went for us kids as well when we were little. He'd like one of us for a time and then hardly at all, but I was generally a favourite; that was not good for the others. Sometimes it was right to stand up to him but if it went too far he didn't want anything to do with you. He is not an easy man.' Anne-Marie shifts away from Aga's caresses. She starts to sob and he is there again with the handkerchief.

A woman, an unknown old woman comes traipsing up to them and gives them the button, Anne-Marie's blouse button, with a broad smile. 'Be careful with each other,' she says. 'One day you're married and then there's no way back.'

Anne-Marie stammers a thank you. 'We are hoping for a way forward together, now that it is spring… and I have some sewing to do. Thanks again. We will be careful, we are careful.' A butterfly, a yellow brimstone, the first butterfly of spring, flutters around them and then settles on Aga's hand – he carefully, extremely cautiously, lifts up his other hand.

'A butterfly! That's promising!' the lady says and smiles. 'This tiny thing, so beautiful. But there shouldn't be butterflies yet. She will die when it gets colder if she doesn't get indoors.'

Aga tries to grab his camera while trying to keep the butterfly hand still, quite still. 'Help me with the camera. Take it out and try to get a photo. You know how to do it. Look up there and then press the lever to the right. Hurry, it is moving.' The butterflies' antennae are moving slightly and it steps forward, feeling the cold, assessing the situation. She presses the lever and he immediately cups his other hand and holds it over the butterfly.

'Are you going to do a magic trick?' Anne-Marie asks, still with her head down over the camera, looking at Helmut seeing him upside down.

He moves very gently to the greenhouse door, lets the butterfly in and closes the door softly behind it. When he gets up closer to her on his way back, Anne-Marie presses the lever a couple of times. Then she wants a picture of the Danish lady who tries to wave her off and quickly goes away. He laughs, takes the camera from Anne-Marie and makes her pose in front of the greenhouse. But she feels cold as a cloud covers the sun. 'Come, hold me again. I need that, just as the butterfly does: warmth and some caring hands.'

Day 6

Next morning she tells him not to hurry down for breakfast but to dress decently. He doesn't understand why, but all of a sudden there's a knock on the door and the waiter comes in with breakfast on a tray that also contains a lit candle.

'What are we celebrating?' he asks. 'My birthday is in December and yours in July.'

'Maybe that Denmark was liberated a year ago; but then you're three days late,' the waiter suggests.

'We noticed!' Aga is still dressing, adjusting the braces that hold his trousers up.

'We had reasons to celebrate don't you think?' the waiter continues. 'Or one could also celebrate that Bornholm is Danish again? The Russians have finally left the island, they did yesterday, almost a year after the liberation of the rest of Denmark.'

'It would have been a good things to celebrate,' Anne-Marie agrees, ' but this' she gestures at the tray, 'is actually to celebrate that we have now been married for a week.'

'Hooray!' the waiter cries, and smiles as he leaves the room, and the two of them to their breakfast and to one another.

When Helmut goes downstairs after breakfast and after some caressing and having leant his head on her belly for at least fifteen minutes, he reads the Danish papers. The war in Denmark is really finally over. It really took time but even the Russians must accept things in the end. They are glad about that. Josephine Baker has come to town on her tour in support of impoverished children who have been the victims of war. Aga wants them to go and see her, he remembers her from when he was young and she was in Stockholm, dancing, wearing only bananas. Anne-Marie doesn't want to, and she tries to joke about it, asking how Josephine Baker would look now when there are no bananas for sale. They decide to go to the aquarium in Charlottenlund to start with. It is quite new and he hasn't had the chance to see it yet.

'Just some shopping first,' she says when they have walked a couple of blocks and she runs ahead down the cobblestone streets towards the centre. It is rather chilly this April morning. As usual he accepts her ideas, tightens his coat and tries to keep up with her faster pace. He finally catches up with her just when they enter Ströget, the pedestrianized street.

'What kind of shopping do you want to do today?' he asks once he's caught his breath and taken her hand.

'Bing and Grøndahl,' she says and they enter the store with all its china. They criss-cross between vases, china dogs, urns and kitchenware. She can't get enough, picking up the fragile pieces, patting small porcelain cats, and trying to lay tables with tureens, letting out small sighs from time to time. He admires a porcelain Columbine and comments on the cats' eyes that they don't look real. He gets bored long before she does and sits down to wait for her, his hands on his knees. When she suggests that they should buy something, he starts to argue about the price and it takes them a while to agree on a small blue vase decorated with some pollarded willows in an agricultural setting. Very typically Danish. They see to that it's properly wrapped and then they find their way to the local railway station, the S-banen.

First they go to Klampenborg and stroll around in the beech forest, he rooting for morels, she fascinated by the magic light; a very weak light filters down through the beech trees and even though the leaves have not yet blossomed the trees create a lattice, allowing only small sprinkles of sunlight to reach the ground. Last year's leaves have formed a litter that is soft to walk on. She could walk around there for hours. Suddenly she notices that he's gone. She calls across the forest and finally sits down on a rock and takes out a cigarette. Then she hears something charging ahead through the forest and looks worried. Is it him? But it is only a fallow deer thundering along, driven by the scent of a doe – the males have one thing only in their heads at that time of year, to chase females without any sideways glances.

It's All Coming Back

She sees several deer but not him. She feels abandoned when he is away for even a couple of minutes; the whole world breaks down without him. This is worse. She walks back to where they came from and there he is, and he has put a hedgehog in his hat. She stops and just looks at him and he tells her to be quiet and points at a restaurant right at the edge of the forest. They go there, he carrying the hedgehog. She gets angry and asks him if a hedgehog is more important than her. But he tells her again to be quiet and enters urbanely, asking the waiter if they have hedgehog beef on the menu as he gives him the hat. 'Of course, hedgehog is our speciality,' the waiter says and takes the hat, grinning at Anne-Marie. 'Hedgehog with liver pâté.' They have a very good lunch, whether it is hedgehog or veal with liver pâté and morels and she absolutely must have the recipe for that pâté. She is surprised that there are anchovies in it, giving it that extra spice. He takes back his hat and they walk to Charlottenlund for the aquarium. She can't get enough of the manatees, and they talk about sirens and mermaids and how we should all live in the sea. It's his element he says and she says she loves swimming and he that he enjoys just strolling along looking for rocks. 'And women,' she says.

'Looking at all the women to see if any one is half as pretty as you,' he replies.

They take the S-banen back to town. Day is moving into night and the city is changing its face; people are going out for a late supper. On they stroll in the light cast by the streetlights and a starting red dusk, looking at statues and window-shopping. They look between the houses to the sea, taking in the light from the big boats destined for Norway or heading out to the oceans. They eat again, this time some smörrebröd at a little restaurant in Sankt Anne's Plads opposite the Swedish embassy. Their stomachs are really better at last, and a couple of drams also go down. Finally they walk past Kongens Nytorv where they can see all the elm trees in the gaslight. It has been a long and intense day and her cheeks are glowing red. They realize there won't be any Josephine Baker tonight.

'I'll make do with you,' he whispers into her ear. 'I would like you wearing bananas.' She tries to fend him off but he murmurs in her ear again. 'You're so beautiful, after today you're shining like a red traffic light or a Danish sausage.' He wants to pat her cheek but she shies away. At Gammeltorv he wants a red hot-dog – now his stomach is working he can't get enough. They sit on a bench by the fountain with a red sausage and a beer each.

'Weren't we going home?' He pinches her ear and then he pinches her sausage – he has already eaten his. His free hand slides inside her jacket and holds her shoulders and she almost drops her food. He kisses her neck. She turns loose and knocks over the beer bottle standing on the bench, wetting his trousers.

'Behave!' she scolds and gets up, adjusting her clothing and checking to see if anybody has been watching her. She sees some people smiling at them. This city is used to people embracing and their reactions vary from tolerance to appreciation.

They slowly walk back to the hotel. It's close to midnight and there is heavy traffic in the area where they are staying. When they ask the porter for the key he tells them that a man called for them and that a cable arrived. She grabs it, reads it and shows Aga.

WILL PASS COPENHAGEN STOP MEET ME STATION STOP 13.30 10 APRIL STOP SVEN

'Damn!' she says. 'That's the day after tomorrow! Why is he coming?'

'I'll get to see him sooner or later. I'll be exciting,' Helmut says though, inside, he is really worried about what might happen. He wonders how he can meet this man and if they could ever be friends, the way he imagined it would be with a father-in-law, someone to play cards or chess with, maybe take a beer with, talk about important matters. Now is the last chance to talk about all the things that haven't been said. They should really be dead tired but instead they sit for half the night, talking in their small hotel room. She asks more about why he stayed in Sweden and why he didn't become a doctor... She hasn't quite grasped that part.

London 1935

'I applied to Oxford to become a doctor. I was accepted and followed my family to England. It was great fun you know; I met Harry who is now married to my cousin Trudy and a lot of other friends there.'

'I can imagine,' she says and her eyes glitter. 'Girls. Cars, Booze.'

'Indeed! And family, and punting on the boats on the river, writing poetry and travelling. I even rowed on one of the teams.'

'You?' she says looking sceptically at his round body.

'Why yes! I wasn't so heavy then, and the force is *here*.' He shows his biceps on his hairy arm. 'I did a trip to Italy and the Middle East. Oh I had my fantasies about killing Mussolini, he always had mass meetings, anyone could have hit him from a balcony. Only fantasies. I was quite left and politically engaged. Perhaps I should have studied more.' He pauses to go to the toilet. When he comes back he continues at once.

*

What really decided things was when he was in London on holiday from his Oxford studies. It was June 1935, and birds were sitting in the trees in front of the house in Aberdare Gardens. The family were living there already then; in Berlin and London they stuck to their houses, but in Stockholm they moved every year almost. He found the bird's singing annoyingly sharp. His mother and sisters and even his grandmother grated on his nerves with their chat about neighbours, relatives, celebrities and shopping. Sigmund was sitting reading and working in his study. Helmut sat by the small telephone table, a list of addresses in front of him: all his pals, girls, family, friends; it was just a case of deciding who to see and what to do. Maybe the movies; he wanted to see *Cleopatra* with Claudette Colbert.

*

'Never saw that one though, did you?'
She shakes her head.
'We'll see it if it comes back. I also wanted to listen to boxing on the wireless; this was when Max Baer was going to fight to defend his heavyweight title, the one he took from Primo Carnera. That little Jew was beating them all; first he beat Schmeling, whom the Nazis supported, then Mussolini's darling Carnera, and this fight was with another American. I glued photographs into albums and wrote small verses next to the pictures, verses mainly about the girl I just left in Oxford. We would meet again in a couple of days; I thought it might be serious. The closest before you.'
'I knew,' she giggles and stretches out over the bedding.
'My relatives' he continues without taking notice of her reaction, 'Were now beginning to arrive in England from Germany, they were talking about persecution, how bad, how frightening life was becoming there…'

*

Karl and his family were in Amsterdam and their daughter, Helmut's cousin Eva, had been in London the same year, but earlier. He had showed her the city. She was so young, but not bad looking, and she admired him, he thought. They had taken Karl's mother to Amsterdam as well.

*

'May she rest in peace.'

'His mother died? In the camps?' Anne-Marie sits up and he nods.

*

He longed to get out, he had been so active in Oxford, but not yet in London.

His father Sigmund had become so feeble: the doctor had told him to cut down on travelling. Now he mainly sat reading in his armchair. Normally his suitcase was always packed; he was often in Sweden for weeks on end. He had fantasies about his father having a second identity there, with mistresses, excitement. Sigmund had enrolled Helmut to help with some work during summer; he had asked him to write some business letters. The young man did that as best he could, and he realised as he did so that a big deal for the business was coming up.

One day, when Helmut was about to go out and taste some of the excitement London had to offer, Sigmund called him from the small study.

'Helmut, can you come, please?' His voice had become hoarse: you could hear that he wasn't well. His son entered the dark study, lit only by a small office lamp; from outside very little light came in,. He looked down at his father; he had become balder, stouter and this man who had always been so dapper had several day's worth of stubble. This larger-than-life figure, who was once so virile, so full of plans and energy, sat in his chair in a pullover, a cigar in the corner of his mouth, his sleeve cuffs unbuttoned. The smoke was thick and pungent. He coughed and put his cigar down.

'*Mein Sohn*,' he said in German but changed quickly to English. 'Your studies, your studies; will you manage, or…?' Now he changed to Swedish: 'I want you to help me, help us.' Helmut looked at this man who had become so much older so quickly; he was only a little past 50. And now, too, he murmured in his German accent without always connecting one thing to another. Helmut sat down cautiously in the office chair.

Sigmund nodded. 'I can't go to Sweden much more,' he said.

'Or in any case, not as often.'

Helmut raised his eyebrows. 'Do you think we should sell the Stockholm office then?'.

Sigmund shook his head – the most vigorous movement his son had seen him make for a while. 'No, no – can't you… can't you… can't you just step in, until I get better?'

Helmut frowned of course, and sat back heavily in his seat. 'Well… but what about my studies? And there's this girl. I haven't told you, but there is…'

'I know: there always is,' Sigmund coughed, a deep, severe cough this time. 'If it's real, then it will happen in it's own time. Otherwise, there will be others.'

'You don't understand my situation!' He stood up abruptly, moved closer to his father, 'You don't understand what's important in my life!'

Sigmund sighed. 'There's the possibility of taking a break, isn't there? I could call your college; speak to headmaster or whoever the relevant people are over there. This is just a temporary thing. You'll become a doctor, don't you worry. But now… now there's an important order coming in, you see.' He took off his reading glasses, the better to communicate his feelings, the better to show his own frailty.

Helmut sat down again, his shoulders slumped. 'I'll look into it. I'll check. Just promise me you'll get well soon. Maybe I can take a few weeks' leave.' Yes, he said all those things though his heart cried the opposite. In fact, he immediately regretted having said yes.

But even so, within days he put everything else aside and went to Stockholm: and stayed there. Once again he had let his father's business govern his life. As if the firm was more important than his own future. He still thought he was going to be a doctor; there was nothing else.

*

Oh, how I regret my decision! But what else could I have done?'

'And you wouldn't have met me either.'

'Oh, that was more to do with my decision to go back to Sweden in 1939 after Käthe's wedding and my father was dead. Otherwise I wouldn't have been there last November.'

The night between days 6 and 7

She is worried about the meeting with her father. She loves Aga; he is everything to her now and she is so worried about what he will think. She looks at that gap between his teeth, his mouth, his hair, she loves all of him but cannot think of anything but the meeting between these two men. She makes a quick inventory; *is there anything more I should have told him?* And he does the same and he realizes now that the whole story of Bergen-Belsen must be told. He is touched by it and it will be difficult to tell her Eva's story as Emmy told it. He wipes his nose and sits himself on the bed that she is already halfway lying in, doing crochet - always something at hand.

'I haven't told you all either,' he says and looks sad.

'I think you have, or is there more, really. We are getting exhausted by all stories, you know.'

'It is more of uncle Karl. Things I didn't realize until a week or two ago in London.'

'You told me he was in Stockholm 1933 and then in a concentration camp. Right?'

'I don't really know how Karl was at the time, how he reacted to the fact that he had to leave Germany in 1933. He was in the spring of 1933. I think my father tried to help him but he couldn't but Karl was aided by some psychoanalysts in Sweden to apply for work in Stockholm. But it didn't work out the way he had hoped. I don't know what happened, what really happened. Over this past year I have imagined, my God, I have imagined, over and over, what might have happened, I can only imagine. I know far too little and will never know.'

'You weren't there?'

'I said I was occupied with other things.'

'I get it.'

'Let me go on. You want to know, don't you? They went to Amsterdam instead of Stockholm. We were all in despair. I am still upset. There was this damn mawkishness in everyone's relationship to Germany at the time. I get furious whenever I think about it.'

When Helmut gets angry like that his eye grow troubled and his mouth looks as if he is smiling, but it's certainly not that. If one looks closer, his mouth is somewhat mysterious and sly and she has learnt to be fascinated and provoked by it. The corner of that mouth is now contracted and those big eyebrows seem to glisten. Jewish eyes. His family seems less Jewish than her mother's father's. And they are only partly Jewish. And yet Helmut's whole family has been so profoundly affected by its Jewish legacy, divided somehow, and the war has struck them brutally, driven them apart. Now she compares him to all the newspaper pictures of Jews, terrible images of haunted people, haggard, destroyed; the 1946 picture of Jewishness. This is not Aga: his eyes are alive, his smile is contagious, and his self-assuredness is striking. She smiles and he smiles back at her, touches her cheek, pulls her close and gives her a quick kiss.

She doesn't wait for the end of his story of Karl but instead she starts telling him about her father, but it is hard, she knows too little. She describes his hectic work in the '30s with politics and the firm. How he was suddenly alone when Siri left him for a year or so and then about her return. How in time he had had enough of some of the Swedish Nazis, but not of the ideas. She keeps talking and though he wants to know more he isn't able to listen. He imagines her as a mother to their children, and pictures her listening to the children as she listens to him, how she will read rhymes to them as she reads poems to him. They will have babies soon. He seldom uses protection. He seldom has done in the past, sometimes leading to an unexpected result. Until now he hasn't wanted to simply for the sensation. Now there is no need for any of that, they are married. They haven't really talked of children. Of course they will have them, they don't have to discuss or plan that; Anne-Marie's and his children. But first he has to know more about Sven. He asks again, he isn't satisfied with her story. He wants to know who he collaborated with, if he was a 'mere' nationalist and anti-communist or if he was a true anti-Semite. He asks, and she wants to give him answers, but she has almost none to give. It's bad enough as it is. She nestles her head into the pillow and is close to weeping. She is dead tired and is having a hard time coping with all his eager questions. 'I must sleep,' she says.

'Why don't you answer? Hell, Anne-Marie, how can we make this work, live together, have children if you can't answer these questions?'

'I've tried my hardest! I don't have his views! Isn't that enough?'

'No it isn't, it bloody well isn't! And I haven't finished *my* story!'

'We can do that later.' She tries to embrace him but he pulls one of the mattresses from the bed, puts it on the floor and lies down on it to mark the distance between them. She cries until she falls asleep.

Day 7

In the morning he goes out again. She is still sleeping. First he passes the Tivoli Gardens. They haven't opened yet. They do on 1st May, to make the Danes choose between demonstrations and a visit to the pleasure park, between socialism and candyfloss. There is construction work going on in the corner near the station where an English bomb came down. He sneaks in between the planks. The first thing he sees is the Pantomime theatre. He closes his eyes and tries to remember all the characters. The truth is Helmut has had problems enjoying the things that they have seen in Copenhagen. The city has at the same time been a sore reminder of the war and a backdrop to his love for Anne-Marie, and then to their stomach troubles and finally to Anne-Marie's father being a mysterious dark phantom blocking Helmut's ability to see things properly. When you are in the midst of the fog you don't grasp how thick the fog is. It's greyish outside, low clouds and some mist.

A humid wind sweeps through the city, helping to rid it of the dust and the sand that has been lingering as a remembrance of winter. The wind makes the fog dissolve in front of him; the clouds get thinner. The sun comes up over the station and finds its way into the Tivoli, making the Pantomime theatre's peacock curtain glimmer. The curtain does indeed look like feathers on a big blue and gold painted peacock, standing in front of the stage with its beak towards the audience. This curtain is designed to be lowered like a fan. It will again this summer and the classic figures will come out on the stage as they have done every summer whether in war or peace; Harlequin, Cassander, Columbine and Pierrot. He remembers the cast and all the central characters. There, in the sun in front of the theatre, he sees them all clearly. In almost every version, Cassander, Columbine's father, is ready to make her take another admirer instead of the one she wants. Sven has not protested against his daughter's admirer, so Anne-Marie has said, but he perhaps doesn't want a Jewish admirer.

'I don't care,' Helmut says to himself, concentrating on the beak of the peacock. 'I will not pity that man. Anne-Marie must be independent enough not to care about him. But who knows?'

He sits down on a bench and falls asleep. He sees the entire act, pompous Cassander with his big belly, his gun and his great self-assuredness, he who can sit in front of the mirror for hours and wants to govern and have his say in the small town or in the country and has the most beautiful daughter in the land. Columbine, that is, and she has so many admirers and wants to choose for herself, but Cassander wants her to marry a nobleman. There is also Cassander's servant, almost his alter ego, Pierrot, who does everything for his master but would like Columbine for his own. Then there is Harlequin who doesn't join Cassander's adventures at all but who has won Columbine's heart, maybe by being such a contrast to her father. All of Harlequin's family comes along. The actors are eager to start; the show is about to begin. In front of the shining peacock the audience have now sat down, some children have candyfloss in their hands and everyone's clothes get smeared. There is a couple on honeymoon, a single refugee, a student of psychology testing out what he's learnt. Some of them were just passing and had sat down through lack of anything better to do. Now the orchestra starts to play, all the peacock's feathers are lowered and the stage appears. In comes Cassander dressed as a baby with a nappy. The audience laughs. He runs after a busty woman, his mother or nanny. Pierrot teases him with a big dummy and Cassander wants to suck it. The student in the audience turns to his companion and looks deep into her décolletage. 'The breasts as lust objects, for you to yearn for eternally.' She shakes his shoulder with a firm grip to make him stop. A man shaking him by the shoulder arouses Aga.

'It is closed, you have to leave' he says and Helmut hurries towards the exit.

It's All Coming Back

He droops and paces out of there, past Glyptoteket and down to the canal and then along it down to the big Royal Library, the old one just off Christiansborg Castle down by the canals, between the parliament building and the sea. Libraries, reading and history are important things for this city and also for Helmut. There, as everywhere, he is a reading man, one who likes to reflect on what he reads and who often writes *Sic!* In the margin with the little green pencil he always keeps in his jacket or shirt pocket. He is still curious, but above all, he is newly married and he wants to know all about her, this woman with whom he is going to spend the rest of his life. It is a sunny but windy spring day, with the sun coming in from Öresund and the copper roofs and car surfaces are glittering, and life mirrors itself in the canals, when the soil lies open and the first green vegetation starts to show.

Sniffing the air, he knows that warm weather will really be coming soon, that there is a new season coming, another face, that the world can change. He knows his wife needs a long morning's sleep and he wants to read. Settling himself in the big library he finds the magazine and newspaper department and takes a seat at a table with the green reading lamps, under huge brick arches and close to spiral staircases. There he reads eagerly, trying to find information from this woman's past. He knows history can be written and it can be made black and white, right and wrong. Some know what depended on what, who the good guy was and who caused the evil and the unfairness. In the present you don't have that opportunity to make finals judgements, not in the same way. He realizes he is forming a more distanced attitude to politics than before; he doesn't take part as much, but rather observes, as one looks into one of those sugar eggs with a small window and a landscape inside. A couple of years earlier he had enjoyed shaking the world, but not now; after the war it's not as important anymore. It isn't that he intends to be passive when a fight is needed – on the contrary, he has always been ready to go under cover if the Nazis come back or the communists – he is ready for that.

But now, in the library, he is getting distracted, absorbed in all the political stuff he is finding, and has almost forgotten what he has come for. It's not so strange; he has not read Swedish newspapers or magazines for weeks. There are also a lot of stories about crime. About that, he had a relaxed attitude: *'As long as you don't injure others.'*

Now, he finds that he's got drawn into the middle of something that he can't manage to understand. He wants to know more than what she has told him. That is why is sitting indoors when the sun is bright outside over Copenhagen's historic centre. He sits inside the big redbrick walls, trying to grasp the context, to get beneath the surface of things, to see them from a new angle or different perspective, and to understand. The room is full of echoes, and every rustle from the newspaper pages is amplified – he has to turn the pages of these Swedish newspapers that he has unearthed very quietly. There he finds the usual gossip about who had really been a Nazi and who had not. There are stories about men, mainly men, who has committed fraud, murder, thefts and real atrocities. Men who has lost normal compassion and let sheer selfishness take over. He hates selfish people. Yet, yet he tries to understand even them; only by understanding can you do something about it, whether it's Nazis, murderers or fraudsters. But now all the evil ones seem to be put together as if they were one. There is evil and there is good. Full stop.

In the midst of all this information he recognizes the name of his father-in-law in an article. *Does anybody else have that name?* He reads and soon his doubts, his questions, and his torments have suddenly all been answered. He stops, clears his throat, glances across the room. His heart is pounding. He has been looking forward to spending time with a father-in-law. His own father has been dead for almost six years. Of course, this tall man, whom he has heard so much about, would never be able to replace his father. His mother's new husband cannot do that either. He has never really believed that they could, but he has hoped that there might be someone to be tied to, to turn to, to talk with about things. He feels himself almost suffocating with all the old junk and lumber coming through the yellowing pages. For a moment his whole existence, his entire future is under attack.

In the article Sven is named as one of the candidates for a putative cabinet, a secret Swedish-Nazi government, set up by a society called Manhem; a potential Swedish Quisling cabinet. The list was handed to the Germans. Helmut reads it and interprets more than just the written facts, and sitting alone in the library he becomes more and more agitated. Of course, from their conversations over the last few days, he knew some of this already and yet the new knowledge about his father-in-law and his potential past role deeply wounds him.

Is the bloody war after me again, haunting me, all the rights and wrongs, all the friends and enemies? Will it come back and ruin everything? The war that pulled my family apart, the war that left me so lonely, so full of hate, destined to work for the cause of liberation?

He feels so inadequate about what he has done, as if he's not in the right place at the proper time. He has stuck to Sweden; it's safe and sort of innocent in a way. He holds his head. The war echoes again, that damn, bloody, fucking war.

He walks around, checks to see if anyone is watching him, tries to look unaffected even though his body is screaming once more. He doesn't know if he should hide or just stand up and announce his discovery. He leaves the paper open and walks down the stairs, wanting to get outside. Once in the fresh air, he looks over the embankment and the canal across to the houses on Christian's Island on the other side. A very old car passes the old barracks; he can even smell it as the sound of a worn down exhaust pipe retorts like a shot, and the noise echoes across the canal. He walks to the embankment and looking down into all the clutter, takes out his last cigarette. A strong and damp breeze comes in from the sea and races over the canal. Finally he manages to light the cigarette. He smokes forcefully

War is over and love has begun. Love is powerful, he knows that, he knows that more than ever: true love, serene, eternal, the kind that he has found this time – but can love really help when it turns out that the one you love isn't the person you thought they were? Or at least, turns out to be close to somebody... different. *Evil. Something inhumane.* It's an easy phrase to fall back on, a template, a mould; he knows that – a mould that excludes comparisons with one's own self. He has learnt to tussle with the war or live through it. He does not, however, know how to deal with this, and he feels strong forces tearing at him. He has never felt this way before.

Suddenly he feels overwhelmed with concern for Anne-Marie and sharply regrets letting her cry herself to sleep last night. Today they haven't talked; they haven't talked since yesterday's quarrel. He is so worried that he can feel it in his stomach.

So he sneaks straight back to the hotel to talk to his wife, to sort it out with her, but in a clearer way now, because he at last he knows the full truth about her father. He doesn't know – and it is making his whole body ache – he doesn't know whether to confront her or simply to make love to her. But she is still asleep, deeply asleep and beautiful. He doesn't have the courage to wake her up. It would make things worse, he knows she does not want to be awakened; it'll only make her angry. He wants to caress her cheek but takes his hand away. He just stops and looks at her fairy tale slumber and goes out onto the streets of Copenhagen again.

Quickly, he walks along Ströget and into Hviid's vinstue around the corner by Kongens Nytorv. The tavern has always been there, a half step down, with its misty windows, its barmen and cigar-smoking women with their salty jokes, and the typical Copenhagen blend of partying townsmen, tourists, merchants and sailors. It's before noon and the place has just opened. It's cleaner, emptier, and less smoky than usual but there are some early birds who have come for the first beer of the day. He has to get back to Anne-Marie soon, she is a late sleeper but will wake up soon, thoroughly rested and full of energy, and hopefully ready to listen. He sits down with a pilsner and some Danish sausage, lights a small cigar and stares over to the corner of the dim bar, with its simple tables and ingrained good nature.

Then he sees a man coming out of the men's room and starts as her realises that he remembers him, recognizes this Danish face from the past. The man passes the bar and looks at Aga for a short moment. He is as shaggy as he was in the boat back then, so Danish with his goatee beard and the pipe that has almost grown into his mouth. Aga hesitates as to whether or not he should say hello. He cannot even remember the man's name, just them rowing together across Öresund. His name was an assumed one of course. Aga just nods.

The other man looks at Helmut with astonishment, and cries out without stopping, 'Jon! Jon, damn, you survived! Damn hell! Me too. Look at me! I survived … for what it's worth.' Helmut has no chance to answer; he is stunned and in a hurry. He can only nod in response and sits on his stool for just a very short while before hurrying back to the hotel.

Anne-Marie is sitting combing her hair and says a short hello when he comes in, as if it was the most natural thing that he was not there when she woke up. She has put the mattress back in its place and made the bed.

'You didn't finish your story about Karl,' she says almost in passing. And so, very well, he tells her at once, though his head is full of Sven. He doesn't apologize for yesterday; he doesn't confront her, not now. He starts talking about his own family's past and waits to deal with the other things. They would hurt and eventually heal, like any time one uses a really strong solution on a wound. You may need the pain to heal. But later.

'They were taken to Belsen, three of them. I discovered this, and you know I tried to get to know more. Then a German airman fell into our army position and I spoke to the Germans about exchanging him for Karl and Lins.'

His story is clearly just skimming the very top of what happened, and she tries to understand what he's leaving out, to read between the lines. She can tell he's clearly not being evasive, he just doesn't seem to have the focus to tell the story in depth as he has at other times with other tales. He obviously tried to exchange his family members in a concentration camp for a German airman, and all this from Sweden. *He is bloody well as foolhardy as my father*, she figures. If he isn't telling a tall story. Sometimes she doesn't know what is true and what not.

'Well, there were three of them and I had said two, so my support was of no help to Karl and I don't know what really happened, if my proposal meant anything.'

She still doesn't know what to believe. The story is too odd.

'Karl died on 27th January, you know, the same day that Auschwitz was liberated. What an irony. Belsen was not liberated for quite some time, but I don't think Eva and Lins saw the final days of it. It was indescribable.' He had believed that this story would be difficult, almost impossible to tell but it's OK: he doesn't sob, doesn't stammer.

Anne-Marie closes her eyes. *What can I say? What can I do? How can I help him?* She assumes that Aga has run through this story a hundred times, figuring out how to tell it. It's all so cold, straight, and simple.

'Why?' she tries. 'Why such a hell?' She tastes the sorrow and tries to express it.

'That was how it was,' he says. 'Exactly as diabolical as that. Eva and Lins got out and headed off on a perilous voyage through the German countryside, with no one there to help them, with a retreating war machine where everybody was just concerned for their own protection. In a bombed land in the middle of winter, finding food was not easy. But they made it.'

'And Karl didn't?'

He just shakes his head.

'By the time Lins and Eva finally found the allied troops, they were torn, ravaged – it took them a long time to recover. In Amsterdam they met Eva's sister – Lins' daughter of course – Suse who had her own terrible hardships in Arnhem where she lived without saying she was Jewish. Now they're all heading for the US where they'll meet everyone again. I gather that the youngest son Paulus is in Palestine… he must be twenty by now. He pretended he was a Dutch worker, and joined the resistance and did a lot of things in the Netherlands, Belgium and France. But he almost starved, almost died of malnutrition. He got to Spain and from there made it to Palestine.' Helmut becomes silent. Anne-Marie creeps up against his coat. He stares at the graphite grey sky and opens the window wide. There's a strong wind and he holds his face up towards it and lets the cold blow through him. He's opened up, is exposed and so vulnerable. 'It is hard to believe all these stories. And yet there are thousands of them and it's good to remember the causes of these things, and what happens next.'

'What do you mean?' she looks anxiously at him. 'Remember what?'

'That Sweden didn't let Karl work as a psychoanalyst; they more or less forced him away. Do you get it? He could have stayed in Sweden! He could have survived!'

'Bloody hell!' She holds her arms around him and nuzzles her sobbing face in under his chin.

She holds him for a long time, completely still; it is so different from her usual frenetic style He falls asleep in her arms and she watches him for a long while.

Day 8

They wake up in the afternoon of 9th April, the day before Sven arrives, the day before 10th April, the first occasion that the liberated Danes are able to remember the German invasion; the five year occupation began six years ago on that date. And the Danes are out with red-white flags. Anne-Marie and Helmut use the day to take it easy, strolling along the embankments, past Nyhavn, past Amalienborg castle and on to Langelinie. There is a light rain, a very weak and warm drizzle. They walk on, fast, as if they were heading somewhere but they aren't. They look at the water at Öresund that now in spring smells better than ever. Helmut only has his father-in-law in mind; the issue comes to him regularly like a bellboy. She also imagines the upcoming meeting but knows she can't do anything about it, the two will either like each other or not. That is the way it is. They walk a bit apart from each other. There is a strong breeze coming in from the sea - spring is like that here; it is warmer but these same strong winds that usher out the old winter also make things less rosy.

Aga stops and steps up on a small bollard just by the embankment. Turning around, he places himself as close to the edge as he can, half his shoe on the outside, and looks straight down into the black water. On another occasion he could have jumped, held his breathe and tried to sink down. The water is cold enough, but that would solve nothing. He looks for fish instead: perch, salmon maybe. He stares down, straight down. The water is both clear and dirty, ropes, algae, contraceptives, old tyres, a board. Dead fish on the surface. So much death, so many dead. If Sven had been dead it would have been all the easier, he figures. He likes having these mean thoughts, evil – no one should die for their views. If Sven really had been minister in an occupation cabinet, a Swedish Quisling government, he probably would have been jailed after the war and maybe executed. That's what they're doing in Norway now. Sven had the good fortune that things evolved the way they did, but he will be forever stamped a Nazi.

Aga looks up at the houses on the other side, towards Christianshavn and all the old military installations. Searches for life, for human beings there. A gull swoops from behind a house and dives at the clutter in the sea, and then a small boat with some intoxicated youngsters passes by. He gets irritated at first but then he realizes that he needs all these things to distract him from thoughts of Sven.

There is traffic on the bridge. *See, there is life.* Anne-Marie is standing a little further away looking at him. He sits down on the rim of the embankment after having wiped it clean for a seat or two with his big square kerchief. Swinging his legs, feeling like Humpty Dumpty, he starts to throw gravel into the sea, over the junk, onto the dead fishes and finally also on his own mirrored image.

Anne-Marie calls and he turns around to rise, but slips with one leg and realises that he's slithering down, gliding over the edge. At the last moment he is able to grab the bollard with his hands and tries to heave himself up; it's heavy and he almost feels he can't make it and is imagining giving in, but Anne-Marie gives him a hand. Some black-headed gulls that are on the water, fighting over a fish, look up at him. He makes a final effort. At last it works. Now other people are also close by. He is left on all fours on the embankment and a couple of men with peaked caps and a lady wearing a fur coat approach him. His hand is bleeding having been scraped on the tar gravel, but he rises slowly and wipes his clothes off. 'No problem, all in order!' he says cheerfully in his best Danish and looks at them and then at his hand. He spits onto the wound, and wipes the kerchief around it. It is not too bad. Soon they walk off towards the city centre again. He is alive, he wants to be alive and live with Anne-Marie even if her father is a Nazi or whatever he was or is.

Day 9

The next day they wake up early. They make love properly. They have to. The sun sneaks in through the hotel window even though they pulled down the blind.

'What a change in the weather,' Anne-Marie says and she lets up the blind too fast. It spins round and jumps out of its hanger straight on to the bed where Aga still is lying. It only just misses him. He picks it up and points with it at Anne-Marie as if it were a lance.

'Now: I must know. I *demand* an answer as to how involved he was. I think he was on a cabinet list, a list of potential Nazi ministers. Those Swedish Quislings.'

'What are you saying?' He can see that Anne-Marie is genuinely shocked. 'Was he on a list? What are you talking about?'

'I don't know what kind of minister he was proposed to become, but he had become involved, and he was guilty! And what would a Swedish Nazi government do with the Jews, with those like me for instance, and everybody else for that matter? I would probably have been able to hide, but the rest? Look at Norway!'

'No! He would never do that!'

'How do you know? Many are corrupted or allow themselves to be corrupted step by step, whether forced or semi-forced. *That's how it works*, you know. I believe you when you talk about his personality but I don't think anyone could abstain, not with all that pressure.'

'Why would he? I don't get it. He is not that kind of man!' She pulls the blind from him, stands on the chair and puts it back in place.

'Maybe he's better than all the rest of us.' Helmut shrugs, a gesture that belies the extreme tension he's feeling. 'I'll judge when I see him.'

'But do not judge him unseen.'

'I know, but I was so upset when I saw him mentioned as one of the Swedish Nazis.' He decides to tell her all. 'You know… I looked at old Swedish papers in the Royal Library the other day?'

Anne-Marie looks at him while dressing, trying to connect to him with her eyes. 'But you've known about his politics for a while; why let this come between us now?'

'No, it's different now. I didn't think about it this way before. I hadn't seen it so clearly, there in black and white.'

'And why now?'

'…and my mother was so proud of your family with a grandfather in the Swedish Academy.'

'But that's on my mother's side, mother La's side.' She feels that she could weep at the sadness in his voice, the ache in her heart. 'And, if somebody put him on a list, you can't judge him for that.'

'No, I won't condemn your father for being put on a cabinet list by others. I'll judge him for his own deeds and what he could have done. And we both know what he stood for. What he stands for. I want to hear his version and then I'll accept him as your father, never ever anything more than that.' He puts on his jacket and rubs off some stains from it, very thoroughly.

'Don't make this situation more irrational than it already is!' Anne-Marie tries. 'These are hypothetical questions. We don't know if he wanted to be a minister or if this was just somebody else's idea. It is all hypothetical, damn hypothetical!'

'I know,' he concedes, but still

'Well, let the bough bend or break.' Her voice is hardening, but she also sounds helpless now.

'I've waited for a long time,' he points out.

They sit with their own thoughts for a while.

A good breakfast and then down to the town centre, hand in hand. *At last*, Helmut thinks. *Bend or break*, Anne-Marie thinks. He swallows, almost retching but collects himself. He doesn't notice her seriousness, her worries. It is sunny but they can see that out by the sea, only a couple of blocks away, it is misty as it has been most of the time. They arrive at the station with its brick vaults. Before entering she holds his hand tight and makes him stop.

'You, do you want to?' she asks, her eyes searching his.

'Yes,' he nods, firmly. 'I have to.'

'No: I mean, do you still want to?'

'Never mind what I want.'

'Do you still want to have a baby?' she pushes, ' With me?'.

'You know I do! With you, as long as he doesn't interfere.'

'Good,' she says and holds her belly. 'You will get this baby with me. Good. I believe it will be a boy.'

He embraces her and smiles. 'A boy? I want a girl, another girl!' He watches her for a long while. A quick kiss and then they move on. Several trains are arriving from Helsingör and he may come on any one of them. To pass the time Aga puts a coin into the electric model train that is situated in the hall: slowly the machine starts and Aga watches the big black and red wheels go round without the train moving. A theatre. Anne-Marie looks at him and likes his childishness. He feels a hand on his shoulder.

'So, a playful son-in-law. Well, it could be worse.' Aga turns around and looks straight into Sven's small, beady eyes that actually somehow appear rather kind. Then he sees his clothes; a brown trench coat with a Swedish flag on the lapel, a brown beret a bit askew, and a smile, maybe a bit patronizing but also a kind smile.

He looks damn kind.

Aga prepares what to say but doesn't make it in time before Sven continues:

'Playfulness, but maybe some seriousness as well? How good that we could meet here. Congratulations to the two of you on your marriage! Hope you find happiness.' He takes some flowers he has had behind his back, tulips, and hands them to Aga. Helmut straightens up, waits a bit with his questions, his decisive questions – he'll save them for later. He dusts off his coat and holds out his hand to take the flowers.

'Thanks. And here is Anne-Marie, now with a new surname,' he pulls her to him, smiling. 'The flowers must be for her.'

'Exactly,' Sven says and smiles again. 'I think it is about time, very much about time for my little daughter to become a Mrs, and she hasn't made a bad bargain.' He still has his eyes fixed on Aga. There is something wild about this man, but he likes him, this *human being* standing before him has honest eyes, you can't be unfriendly with him. He puts his arm around Aga who doesn't know how to react, but he manages to ward him off by holding Anne-Marie instead, which makes Sven drop his arm. Then the older man goes on eagerly:

'I'm hungry! Let's go and eat, or what do you suggest? We have two hours before I have to get going. I took an early train to have some time here. I am heading on to south Sweden again to Österlen, and you wouldn't want me to disturb your happiness too long, would you?'

They hadn't thought about what they would actually do with him. They walk together to the station restaurant. Helmut is silent, still planning his words in his mind. He finds it ever more difficult to think of how to say it. Sven takes the lead and orders lunch for the three of them. The fish lunch is what he suggests and with a small dram. 'You need a shot for the fish, isn't that so?' and he jabs Aga in his belly. Then he starts to talk, without pausing, about his new wife, about all their relatives, about Umeå. 'You know that is why I am in a hurry. Lisa and I are going to meet up in south Sweden. Happiness is not just for the young. This is my third time. Third time lucky, I hope!'

Ann-Marie looks concerned. 'Congratulations,' she says. '*Skål*, Father. I hope this time will be good for you. I know it will.'

Helmut excuses himself and leaves the table. He has seen a man outside the restaurant, through the glass walls into the station hall, one with a goatee beard and a pipe, the man he bumped into at Hviid's yesterday and then didn't say very much to, didn't know what to say. Now Helmut runs to see him out of sight of the restaurant, holds him and asks what he meant. He is going to ask what the man knows of other people from the resistance; he wants to know what happened to them. He wants to talk about the resolution of his own war. In fact he wants to be saved from his father-in-law's grip. *Can we start anew?* is another question he would like to ask. Can one start anew without caring what side people were on during the war and before? He paces up to the man and puts his arm around him. Then he sees: it's not the same person. He quickly withdraws but now he is on the receiving end of a very perplexed look.

'Sorry! I thought... I thought you were someone else,' Helmut tries to explain while quickly backing away towards the men's room and not noticing the people gathering around them. He goes in fast as if he is in some desperate need and stays there until the people have dispersed. When he comes back, somewhat dejected, Sven is still in the middle of a monologue, maybe the same one as when he left, but this time about how he took Paulie and left him with his mother in Lund. He speaks about Paulie's mother and how she is doing, he speaks of Germany and what he has read about the conditions there, what he saw two years ago when he was last there, and says that he would have liked to go now but doesn't dare because of his angina. He speaks of ruins and of dusk for a country and its culture, about poor people who have to walk around searching for food and shelter, people have become like rats, about diseases and the lack of hygiene.

'How could they do it?' he says and turns towards Helmut, 'How could they do it to your country? Do you see how they ruined your fatherland, how they ruined European culture?' Helmut does not know how to respond. For once he is lost for words. 'The war was one long misery,' Sven continues after some silence.

'Do you think so, depends of course how you see it. But it is all over now at least – ' Helmut starts and is about to continue but Sven interrupts him.

'Well, it's over only if you can stop the Cossacks' progress,' he says. He has put the last piece of fish on a slice of rye bread. 'That other governments trust the Russians is what I understand the least.' He chews for a moment. 'But now

Germany has to be rebuilt and without delay. There must be room for forgiving. *Skål!* For the rebuilding of Germany, your Germany!' he declares, and waits to empty the glass. Helmut hesitates before raising his.

'*Skål*' he replies. 'Cheers! For a completely different Germany, a Germany like the one I remember from my childhood. Where everybody of all sorts can live and enjoy their lives, decide for themselves about how they live and have any opinion or religion or skin colour they like,' he says, 'And cheers to Stockholm and Sweden, Anne-Marie's and my home, the place my father chose before the Germany of the '20s. The decade when all the devilry came forward.'

'We were too bloody cowardly,' Sven says prudently. 'We should have stated a clear position, like the Finns did.'

'Not everyone was a coward,' Helmut replies quickly. 'Though God knows I should have done more for those that were left, for my relatives. How come so many didn't understand what was happening?' He turns to Sven with that question and is ready to continue with what he had planned to say but hasn't yet said.

'Cheers, whatever,' his father-in-law interrupts, distracted. With his free hand, the one not holding a glass, he looks at the watch in his waistcoat. 'Oh, I am almost late!' he exclaims as the glasses are lowered, 'Oh yes the present: this is something fine for you.' He pulls a small envelope from his jacket pocket. 'Well I, or we, have left the red house and therefore my idea is that you take the empire-style sofa, chair and table. This is a deed of the gift.'

'Thank you, Dad. But before you go, there was something Helmut was going to ask you, about the war and how come you were on that list. He would like to...'

Sven frowns. 'Can't it wait? I have to run, we can talk when we see each other next time, and it will be soon I am sure. Could you come to Österlen? We will be there for a couple of weeks; it would be nice. You look so happy.' And with that, he dashes, or maybe runs, away.

Afterwards when Anne-Marie wants to drag Helmut back to the hotel, he is quiet and slow, he doesn't move from his place at once and then he doesn't follow at her pace. Preoccupied, he's ashamed about all he hasn't said, all the words that he had had on the tip of his tongue but couldn't spit out. He feels like a coward. He had planned to say that everyone should have understood, that everyone ought to have understood long before where it was going and that democracy must be defended at any price and that no one is worth more than anybody else and that everyone has a right to exist.

He wanted to say that nationalism is dangerous.

He wanted to ask what Sven knew about the Holocaust and why he continued to support Hitler.

And he had wanted to know whether he would have said 'yes' to an offer to sit in a Swedish Quisling government.

Anne-Marie once told the story of how vain Sven was when he had a cable from the Prime Minister-to-be during the First World War, a telegram asking about his political views. Probably a tall tale but like all of those usually with some truth in it, and Helmut wants to know what Sven's reactions would have been to a similar telegram if the Germans had attacked Sweden… and of course also what he would have done to make the Germans happy. Would he have sent off Jews or not? That is the most important issue. Aga knows that Sven likely would say that these were hypothetical questions. Aga knows that. The Nazis were not even close to taking Sweden. The government, the coalition that was, even they were far too cooperative with the Germans, Aga thinks. That's his opinion.

He should have asked these questions, taken the opportunity. He beats his legs in frustration.

But Anne-Marie doesn't have the same concerns. She's glad that there was no conflict and she laughs and is pleased and pushes him along to go faster.

'Why was I so silent? Why? Why? I would have liked to talk about how everyone has good and evil within them and that things will go wrong if you make the wrong choices,' Helmut laments slowly, 'I had wanted to speak of evil and love and that you should dissociate yourself from those that hurt others! I wanted to talk about the need to show personal courage and not least to be able to change your mind, to dare to change your mind. You know exactly what I meant to say!'

Anne-Marie only smiles her best smile and her dimples show. She is satisfied with the two having met and that no confrontation occurred. She is glad that they didn't become enemies. She is happy, she now knows she is pregnant. 'I don't know what he supported then nor what his opinion is now.'

'Well,' he continues, 'I would have liked to say that there is no defending those who took the wrong stand. The only thing you can do now is to change your mind and reconcile, to dare to think anew. And then I would have liked to talk about the need for a new beginning.' Helmut is silent when he sees that he is only getting short answers and sees that she just wants to move on. He knows they must move on – but if she could just wait for a little while, be in the moment for once.

'How about a cup of coffee?' he sighs, and they are soon sitting, each with a cup, at a small café by the station with music playing in the background. She has found a magazine to flick through. He just sits still, breathing and thinking. His rage over his failure to confront his father-in-law is slowly ebbing away and he's getting more and more composed. He realizes that he just has to understand that the war is over, that now is time for rebuilding, for building a new life. He would have liked to talk about that as well but now the dissecting is over with for the time-being.

He knows enough about her and her father, about Sven. The father-in-law is on the losing side, he belongs to the past, to those who were wrong, those to be judged.

As if there were any victors.

We are all losers, aren't we? Aga figures. He knows that defeat and loss is the essence for the restart and rebuilding. *We will not forget.* But the time for dwelling on the past is over. He had the meeting, after all, the meeting he had feared for so long. And Sven is nothing but a father-in-law. Aga hasn't married him. He looks at Anne-Marie who is still reading her magazine and who, he suddenly remembers with an electric thrill, is pregnant with their baby. There is a future for them. In Stockholm their new flat awaits them. Now they must build their future without glances back at what has been. It is time for spring to come for real at last.

They walk home and for a moment he sees out to Öresund. It had been a fog out there most of their week and a half in Copenhagen. This morning it was all misty. Now it has cleared a bit and moved to the Swedish side. He hopes it clears for the crossing.

V.
Reflections and facts

Afterthoughts

The past finds its way back with all its smells, the entire gloomy shimmer and its distant sounds, all its hidden lives. It rolls to the forefront of my thoughts at times, prising things apart, grubbing around and finally looks me in the face although I have fended it off for so long. Before, I didn't dare to pose the right questions, didn't dare look behind closed doors and into forgotten crannies. But all the small fragments of things said and unsaid have clamoured so long for my attention, to be interpreted and explained. I can no longer hold out against the questions of what was so special, so out of the ordinary. It's only through trying to live the past, by entering into the past, that we can begin to get a sense of it, and start the hard work of explaining. Try to pry into their thoughts even though we know nothing. We don't know anything other than that they were humans; all of them were. We can mourn and we can explain but we will not understand, we will never ever understand; at least I never will.

My parents stayed together all their life, for more than forty years. And when he finally died first I rushed to their home by car, train and taxi and my mother met me on the porch and she said 'I cannot cry, I cannot cry' and she almost wept for not being able to cry. We hugged and sat silently.

I have seen the pictures from their wedding. They were so lucky there in West Hampstead when they got married. You can see so much joy in their faces in the pictures. That was their first short stop after the wedding. The same smiles on the photos of them and of us children when we were small. And still.

When they weren't travelling, he sat there kneeling in his chair, leaning on his desk, reading and combing his moustache and digesting, and he was silent. As silent as she was when driving hundreds of kilometres in deep concentration on vacations, despite his swearing and his comments. He went to the aquariums he kept in the basement with all those odd species, to his cat breeding, his other women, chose to tenderly plant new sprouts in the garden and sort fossils. And she often went out alone mushroom picking in the woods. They had that interest in common but she often did it alone.

I think he changed a lot when he broke his leg under a bus some years after the war. This and his obesity made him uncomfortable and sometimes gruff and insular and left him wanting to sit at home. Sometimes there was a presence however and the words flew.

You should have seen them on their travels in England, she with his family, and he with hers. Talking the nights through. Sometimes it was as if a catalyst was needed to wake him from his slumber. And she accepted all his escapades on the side – those were never concealed either, on the contrary. In matters of that kind they were extremely liberal and at the same time so direct. He eventually took up his studies again, not medicine but English, German, Ethology, Genetics, Yiddish and Dutch and became a teacher in high schools, happy and successful in that.

She also went into teaching of young adults; in economics and accounting and that sort. They lived in the present but probably the past made a lifelong resonance in the background somewhere. How it really felt, I do not know.

He accepted her going to all the meetings with various organizations, unions and even political groups, but finally could no longer hide a helpless loneliness and begged her to stay at home where they had little communication. But they really stayed together all their lives, despite everything. She died only three years after him.

When it is too late to start asking the proper questions I start adding things up, combining silence and some murmurs from conservations with newspaper articles, what I read in books and the memories of others. Then it becomes clear that it wasn't quite as they told me. A tide comes in with all the junk. I hold out my hands and try to fend it off but it all comes in unsorted, lovely and awful, edgy and broken, soft and incisive. Then it all lies spread out and I try to sort it, choose and throw away, build patterns and search for pieces

It's All Coming Back

I cannot find. I build and rebuild again and again. New patterns, new possibilities, new scenarios. I realize I never will have the full picture, as it really was. I realize I will not have all the pieces, the right pieces

I started recognizing patterns, patterns that are seen again and again, those eternal patterns. Finally some kind of truth can be brought to light in all this strangeness. Their story finally looms; their joint past is recreated and I myself become a fragment of their story. Like a double-exposed or even triple-exposed photograph in a developing solution, the picture comes alive. The weak and plain light makes the sight strange; first you recognize nothing, and then more and more details come to the fore.

Where to start?

What am I proud of and what makes me ashamed?

I haven't processed this fully. I will never be able to process it, will never be able to understand: I don't want to understand. I have to add some and paint in brighter colours and it becomes clearer; probably even clearer than it was. I could have kept the blurred image; I could have chosen to hide and keep silent. But, could I have continued my life without caring about what had been before? It's one thing is to know about all this old business. The real issue comes in the next step: should I accept or let feelings of guilt of what my grandfather did or could have done take over; be cut back by the past and in my life; or in fact in their lives. Another option is to choose to reject, throw out, condemn, and to position myself for a new starting point. Then I must dare to see the background and refuse to become part of it.

The big problem for me is of course Sven my Swedish grandfather.

When we were still kids my sister and I went up north, bedded down in a train compartment, alone, small – we had barely started school. It was once or twice; I believe it had to do with my mother's abortions or scrapings and/or when my small sister was born. We stayed with the cousins in Umeå, the cousins we barely knew, with uncle Ivar and his children. One was a teenager and had painted toenails and swallowed swords and was later a soldier's widow in the United States after another war. We went to movies and went on the kick-sleigh. It was my sister and I, but it still felt lonely and awkward. We were at our granddads; he had invited a magician just for us. It was cold and we went to watch horse jumping at the local regimental headquarters where we met our uncle in uniform. Some of the military men greeted Granddad very politely – it was all somewhat tedious and ceremonious. Others didn't see him or pretended not to. Another time we went to the mountains up north with our parents. They wanted to be reconciled, to come back together after some problems. The cows walked in the forest during the daytime and came back at night to stand under the corrugated roof. The folks we stayed with made pudding from the first milk and the long-sour milk and fished and prepared char in various ways. The Sami woman made the thin soft unleavened bread. The raven on the hill called out warnings. The water was clear and I believed I could swim but understood neither how cold it was nor how deep it was. As a child I did not see the deep. I was lucky not to go in. The farmlands were not under cultivation; farmers were paid both for putting new land to the plough and next year or closing old fields. It was the '50s. My granddad came there to Klimpfjäll one day. The farmers greeted him with straight backs, slightly tense and they talked hydropower development all night. He would defend them against the superiors who would put the river outlets where the char were spawning underwater. He was liked out there. I never had the opportunity to ask him about his Nazism. There was something between him and Dad, tenseness. I think my father Aga felt awkward with that family didn't know if he would confront them with the past or just pretend as if that was nothing to really make a fuss about.

I remember the first time I told this story for outsiders. I worked close to the northern cemetery of Stockholm, in Solna where my maternal grandmother was buried in her husband's family grave after her suicide in 1919 and my paternal grandfather was buried in the Jewish graveyard in June 1939, when World War II was only a threat on the horizon. We walked there, me and some friends from work, during our lunch break one sunny spring day and we talked of our respective families who had been buried in different places, and made a joke of our view of our future from our office windows facing the cemetery. I told them about my family lying there and touched on the fact that my grandfather was a Nazi. I remember first the silence then the reactions; someone didn't believe me and I had to convince him, another was surprised, another didn't dare to make any comment or didn't care, one was indignant and one tried to explain: 'That was what it was like then, they couldn't know.' I hated that reaction and still hate it. *Everybody ought to have understood.* Many have looked at me as a Jew: a true Jew. But then I revealed this, quite another reality. Of course they wondered who I really was. I do myself.

Suddenly everything was so clear for me. My grandfather stood for all I had fought against in my political life. I should have understood that much earlier. They mentioned it at home, passing over it, like an anecdote. I pushed it away, understood but didn't want to see. Finally I mustered the courage and examined how it really was. And it was worse than I had thought.

It wasn't until the 1980s that I understood the breadth of his engagement.

It was in the 1990s, when they were all dead, that I began my research, and the picture became clearer. That was when I read all the new books about Swedish Nazis and found him there; I began to compile facts. Sven my grandfather, this man who was a bit aloof but was loved by the farmers and who liked his grandchildren but had problems showing his feelings, was the same man who was a Swedish Nazi.

Truth gets you sooner or later.

I've wondered why this wasn't spoken about more in my family. Nothing was concealed, but no one ever mentioned it spontaneously. Maybe that's how it is in all families – if the closets remain closed, you can't smell what's been lying in there for years and years. Perhaps they didn't know it all.

Perhaps they didn't want the Jewish relatives to know. Or maybe it wasn't such a big deal to them.

But I believe it is a big deal. Only by talking and poking one's nose into things will you be able to understand, accept or reject. Nothing can be put behind you until it is properly ventilated and sorted through.

I was also a politician and active in the Centre Party at the time and sometimes people taunted me for being a member of that party with its past in the '30s and my Jewish name. They said it was a Brown history of a Green party. If I had known that history when I entered the party, the story from the '30s when some party men said things that no one can defend, if I had known then, I might have taken a different stand to begin with. Instead I made every effort to make the party take a clear stand for immigration against oppression and racism. And then all of a sudden it was clear to me that this past, the terribly wrong and brown past was not just about a few party men in the '30s but even more about my own grandfather.

This clarity was agonizing.

My life has been coloured to a great extent by this story; all the choices, all the positions I have taken. It is as if I inherited the entire century, all of the 1900s. It has forced me into choices, who should I be, what should I take a stand for or against. In later years when this truth has been even clearer this has become intrusive. I must get free from this; the past entraps me. I cannot do that without telling the story, being ashamed and yet telling it, calling out my shame and sorrow in order to somehow get free from it, or soothe it, or show that I will never accept the past as it really was. I heard that after the war he still met his old party friends and some of them even made the old salute. But at that time he blamed Hitler for the result of the war.

In my teenage years I travelled in another direction, to England, to my grandmother's hotel that she acquired with her husband a couple of years after the war. Cider, shandy, lager and lime. I tried to find a place for myself; somewhere

I could find ground to stand on but without religion or tradition. It was a Jewish family. So? And urbane. I went riding on the beach because of the girls looking after the horses and listened to beat music and blues. I discussed things, knew everything, and yet was so shy. I dreamt, made fantasies.

And then one day the juvenile days were over. One day I knew. Sven and his brother Erik did, for instance, go to a meeting at the beginning of the war with the Swedish National League. Neither of them was a member there, but they wanted to go; many of the German-friendly Swedes wanted to tell the Germans who would be best to rule Sweden – that was the issue of the meeting. Sven asked for the floor and demanded a clear stand from the National League if they were ready to attach themselves fully to a new political order and to the axis. 'Then you have to accept an Aryan paragraph,' he said, 'that Aryans would have the first option on all official tasks, as they do in Germany.' He believed that this was right then. This is the closest I come to seeing him as an anti-Semite

My father never returned to Berlin. He never saw that his parents' house in Trautenaustrasse was one of the few ruined by the war in that street. He didn't see that the synagogue in Fasanenstrasse had been turned into a Jewish *Gemeindehaus* with only a fragment left of the old building after the *Kristallnacht* and the war. Both my parents went back to Copenhagen many times over the years always with the same delight. England was their refuge. And finally we made him return to the family's Heilbronn. He sighed then. I never saw him cry.

Where is the real story? Where is the truth of what was? I go back to my memories of someone sobbing, a vibrating nostril, a glance into the future which is now, a glance close and yet passing me by, looking at the things I will never find.

On a street corner in Copenhagen an elusive shadow looks at me eating a cake perhaps similar to what they may have eaten and at Hviids I try to listen and sense the conversation at the next table to imagine what it sounded like seventy years ago. Are these things only ideas that have come up in my mind, those I think I know but do not? I also wonder if some of this is built on my parents' boasting.

But, wait, who is that stout but steady person walking outside the Tivoli Garden with an old camera on his chest? I must run after him. When I get there he is completely different from what I expected. At the next street corner I see some kids slipping into a café. I sneak after them and try to listen in. Children have always been the same and different. I try to hear. And I see a tall bald-headed man outside the window.

At one time we had uncle Björn's ashes in our corner cupboard, the one that was crowned by my mother's plaster head, a refuge for all sorts of relics from the past. When you turned the brass key and carefully opened the door, this cupboard smelled of history, camphor, cigars and old silver. The urn with my uncle stood there for months. Every time you came close to the cupboard you could see him smiling like a gamin, the way he did in the first of May marches in the north or later when he was going to the Queen's tea party in London. He had died somewhere on a train from England to Sweden. Was cremated in England but was to be put in the family grave in Stockholm. Like all of them in my mother's family, he was always on the go, on the way to somewhere else, always as eager and open to new ideas and impressions, and you always knew there were some family secrets that were not told.

By the side of the cupboard there was an illustrious painting. If you looked for a long while you could see a man with tied hands, kneeling and looking to the sky. The artist had given it as payment for therapy to my father's uncle, Karl. That room contained our family history. The empire-style furniture finally came from Umeå but when Granddad was dead. My grandmother Emmy once sat in it, she came all the way from England, but only once although she lived a long life, into her late 80s.

Sven was the model for another painting; this egg-shaped, bald man was the model for this painting in our house. I still don't understand why my father let it hang there. We children were a little afraid of the corner cupboard. It was not to be touched. It contained liquor and medicine. My water gun was placed behind the plaster head after I shot at Daddy. Björn's ashes made the cupboard even weirder but also exciting. When we made explorations into its interior we found Granddad's old gold tooth, some dry cigars that turned into dust when touched, yellowed letters, old menus, pendants my mother never wore that she had received from some German boy, even with German symbols which she hadn't thrown away, a prayer book with incomprehensible Hebrew writing which we didn't know if it was to be read from the front or from the back, a Jewish shawl which was a little damaged and some English wedding cake. The cake was decades old but I took a chew – it tasted sweet and I didn't get ill. These strange, antiquated articles were saved and yet forgotten. The remainder of something we had not been involved in. It all comes back now. Memories that now fill me.

It is important to condemn all right wing extremists, denounce them, hate them for what they do and for what they did, hate them for what they could have done, hate them for what they want to do, hate them for what they did not understand they could be made to do. What makes them like that? There is an old photograph from the Herrhamra manor house at Torö in the Stockholm archipelago, a place my grandfather's grandfather built and his father (Sven's grandfather) owned in the nineteenth century and which also my great grandfather, Sven's father, was part-owner of. There are some boys in that photo: Sven and Erik's other brothers who look frisky. There is also their cousin Set who was on the same Nazi cabinet list as Sven during the war, some 50 years after the picture was taken. And you can see the good-tempered and bearded uncle of theirs who ran the place. It looks like idyllic countryside life. And yet, was this where the first seeds grew? Three small boys who became Swedish Nazis. Who could have become so much more if history had made another turn. I am glad it didn't.

The analysis of what was – of human action, feelings and thoughts about the past – always comes afterwards. Before, you know nothing about anything, and above all not about what will come later. But I have to begin exactly there, when people didn't understand the consequences of their behaviour and their actions. When they, my ancestors, *ought* to have understood. They should have understood at least something. It's hard for me to accept that they didn't foresee at all or at least sense the consequences of what they were doing. And I cannot understand without knowing what happened beforehand. Or, rather, I don't want to understand if that means accepting. I will never accept it. But I have to somehow grasp it. I have at least to go through it. There is no other way of getting a grip on things, getting a grip on people, grasping it all.

Did my father and mother reason the same way and did they explain?

I believe that my father's relatives mostly tried to be like everybody else: build businesses, and live decent lives. Some of them wanted to help others to have good lives. My mother's family was more complicated. I know that much. There were many of them who wanted to change society to what they thought would be better but also to be recognised themselves, to show off. But maybe that is something we all yearn for. The problem occurs when others are hit, when those nearby and far away are stricken.

In 1924, Karl Landauer, one of my relatives and one of the characters in this book, wrote:

'Ambitions that you aim for consciously lose their force, those aspirations that are happening unconsciously will become powerful.'

He also wrote in 1939:

'In the mental therapy of more than one disorder it is important that the patient learns anew what it is to feel; feel real rage, feel real sorrow; it is first after that that real joy, true love returns to him.'

(My free translations)

It's All Coming Back

We are all peculiar and strange, each one in his own manner. Landauer wanted to see how Sigmund Freud's theories worked on more ordinary people than Freud's nervous patients.

My reason for writing this book isn't purely historic. I wonder what we, we who live today, will be judged for, be condemned for and hated for. There are some who perform inhuman acts that will be judged of course. How about the rest of us? We believe that we have achieved a much greater degree of humanism and knowledge. What standpoints can lead to us encouraging those who destroy nature or that we merely remain passive when mass murders and starvation occur or that we just don't help the weak to get proper care? We live in a time when the tempo is much faster, with no time for reflection. We may be criticized for the big and the small, for being active or for being passive. People still cannot live where they want to in this world. Maybe it will primarily be for doing nothing that we will be charged; for cowardly sitting on our behinds, most did then, most do now.

Have I changed in writing this book? I believe I have. I know so much more and I am able to judge. It has been a journey into the unknown. Some things I don't know more about, like who said what and when, but I know much more about my parents and grandparents and how it all came to be. And I don't excuse them. I just realize how it all was. I have understood it is all not just an anecdote.

What I know and do not know

This is not a documentary, but it is about real people and real times. This of course poses the question of what is really true? This book is my view of things, and other people's perspectives and their feelings of how it was and their interpretations of facts may be different but in a way just as true. I believe that history very often is subjective. We look at things differently; that is very natural.

What I don't know and what this book is about, is when my father got to know all about his father in law. If he ever knew everything. Or how he reacted and how it affected their marriage. I really do not know. Perhaps it wasn't as big a deal to him as it is to me. Did she try to tell him the whole story, trying to explain how her father had become the way he was? Did she know? Did he try to explain why his business was in the state it was?

Did they start from the beginning, or was almost everything unsaid and unknown and unfinished? Explaining, rationalizing, I mean they must have asked, mustn't they? But on the other hand, no one gains anything from rationalizing, especially not retrospectively; I know that is what he would have told me that if I had asked. But they must have talked, surely? And then it would all have been exposed, undressed; open like the soil in springtime. And they could have been forgiven or been blocked forever. I don't know. It is easy to believe that you know how it all happened and to find explanations. These are things I will never know.

All the people described are real people and were in the places I describe at those times in history. I have added a lot of feelings and reasoning to create the right sense of the time but I have really tried to describe things as close to what really happened or to what I know of as I can and I have put in things that would be plausible knowing their characters. The letters in facsimile are exactly the ones I have found and translated. The one from Eva and Lins is on thin glossy paper, when I found it it was still smelling of something sixty years after being sent but now only vaguely. I think it is perfume behind old wood and detergent. The letter had been lying for decades in my parents' corner cupboard. I have imagined some other letters like the one about the Landauers going to concentration camp in 1943. But Helmut knew about it, he really did. I have found an envelope with exactly the censorship remarks I described there. The last words of Sigmund and of Karl are the ones they spoke, or what those present said they did. The story of the handling of Swedish authorities of Karl Landauers application is indeed true and he really was in Sweden at least in May 1933 before he went to Holland. There are letters of his from my grandparents flat in Östermalm, Stockholm from that date and he really decided against Sweden first when he knew he wouldn't get the permit to work as a doctor in Sweden.

My parent's wedding trip was to Copenhagen after they were married in West Hampstead on 30th March 1946 and they had stomach problems on their honeymoon. I don't know though where they went in Copenhagen or what they said to each other then. But the story of the old bomb plane with hatches is true, just as an example. Everybody is pictured the way I remember them or the way I have heard by other relatives that they were. What I really know least of is when or if my father was taken into the psychiatric ward, this is just a vague memory of something being said and I do not know what he did in Copenhagen during the war. His mother Emmy did write that he took photographs in Copenhagen for the English, she also said he got beaten up by the Danish police; another story is that he helped in getting Danish Jews over to the Swedish side. I have found no way to check this. But he said he had a passport with the name Jon.

Regarding Bergen-Belsen I have taken some of what Emmy wrote in her unpublished memoir, complemented with what I learnt from the now Sigmund Freud institute in

Frankfurt am Main and other facts. The castration of Eva's boyfriend or fiancée is only described in Emmy's memoirs.

Sven was a complex character about whom there may be many views. But he really shot at the milk transport.

I have read my father's cousin Gerald's description of Sachsenhausen. I have read old letters and other material left behind; there are still loads more. Interesting is for instance the letters Laura and Sven wrote when they fled to Germany and him further to Cuba. The threats and feelings you find there are much starker than what I have been able to describe. But the real sensitive things were never written down or were already transformed when they got to the paper. There is also much more to know. I know of letters I haven't read like the ones from Anna Freud to Karl Landauer, and the ones Sven wrote at least once a week throughout the years to the anthropologist Gustaf Hallström, a friend of his. There is always more to know and to research. I might be wrong about things. I will be happy if facts can be corrected or complemented.

I have tried to remember all the pieces of stories given by relatives. I don't remember everything and some tales are probably not true. Maybe someone has wanted to take on a greater or smaller role than was actually the case. That may be true for my father's story of how he tried to help the Landauers when they were in Bergen-Belsen. Historical fraud can also be a problem. There is no point in telling a false story. I want to look at it straight on. Even if it sometimes closes its eyes or just giggles with me. Then I will twinkle back.

Thanks

Finally I wish to thank all those who contributed, not least my close family, and tell a little about where I gathered all the material.

I have read many books and essays on Swedish Nazism and on the attack on the communist newspaper Norrskensflamman and a lot of other books and articles on Sweden and England and the war. I owe a great deal to Professor Hans-Joachim Rothe at the Sigmund Freud Institut in Frankfurt that tries to preserve Karl Landauers legacy, and I have read his books on Karl Landauer and he has also lead me to other material.

I have read eyewitness accounts from Bergen-Belsen. I have been to most places mentioned in this book and I owe thanks to the Jewish museum in Amsterda, to the Dutch Red Cross and to those helping me with Copenhagen history and others.

A special thank to the Umeå university archive. I have gone through my grandfather Sven's archive there.

Cousins have contributed with stories of the past and I have of course been through all that my parent's left. A second cousin in the US on my father's side have read and given advice and corrections and so has the wife to a cousin on my mother's side. My cousin Sally have read and commented several rounds and has been a good coach and she has done most of the help with the book. I have listened to tapes with my grandmother Emmy and my aunt Ilse, recorded by Sally. She started to record those tapes when Emmy came to life after having been in a coma - she was over ninety at the time. When she woke up she said to my aunt Ilse: 'I have been dead, it was wonderful.'

Thanks to Karl French who did a professional language check. Thanks to friends and professional readers not least Erik Grundström. Worth mentioning are also my friends Simon Linter and Göran Parner.

My Chronology of the first 45 years of the twentieth century

1903-1905
My grandparents Laura and Sven meet in Lago Maggiore and are married in Uppsala.
The entente cordiale between France and England is created, the first alliance before World War I.
Emmy moves to Berlin from Silesia. (around this time)
The union between Sweden and Norway is dissolved.

1909
Laura and Sven move to Umeå.

1911
Emmy and Sigmund are married in Berlin.

1913
Helmut is born.

1914
The shot in Sarajevo. World War I is declared. Sweden is neutral.

1915
Sigmund is sent to the eastern front.

1916
Sigmund is wounded. (around this time)

1917
Anne-Marie is born.
Peace between Germany and Russia in Brest-Litovsk.

Revolution in Berlin.
Famine in Stockholm.

1918
Sven in Tampere.
Peace on the western front. WWI ends.

1919
Peace accord signed in Versailles.
Laura dies.

1924
Sigmund, Emmy, Helmut and his sisters Käthe and Ilse move to Stockholm. (around this time)
Siri and Sven marry.

1933
Adolf Hitler and the NSDAP take power in Germany.
Sigmund, Emmy, Käthe and Ilse move to London.
Sven to and fro to Berlin for the court case on the fire at the German Reichstag.
The Frankfurt Psycho-analytisches Instituts is closed. Karl Landauer to Sweden and then to Holland where his family is united with him.
Anne-Marie's brother Paul dies.

1934
Sven is elected as national socialist to Umeå town council.

1936
Helmut returns to Sweden for good.
Berlin Olympics.

1938
England accepts Germany's annexations of neighbouring areas. Peace in our time.
Anne-Marie gets tuberculosis. (around this time)
Kristallnacht, internations in Dachau and Sachsenhausen

It's All Coming Back

1939

Most of Helmut's relatives are able to leave Germany.
Sigmund dies in Stockholm.
Anne-Marie's brother Björn leaves communism behind and moves to London. Anne-Marie moves to Göteborg to study.
Germany and Russia attack Poland and World War II is a fact.

1941

Germany invades Russia.
Pearl Harbour is attacked and USA joins the war.

1942

Germany loses in Stalingrad and El Alamein
Emmy and Hans are married.

1943

Helmut undercover in Copenhagen.
Landauers to Westerbork.
War is turning.
Sven is in Germany meeting ministers.

1944

Landauers to Bergen Belsen
Allied troops lands in Normandy

1945

Karl Landauer dies.
Bombings of Germany. Atomic bomb over Japan.
Peace on the western front and later also on the eastern front.
Anne-Marie and Helmut meet.

Persons occurring in the book

Anne-Marie's family
1. Paul Otto,
Paul Otto's children:
1.1 **Sven**
Sven's first wife:
Laura daughter to Herman Schück
Sven's and Laura's children:
1.1.1 **Björn**,
Björn's son Paul (Paulie) with his first wife Margit
1.1.2 Ivar
1.1.3 **Paul**
1.1.4 Harriet
1.1.5 **Anne-Marie**
Sven's second wife:
Siri
1.2 Erik and more sisters and brothers
Helmut's family

2 Moses
His wife:
Regina
Moses' and Regina's children:
2.1 Anselm
Anselm's son Stephan
2.2 Josef
Married to Erna.
2.3 Leopold
2.4 Julius
2.5 **Sigmund**
Married to **Emmy**,
Emmy's mother Flora
Emmy's brother Erich

his daughter Trudy married to Harry

Emmy's and Sigmund's children:
2.5.1 Fritz (died as a baby)
2.5.2 **Helmut (Aga)**
2.5.2 Käthe
2.5.3 Ilse

2. 6 Fritz Sally called Fred
his son Walter
2.7 **Lina (Lins)**
Married to **Karl**
Lins' and Karl´s children:
2.7.1 Eva
2.7.2 Paul (Paulus in this book)
2.7.3 Susan (Suse in this book)

www.ingramcontent.com/pod-product-compliance
Lightning Source LLC
Chambersburg PA
CBHW031055080526
44587CB00011B/700